William A. Muhlenberg

The People's Psalter

being the Psalms of David arranged for chanting - with an appendix, containing

hymns from Holy Scripture, and a selection of chants

William A. Muhlenberg

The People's Psalter

being the Psalms of David arranged for chanting - with an appendix, containing hymns from Holy Scripture, and a selection of chants

ISBN/EAN: 9783337286675

Printed in Europe, USA, Canada, Australia, Japan

Cover: Foto ©Lupo / pixelio.de

More available books at **www.hansebooks.com**

THE

PEOPLE'S PSALTER.

BEING

THE PSALMS OF DAVID

ARRANGED FOR CHANTING.

WITH AN

APPENDIX,

CONTAINING HYMNS FROM HOLY SCRIPTURE,

AND A SELECTION OF CHANTS.

REVISED AND ENLARGED.

NEW YORK:
PUBLISHED BY F. D. HARRIMAN,
No. 762 BROADWAY.
1866.

Stereotyped by SMITH & McDOUGAL, 82 & 84 Beekman St., N. Y.

PREFACE.

The Choir and Family Psalter is here reduced to a size convenient for the pocket. The division of the words being, of course, the same, when that work is used by the organist and choir of a church, this may be used by the people. The single and double marks in each verse correspond to the single and double bars of a chant. When a hyphen follows a word or syllable, it signifies that that word or syllable is to be continued through another note. Thus: *I will call upon Him as | long - | as I live,*—here the word *long* is to be sung to the 2nd and 3rd note of the first part of a chant. Again: *Forever | praise - | - the Lord.* Here the word *praise* is to be sung to the 3d and 4th notes of the second part of a chant. Further explanations are not given, seeing they would be superfluous for those who understand chanting, and not intelligible to those who do not. For the same reason, no directions are here laid down for the proper execution of this kind of music. Chanting can be learned only from the oral teacher.

In regard to the pointing, the subscriber repeats what is said in the preface to the Choir and Family Psalter—"It was intended at first to be a copy of his figured Psalter, published some three years since. But in correcting the faulty readings of that book, he found himself gradually departing from the syllabic, and falling into the accentuated, particularly in concluding words of three syllables; hence the latter method prevails throughout the present Psalter. Although it is liable to some objections, it is more spirited, occupies less time in the performance, is more in accordance with correct reading, and is therefore likely to be generally adopted."

In the pointing, ease of execution in the singing has been

chiefly studied, though this has sometimes yielded to correct accentuation. Between the claim of accent on the one hand, and of an easy flow of sound on the other, the preference, it will be found, has in some instances been given to the one, and in others to the other; not, indeed, altogether arbitrarily, yet for reasons which, it cannot be hoped, will always appear. On the whole, it is believed that a pointed Psalter is here presented to the Church which will do something towards uniformity in our chanting, as far as the division of the words is concerned. Such uniformity ought, if possible, to be attained. A worshipper coming into a church, anywhere, should be able to unite as readily in this part of the service, as in the metre psalms and hymns. But at present, there is so great a variety of readings, that one can scarce join in a canticle, except in the particular congregation to which he belongs. Sameness in the music, indeed, is equally desirable. It would be very beautiful if throughout our borders each psalm were invariably associated with a certain melody, so that one would not fail to suggest the other. But it may be long before that is accomplished. In the meanwhile, a great deal will be gained if we come to some agreement in the disposition of the words. When that is everywhere the same, the worshipper, wherever he be, will find no difficulty in bearing his part of the chants, the melody of which is, or ought to be, so simple as to be easily followed as soon as heard.

The present book will be found useful, not only where the whole Psalter is chanted, but when there is a desire to substitute for a metre psalm, one of the psalms in prose. A much larger portion than the usual three or four verses in metre, could thus be sung, and a congregation would be thereby accustomed to chanting, and would grow fond of it. Clergymen who would encourage this kind of music among their people, might do it by occasionally giving out from the Psalter, instead of the metrical selections. They would find the congregation following the choir, or leader, as readily as in the ordinary psalm and hymn tunes.

Further, a book like this is a help to congregational *reading*, as well as chanting. We need one as much as the other; for nothing can be more undevotional than the careless manner in which the alternate verses of the Psalter are generally uttered by the people,—some speaking scarcely above their breath, others hurrying over the words and finishing a verse before their neighbors have got through half of it, and none having any idea that there should be a concert of utterance among them. How much more like united worship would it be, if all kept the same time in reading together. In order to this, there must be a simultaneous pause about the middle of the verse, the place for which in the Psalter of the English Prayer Book is indicated by the colon. In our American Book, that pause has been omitted, probably from its sometimes interrupting the sense. It is an old musical stop, (for the most part coinciding with grammatical punctuation,) to show where the first half of the chant ends, and in the present Psalter is restored in the double bar.* By observing this as a slight rest for the voice, a congregation will find it easy to keep company in their reading, and so glorify God with one mouth, as well as with one heart and mind.

To the Psalter are appended a number of Scripture passages, also pointed for chanting, and which of course may be sung as easily as any of the psalms. This is only a small portion of the treasures of Holy Writ with which our worship might be enriched, and varied according to the different periods of the Ecclesiastical year. There is both precedent and authority for such a use of the sacred text other than the psalms. Precedent: in the *Magnificat* and *Nunc Dimittis* of the English Prayer Book, and in the *Benedictus* of our own; and what is more analogous in its character to most of the passages in the Appendix, the anthem for Easter Day, taken from St. Paul's

---

* This, except in some three or four cases in the "Selections of Psalms," will always be found in the same place in the verse, at which the colon in the English Psalter occurs. Had the liberty been taken to alter its position, the readings in many places might have been improved.

Epistles. Authority: in the express allowance of the House of Bishops.

The selection of chants at the end consists of such as, from their simplicity, are best adapted to the common voice and ear. For antiphonal singing, single chants are to be preferred. When double ones are thus used, they should be those in which the second part is somewhat of answer to the first. Let a congregation be familiar with only the few here presented, and they will be always ready to take their part, in what are eminently the "Songs of Zion." For further observations on congregational chanting, the reader is referred to the *Choir and Family Psalter.*

W. A. MUHLENBERG,
Pastor of the Church of the Holy Communion, New York.

JUNE, 1851.

NOTICE.

This edition of "The People's Psalter" has been carefully revised and corrected. The Divisions of the Canticles and Selections have, in many places, been rendered much smoother, and those Psalms which occur both in the Selections and Psalter, have been carefully compared and pointed alike.

The Harmonies of the Chants, at the end of the work, have been revised by Mr. James A. Johnson, chorister of the church of the Holy Communion. A number of Chants have also been selected and added, and no pains have been spared to make the present edition *perfect.*

THE GENERAL PROTESTANT EPISCOPAL SUNDAY SCHOOL UNION AND CHURCH BOOK SOCIETY was organized at a meeting of the General Convention and others, in November, 1826, for the purpose of providing approved books for Church Sunday School Libraries, and approved books of Instruction for Church Sunday Schools.

This Society consists of the Bishops of the Protestant Episcopal Church, of the Clergy of the same, of the Lay Deputies of the General Convention, and all other members of the Church who shall contribute not less than One Dollar annually to its funds.

Every member of the Church who contributes Thirty Dollars in one payment, is a Life Member; one who contributes Fifty Dollars at one time, is an Honorary Manager; one who contributes One Hundred Dollars in one payment, is a Patron of the Society.

Every Life Member is entitled to Two Dollars' worth of Books; every Honorary Manager to Three and a Half Dollars' worth; every Patron to Seven Dollars' worth of Books. The Books must be drawn each year, as arrearages are not allowed to accumulate.

Meetings are held triennially, during the session of the General Convention.

The Board of Managers consists of all the Bishops, and one hundred members elected triennially by the Society.

The Executive Committee consists of all the Bishops, and twelve Clerical and twelve Lay members, elected annually by the Board of Managers, who, together with the Secretary, Editor, and Treasurer, *ex officio*, conduct the business of the Society.

The Union publishes Sunday School and Parish Library Books, Cards, Tracts, Books of Family and Private Devotion, Sunday School Requisites and Books of Instruction; also the CHILDREN'S MAGAZINE and CHILDREN'S GUEST. Depository, No. 762 Broadway, New York.

The Annual Meeting of the Board of Managers is held on the second Thursday in October.

FORM OF BEQUEST.

I give and bequeath to "The General Protestant Episcopal Sunday School Union and Church Book Society," organized in the city of Philadelphia, in the year of our Lord 1826, and incorporated by the Legislature of the State of New York, April 15, 1854, the sum of.......

Dollars, to be applied to the uses and purposes of said Society.

MORNING PRAYER.

VENITE, EXULTEMUS DOMINO.

O COME, let us sing un | to the | Lord || let us heartily rejoice in the | strength of | our sal | vation.

Let us come before his presence | with thanks | giving || and show ourselves | glad in | him with | psalms.

For the Lord is a | great - | God || and a great | King a | bove all | gods.

In his hand are all the corners | of the | earth || and the strenth of the | hills is | his - | also.

The sea is his, | and he | made it || and his hands pre | pared the dry - | land.

O come, let us worship | and fall down || and kneel be | fore the | Lord our | Maker.

For he is the | Lord our | God || and we are the people of his pasture, | and the | sheep of his | hand.

O worship the Lord in the | beauty of |

MORNING PRAYER.

holiness ‖ let the whole earth | stand in | awe of | him.

For he cometh, for he cometh to | judge the | earth ‖ and with righteousness to judge the world, and the | people | with his | truth.

Glory be to the FATHER | and to the | SON ‖ and to the | HOLY | GHOST.

As it was in the beginning, is now, and | ever shall | be ‖ world without | end - | A - | men.

GLORIA IN EXCELSIS.

GLORY be to | GOD on | high ‖ and on earth | peace, good | will towards | men. We praise thee, we bless thee, we | worship | thee ‖ we glorify thee, we give thanks to | thee for | thy great | glory ‖ O LORD GOD | heavenly | King ‖ GOD the | Father | Al - | mighty.

O LORD, the only-begotten SON | JESUS CHRIST ‖ O LORD GOD, Lamb of | GOD, SON | of the | FATHER ‖ that takest away the | sins of the | world ‖ have mercy | upon | us. Thou that takest away the | sins of the | world ‖ have mercy | upon | us. Thou that takest away the | sins of the | world ‖ re | ceive our | prayer. Thou that sittest at the right hand of | GOD the | FATHER ‖ have mercy | upon | us. ‖

For thou | only art | holy ‖ thou | only | art the | LORD; thou only, O CHRIST, with the | HOLY | GHOST ‖ art most high in the | glory of | GOD the | FATHER ‖ A - | men.

MORNING PRAYER.

TE DEUM LAUDAMUS.

WE prai=e | thee, O | God ‖ we acknowledge | thee to | be the | Lord.

All the earth doth | worship | thee ‖ the | Father | ever | lasting.

To thee all Angels | cry a | loud ‖ the Heavens, and | all the | Powers there | in.

To thee Cherubim, and | Seraph | im ‖ con | tinual | ly do | cry,

Holy, Holy, Holy, Lord | God of | Sabaoth. ‖

Heaven and earth are full of the | Majesty | of thy | Glory.

The glorious company of the Apostles | praise - | thee ‖

The goodly fellowship of the | Prophets | praise - | thee.

The noble army of Martyrs | praise - | thee ‖

The holy Church throughout all the world | doth ac | knowledge | thee.

The | Fa - | ther ‖ of an | infinite | Majes | ty;

Thine adorable, true, and only | Son ‖

Also the | Holy | Ghost, the | Comforter

Thou art the King of Glory, | O - | Christ ‖

Thou art the everlasting | Son - | of the | Father.

When thou tookest upon thee to de | liver | man ‖ thou didst humble thyself to be | born ·| of a | Virgin.

When thou hadst overcome the | sharpness of | death ‖ thou didst open the Kingdom of | Heaven to | all | be | lievers.

Thou sittest at the right | hand of | God | in the | Glory | of the | Father.

We believe that thou shalt come to | be our | Judge ||

We therefore pray thee, help thy servants, whom thou hast redeemed | with thy | precious | blood.

Make them to be numbered | with thy | Saints || in | glory | ever | lasting.

O Lord, | save thy | people || and | bless - | thine - | heritage.

Gov | · ern | them || and | lift them | up for | ever.

Day by day we | magnify | thee ||

And we worship thy Name ever, | world with | out - | end.

Vouch | safe, O | Lord || to keep us this | day with | out - | sin.

O Lord, have | mercy up | on us || have | mer - | cy up | on us.

O Lord, let thy mercy | be up | on us || as our | trust is | in - | thee.

O Lord, in thee | have I | trusted || let me | never | be con | founded.

BENEDICITE, OMNIA OPERA DOMINI.

O ALL ye works of the Lord, | bless ye the | Lord || praise him, and | magnify | him for | ever.

O ye angels of the Lord, | bless ye the | Lord || praise him, and | magnify | him for | ever.

MORNING PRAYER.

O ye Heavens, | bless ye the | Lord ‖ praise him, and | magnify | him for | ever.

O ye Waters that be above the firmament, | bless ye the | Lord ‖ praise him, and | magnify | him for | ever.

O all ye Powers of the Lord, | bless ye the | Lord ‖ praise him, and | magnify | him for | ever.

O ye Sun and Moon, | bless ye the | Lord ‖ praise him, and | magnify | him for | ever.

O ye Stars of Heaven, | bless ye the | Lord ‖ praise him, and | magnify | him for | ever.

O ye Showers and Dew, | bless ye the | Lord ‖ praise him, and | magnify | him for | ever.

O ye Winds of God, | bless ye the | Lord ‖ praise him, and | magnify | him for | ever.

O ye Fire and Heat, | bless ye the | Lord ‖ praise him, and | magnify | him for | ever.

O ye Winter and Summer, | bless ye the | Lord ‖ praise him, and | magnify | him for | ever.

O ye Dews and Frosts, | bless ye the | Lord ‖ praise him, and | magnify | him for | ever.

O ye Frost and Cold, | bless ye the | Lord ‖ praise him, and | magnify | him for | ever.

O ye Ice and Snow, | bless ye the | Lord ‖ praise him, and | magnify | him for | ever.

O ye Nights and Days, | bless ye the | Lord ‖ praise him, and | magnify | him for | ever.

O ye Light and Darkness, | bless ye the | Lord ‖ praise him, and | magnify | him for | ever.

MORNING PRAYER.

O ye Lightnings and Clouds, | bless ye the Lord ‖ praise him, and | magnify | him for ever.

O let the Earth, | bless the | Lord ‖ yea, let it praise him, and | magnify | him for | ever.

O ye Mountains and Hills, | bless ye the Lord ‖ praise him, and | magnify | him for | ever.

O all ye Green Things upon the earth, | bless ye the Lord ‖ praise him, and | magnify | him for | ever.

O ye Wells, | bless ye the Lord ‖ praise him, and | magnify | him for | ever.

O ye Seas and Floods, | bless ye the Lord ‖ praise him, and | magnify | him for ever.

O ye Whales, and all that move in the Waters, | bless ye the Lord ‖ praise him, and | magnify | him for | ever.

O all ye Fowls of the Air, | bless ye the | Lord ‖ praise him, and | magnify | him for | ever.

O all ye Beasts and Cattle, | bless ye the | Lord ‖ praise him, and | magnify | him for | ever.

O ye children of Men, | bless ye the | Lord ‖ praise him, and | magnify | him for | ever.

O let Israel | bless the | Lord ‖ praise him, and | magnify | him for | ever.

O ye Priests of the Lord, | bless ye the | Lord ‖ praise him, and | magnify | him for | ever.

O ye Servants of the Lord, bless ye the | Lord ‖ praise him, and | magnify | him for | ever.

O ye Spirits and Souls of the Righteous, | bless ye the | Lord ‖ praise him, and | magnify | him for | ever.

MORNING PRAYER.

O ye holy and humble Men of heart, | bless ye the | Lord || praise him, and | magnify | him for | ever.

Glory be to the Father, | and to the | Son || and | to the | Holy | Ghost;

As it was in the beginning, is now, and | ever shall | be || world without | end - | A - | men.

JUBILATE DEO.—Psalm C.

O BE joyful in the Lord, | all ye | lands || serve the Lord with gladness, and come before his | presence | with a | song.

Be ye sure that the Lord | he is | God || it is he that hath made us, and not we ourselves; we are his people, | and the | sheep of his | pasture.

O go your way into his gates with thanksgiving, and into his | courts with | praise || be thankful unto him, and speak | good - | of his | Name.

For the Lord is gracious, his mercy is | ever | lasting || and his truth endureth from gener | ation to | gener | ation.

Glory be to the Father, | and to the | Son || and | to the | Holy | Ghost;

As it was in the beginning, is now, and | ever shall | be || world without | end - | A - | men.

BENEDICTUS.—St. Luke i. 68.

BLESSED be the Lord | God of | Israel || for he hath visited | and re | deemed his | people;

MORNING PRAYER.

And hath raised up a mighty sal | vation | for us || in the house | of his | servant | David;

As he spake by the mouth of his | holy | Prophets || which have been | since the | world be | gan;

That we should be saved | from our | enemies || and from the | hand of | all that | hate us.

Glory be to the Father, | and to the | Son || and | to the | Holy | Ghost;

As it was in the beginning, is now, and | ever shall | be || world without | end - | A - | men.

EVENING PRAYER.

CANTATE DOMINO.—Psalm xcviii.

O SING unto the Lord a | new - | song || for he hath | done - | marvellous | things.

With his own right hand, and with his | holy | arm || hath he | gotten him | self the | victory.

The Lord declared | his sal | vation || his righteousness hath he openly showed in the | sight - | of the | heathen.

He hath remembered his mercy and truth toward the | house of | Israel || and all the ends of the world have seen the sal | vation | of our | God.

Show yourselves joyful unto the Lord, | all ye | lands || sing, re | joice, - | and give | thanks.

Praise the Lord up | on the | harp || sing to the harp with a | psalm - | of thanks | giving.

With trumpets | also and | shawms || O show yourselves joyful be | fore the | Lord, the | King.

Let the sea make a noise, and all that | therein | is || the round world, and | they that | dwell there | in.

Let the floods clap their hands, and let the hills be joyful together be | fore the | Lord || for he | cometh to judge | the | earth.

EVENING PRAYER.

With righteousness shall he | judge the | world || and the | people | with - | equity.

Glory be to the Father, | and to the | Son || and | to the | Holy | Ghost;

As it was in the beginning, is now, and | ever shall | be || world without | end - | A -men.

BONUM EST CONFITERI.—Psalm XCII.

IT is a good thing to give thanks un | to the | Lord || and to sing praises unto thy | Name, - | O Most | Highest;

To tell of thy loving-kindness early | in the | morning || and of thy truth | in the | night - | season;

Upon an instrument of ten strings, and up | on the | lute || upon a loud instrument, | and up | on the | harp.

For thou, Lord, hast made me glad | through thy | works || and I will rejoice in giving praise for the oper | ations | of thy | hands.

Glory be to the Father, | and to the | Son || and | to the | Holy | Ghost;

As it was in the beginning, is now, and | ever shall be | world without | end - | A - | men.

DEUS MISEREATUR.—Psalm LXVII.

GOD be merciful unto | us, and | bless us | and show us the light of his countenance, and be | merciful | unto | us:

EVENING PRAYER.

That thy way may be | known upon | earth | thy saving | health a | mong all | nations.

Let the people praise | thee, O | God || yea, let | all the | people | praise thee.

O let the nations re | joice and be | glad || for thou shalt judge the folk righteously, and govern the | nations | upon | earth.

Let the people praise | thee, O | God || yea, let | all the | people | praise thee.

Then shall the earth bring | forth her | increase || and God, even our own God, shall | give - | us his | blessing.

God | shall - | bless us || and all the ends of the | world shall | fear - | him.

Glory be to the Father, | and to the | Son || and | to the | Holy | Ghost;

As it was in the beginning, is now, and | ever shall | be || world without | end - | A - | men.

BENEDIC ANIMA MEA.—Psalm CIII.

PRAISE the Lord, | O my | soul || and all that is within me, | praise his | holy | Name.

Praise the Lord, | O my | soul || and for | get not | all his | benefits:

Who forgiveth | all thy | sin || and healeth | all - | thine in | firmities;

Who saveth thy life | from de | struction || and crowneth thee with | mercy and | loving | kindness.

O praise the Lord, ye Angels of his, ye that

EVENING PRAYER.

ex | cel in | strength || ye that fulfil his commandment, and hearken unto the | voice - | of his | word.

O praise the Lord, all | ye his | hosts || ye servants of | his that | do his | pleasure.

O speak good of the Lord, all ye works of his, in all places of | his do | minion || praise thou the | Lord, - | O my | soul.

Glory be to the Father, | and to the Son, | and | to the | Holy | Ghost;

As it was in the beginning. is now, and | ever shall | be | world without | end - | A - | men.

SELECTIONS OF PSALMS.

TO BE USED INSTEAD OF THE PSALMS FOR THE DAY, AT THE DISCRETION OF THE MINISTER.

Selection First.

PSALM xix.—*Cœli enarrant.*

THE heavens declare the | glory of | God || and the firmament | showeth his | handy | work.

One day | telleth an | other || and one night | certi | fieth an | other.

There is neither | speech nor | language || but their | voices are | heard a | mong them.

Their sound is gone out into | all - | lands || and their words into the | ends - | of the | world.

In them hath he set a tabernacle | for the | sun || which cometh forth as a bridegroom out of his chamber, and rejoiceth as a | giant to | run his | course.

It goeth forth from the uttermost part of the heaven, and runneth about unto the end of | it a | gain || and there is nothing | hid from the | heat there | of.

The law of the LORD is an undefiled law, con | verting the | soul || the testimony of the

Lord is sure, and giveth | wisdom | unto the | simple.

The statutes of the Lord are right, and re | joice the | heart ‖ the commandment of the Lord is pure, and giveth | light un | to the | eyes.

The fear of the Lord is clean, and en | dureth for | ever ‖ the judgments of the Lord are true, and | righteous | alto | gether.

More to be desired are they than gold, yea, than | much fine | gold ‖ sweeter also than honey, | and the | honey | comb.

Moreover by them is thy | servant | taught ‖ and in keeping of them | there is | great re | ward.

Who can tell how | oft he of | fendeth ‖ O cleanse thou me | from my | secret | faults.

Keep thy servant also from pre | sumptuous | sins ‖ lest they get the do | minion | over | me.

Let the words of my mouth, and the meditation | of my | heart ‖ be always ac | ceptable | in thy | sight.

O | -- | Lord ‖ my | strength, and | my re | deemer.

Psalm xxiv. *Domini est terra.*

THE earth is the Lord's, and all that | therein | is ‖ the compass of the world, and | they that | dwell there | in.

For he hath founded it up | on the | seas ‖ and prepared | it up | on the | floods.

Who shall ascend into the | hill of the | Lord ‖ or who shall rise up | in his | holy | place?

Even he that hath clean hands, and a | pure - | heart ‖ and that hath not lift up his mind unto vanity, nor | sworn to de | ceive his | neighbor.

He shall receive the blessing | from the | Lord ‖ and righteousness from the | God of | his sal | vation.

This is the generation of | them that | seek him ‖ even of them that | seek thy | face, O | Jacob.

Lift up your heads, O ye gates; and be ye lift up, ye ever | lasting | doors ‖ and the King of | glory | shall come | in.

Who is the | King of | glory ‖ It is the Lord, strong and mighty, even the | Lord - | mighty in | battle.

Lift up your heads, O ye gates; and be ye lift up, ye ever | lasting | doors ‖ and the King of | glory | shall come | in.

Who is the | King of | glory ‖ Even the Lord of hosts, | he is the | King of | glory.

Psalm ciii.—*Benedic anima mea.*

PRAISE the Lord, | O my | soul ‖ and all that is within me, | praise his | holy | Name.

Praise the Lord, | O my | soul ‖ and for | get not | all his | benefits.

Who forgiveth | all thy | sin ‖ and healeth | all - | thine in | firmities;

Who saveth thy life | from de | struction ‖ and crowneth thee with | mercy and | loving | kind- | ness.

Who satisfieth thy mouth with | good - | things ‖ making thee young and | lusty | as an | eagle.
The Lord executeth righteousness | and - | judgment ‖ for all them that | are op | pressed with | wrong.
He showed his ways | unto | Moses ‖ his works unto the | children of | Isra | el.
The Lord is full of com | passion and | mercy ‖ long-suffering, | and of | great - | goodness.
He will not | alway be | chiding ‖ neither keepeth | he his | anger for | ever.
He hath not dealt with us | after our | sins ‖ nor rewarded us according | to our | wicked | ness.
For look how high the heaven is in compari- son | of the | earth ‖ so great is his mercy also toward - | them that | fear - | him!
Look how wide also the east is | from the | west ‖ so far hath he | set our | sins - | from us.
Yea, like as a father pitieth his | own - | chil dren ‖ even so is the Lord merciful | unto | them that | fear him.
For he knoweth where | of we are | made ‖ he remembereth | that we | are but | dust.
The days of man are | but as | grass ‖ for he flourisheth as a | flower | of the | field.
For as soon as the wind goeth over it, | it is | gone ‖ and the place there | of shall | know it no | more.
But the merciful goodness of the Lord endur- eth for ever and ever upon | them that | fear him | and his righteousness up | on - | children's | chil- dren;

Even upon such as | keep his | covenant ‖ and think upon his com | mand - | ments to | do them.

The LORD hath prepared his | seat in | heaven ‖ and his kingdom | ruleth | over | all.

O praise the LORD, ye angels of his, ye that ex | cel in | strength ‖ ye that fulfil his commandment, and hearken unto the | voice - | of his | word.

O praise the LORD, all | ye his | hosts ‖ ye servants of | his that | do his | pleasure.

O speak good of the LORD, all ye works of his, in all places of | his do | minion ‖ praise thou the | LORD, - | O my | soul.

Selection Second.

FROM PSALM cxxxix.—*Domine, probasti.*

O LORD, thou hast searched me | out, and | known me ‖ Thou knowest my down-sitting, and mine up-rising; thou understandest my | thoughts - | long be | fore.

Thou art about my path, and a | bout my | bed ‖ and | spiest out | all my | ways.

For lo, there is not a word | in my | tongue ‖ but thou, O LORD, | knowest it | alto | gether.

Thou hast fashioned me behind | and be | fore ‖ and | laid thine | hand up | on me.

Such knowledge is too wonderful and | excellent | for me ‖ I cannot at | tain - | unto | it.

Whither shall I go then | from thy | Spirit ‖ or whither shall I | go then | from thy | presence?

If I climb up into heaven, | thou art | there ‖ if I go down to hell, | thou art | there - | also.

If I take the wings | of the | morning || and re-main in the uttermost | parts - | of the | sea;

Even there also shall | thy hand | lead me || and thy | right - | hand shall | hold me.

If I say, Peradventure the | darkness shall | co-ver me || then shall my | night be | turned to | day.

Yea, the darkness is no darkness with thee, but the night is as clear | as the | day || the darkness and light to | thee are | both a | like.

For my | reins are | thine || thou hast covered me | in my | mother's | womb.

I will give thanks unto thee, for I am fearful-ly and | wonderfully | made || marvellous are thy works, and that my soul | knoweth | right - | well.

My bones are not | hid from | thee || though I be made secretly, and fashioned be | neath - | in the | earth.

Thine eyes did see my substance, yet | being im | perfect || and in thy book were | all my | members | written;

Which day by | day were | fashioned || when as | yet there was | none of | them.

How dear are thy counsels unto | me, O | God || O how | great is the | sum of | them!

If I tell them, they are more in number | than the | sand || when I wake up, | I am | present | with thee.

Try me, O God, and seek the ground | of my | heart | prove me, | and ex | amine my | thoughts.

Look well if there be any way of wickedness | in - | me || and lead me in the | way - | ever | lasting.

PSALM cxlv.—*Exaltabo te, Deus.*

I WILL magnify thee, O | God, my | King ‖ and I will praise thy | Name for | ever and | ever.

Every day will I give thanks | unto | thee ‖ and praise thy | Name for | ever and | ever.

Great is the LORD, and marvellous worthy | to be | praised ‖ there is no | end - | of his | greatness.

One generation shall praise thy works un | to an | other ‖ and de | clare - | thy - | power.

As for me, I will be talking | of thy | worship ‖ thy glory, thy | praise and | wondrous | works;

So that men shall speak of the might of thy | marvellous | acts ‖ and I will also | tell - | of thy | greatness.

The memorial of thine abundant kindness | shall be | showed ‖ and men shall | sing - | of thy | righteousness.

The LORD is gracious and | merci | ful ‖ longsuffering, | and of | great - | goodness.

The LORD is loving unto | every | man ‖ and his mercy is | over | all his | works.

All thy works praise | thee, O | LORD ‖ and thy saints give | thanks - | unto | thee.

They show the glory | of thy | kingdom ‖ and | talk - | of thy | power;

That thy power, thy glory, and mightiness | of thy | kingdom ‖ might be | known - | unto | men.

Thy kingdom is an ever | lasting | kingdom ‖ and thy dominion en | dureth through | out all | ages.

The Lord upholdeth all | such as | fall |
and lifteth up all | those - | that are | down.

The eyes of all wait upon | thee, O | Lord |
and thou givest them their | meat in | due - |
season.

Thou openest | thine - | hand || and fillest all
things | living with | plenteous | ness.

The Lord is righteous in | all his | ways |
and | holy in | all his | works.

The Lord is nigh unto all them that | call
up | on him || yea, all such as | call up | on him |
faithfully.

He will fulfil the desire of | them that |
fear him || he also will hear their | cry, - | and
will | help them.

The Lord preserveth all | them that | love
him || but scattereth a | broad all | the un | godly.

My mouth shall speak the praise | of the |
Lord || and let all flesh give thanks unto his holy|
Name for | ever and | ever.

Selection Third.

From Psalm li.—*Miserere mei, Deus.*

HAVE mercy upon me, O God, after thy || great-|
goodness || according to the multitude of thy
mercies do a | way - | mine of | fences.

Wash me throughly | from my | wicked-
ness || and | cleanse me | from my | sin.

For I ac | knowledge my | faults || and my |
sin is | ever be | fore me.

Against thee only have I sinned, and done

this evil | in thy | sight ‖ that thou mightest be justified in thy saying, and | clear when | thou art | judged.

Behold, I was | shapen in | wickedness ‖ and in sin hath my | mother con | ceived | me.

But lo, thou requirest truth in the | inward | parts ‖ and shalt make me to understand | wisdom | secret | ly.

Thou shalt purge me with hyssop, and I | shall be | clean ‖ thou shalt wash me, and I shall be | whi - | ter than | snow.

Thou shalt make me hear of | joy and | gladness ‖ that the bones which thou hast | broken | may re | joice.

Turn thy face | from my | sins ‖ and put out | all - | my mis | deeds.

Make me a clean | heart, O | God ‖ and renew a | right - | spirit with | in me.

Cast me not away | from thy | presence ‖ and take not thy | Holy | Spirit | from me.

O give me the comfort of thy | help a | gain ‖ and stablish me | with thy | free - | Spirit.

Then shall I teach thy ways un | to the | wicked ‖ and sinners shall be con | verted | unto | thee.

Deliver me from blood-guiltiness, O God, thou that art the God | of my | health | and my tongue shall | sing - | of thy | righteousness.

Thou shalt open my | lips, O | Lord ‖ and my | mouth shall | show thy | praise.

For thou desirest no sacrifices, else would I | give it | thee ‖ but thou delightest | not - | in burnt | offerings.

The sacrifice of God is a | troubled | spirit | a broken and contrite heart, O God, | shalt thou | not de | spise.

From Psalm xlii.—*Quemadmodum.*

LIKE as the hart desireth the | water | brooks | so longeth my soul | after | thee, O | God.

My soul is athirst for God, yea, even for the | living | God || when shall I come to appear be | fore the | presence of | God?

My tears have been my meat | day and | night || while they daily say unto me, | Where is | now thy | God?

Now when I think thereupon, I pour out my heart | by my | self || for I went with the multitude, and brought them forth in | to the | house of | God;

In the voice of | praise and | thanksgiving | among such as | keep - | holy | day.

Why art thou so full of heaviness, | O my | soul || and why art thou so dis | quieted | within me?

Put thy | trust in | God || for I will yet give him thanks for the | help - | of his | countenance.

The LORD hath granted his loving-kindness | in the | day-time || and in the night-season did I sing of him, and made my prayer | un | to the | God of my | life.

I will say unto the God of my strength, Why hast thou for | gotten | me || why go I thus heavily, while the | enemy op | presseth | me?

Namely, while they say daily | unto | me ‖ Where | - is | now thy | God?
Why art thou so vexed, | O my soul ‖ and why art thou so dis | quieted | with | in me?
O put thy | trust in | God ‖ for I will yet thank him, which is the help of my | countenance, | and my | God.

Selection Fourth.

PSALM xxxvii.—*Noli æmulari.*

FRET not thyself because of the | un- | godly ‖ neither be thou envious a | gainst the | evil | doers.

For they shall soon be cut down | like the | grass ‖ and be withered even | as the | green | herb.

Put thou thy trust in the LORD, and be | doing | good ‖ dwell in the land, and | verily thou shalt be | fed.

Delight thou | in the | LORD, and he shall | give thee thy | heart's de | sire.

Commit thy way unto the LORD, and put thy | trust in | him ‖ and | he shall | bring it to | pass.

He shall make thy righteousness as | clear as the | light ‖ and thy just | dealing | as the | noonday.

Hold thee still in the LORD, and abide | patiently up | on him ‖ but grieve not thyself at him whose way doth prosper, against the man that doeth | after | evil | counsels.

[Sel. 4.]   SELECTIONS OF PSALMS.

Leave off from wrath, and let | go dis | pleasure || fret not thyself, else shalt thou be | moved | to do | evil.

Wicked doers shall be | rooted | out || and they that patiently abide the Lord, | those shall in | herit the | land.

Yet a little while, and the ungodly shall be | clean - | gone || thou shalt look after his place, and | he shall | be a | way.

But the meek-spirited shall pos | sess the | earth || and shall be refreshed in the | multi | tude of | peace.

The ungodly secketh counsel a | gainst the | just || and gnasheth up | on him | with his | teeth.

The Lord shall | laugh him to | scorn || for he hath | seen that his | day is | coming.

The ungodly have drawn out the sword, and have | bent their | bow || to cast down the poor and needy, and to slay such as are of a | right - | conver | sation.

Their sword shall go through their | own - | heart || and their | bow - | shall be | broken.

A small thing that the | righteous | hath || is better than great | riches of | the un | godly.

For the arms of the ungodly | shall be | broken || and the | Lord up | holdeth the | righteous.

The Lord knoweth the days | of the | godly || and their inheritance | shall en | dure for | ever.

They shall not be confounded in the | perilous | time || and in the days of dearth | they shall | have e | nough.

As for the ungodly, they shall perish, and the

enemies of the Lord shall consume as the | fat of | lambs || yea, even as the smoke shall | they con | sume a | way.

The ungodly borroweth, and payeth | not a | gain || but the righteous is | merci | ful and | liberal.

Such as are blessed of God shall pos | sess the | land || and they that are cursed of him, | shall be | rooted | out.

The Lord ordereth a | good man's | going || and maketh his way ac | ceptable | to him | self.

Though he fall, he shall not be | cast a | way || for the Lord up | holdeth him | with his | hand.

I have been young, and | now am | old || and yet saw I never the righteous forsaken, nor his | seed - | begging their | bread.

The righteous is ever merciful, | and - | lendeth || and | his - | seed is | blessed.

Flee from evil, and do the thing | that is | good || and | dwell for | ever | more.

For the Lord loveth the thing | that is | right || he forsaketh not his that be godly, but they | are pre | served for | ever.

The unrighteous | shall be | punished || as for the seed of the ungodly, it | shall be | rooted | out.

The righteous shall in | herit the | land || and | dwell there | in for | ever.

The mouth of the righteous is exercised | in - | wisdom || and his tongue | will be | talking of | judgment.

The law of his God is | in his | heart || and his | goings | shall not | slide.

[Sel. 5.]   SELECTIONS OF PSALMS.

The ungodly | seeth the | righteous || and | seeketh oc | casion to | slay him.

The Lord will not leave him | in his | hand || nor con | demn him | when he is | judged.

Hope thou in the Lord, and keep his way, and he shall promote thee, that thou shalt pos | sess the | land || when the ungodly shall | perish, | thou shalt | see it.

I myself have seen the ungodly in | great - | power || and flourishing | like a green | bay tree.

I went by, and | lo, he was | gone || I sought him, but his place could | no - | where be | found.

Keep innocency, and take heed unto the thing | that is | right || for that shall bring a man | peace - | at the | last.

As for the transgressors, they shall | perish to | gether || and the end of the ungodly is, they shall be | rooted | out at the | last.

But the salvation of the righteous cometh | of the | Lord || who is also their strength | in the | time of | trouble.

And the Lord shall stand | by them and | save them || he shall deliver them from the ungodly, and shall save them, because they | put their | trust in | him.

Selection Fifth.

Psalm i.—*Beatus vir, qui non abiit.*

BLESSED is the man that hath not walked in the counsel of the ungodly, nor stood in the |

way of | sinners ‖ and hath not sat in the | seat - | of the | scornful.

But his delight is in the law | of the | LORD ‖ and in his law will he exercise him | self - | day and | night.

And he shall be like a tree planted by the | water | side ‖ that will bring forth his | fruit - | in due | season.

His leaf also | shall not | wither ‖ and look, whatsoever he | doeth, | it shall | prosper.

As for the ungodly, it is not | with | them ‖ but they are like the chaff, which the wind scattereth away | from the | face of the | earth.

Therefore the ungodly shall not be able to stand | in the | judgment ‖ neither the sinners in the congre | gation | of the | righteous.

But the LORD knoweth the way | of the | righteous ‖ and the way of the un | godly | shall - | perish.

PSALM XV.—*Domine, quis habitabit?*

LORD, who shall dwell | in thy | tabernacle ‖ or who shall rest up | on thy | holy | hill?

Even he that leadeth an | uncorrupt | life ‖ and doeth the thing which is right, and speaketh the | truth - | from his | heart.

He that hath used no deceit in his tongue, nor done evil | to his | neighbour ‖ and | hath not | slandered his | neighbour.

He that setteth not by himself, but is lowly in | his own | eyes ‖ and maketh much of | them that | fear the | LORD.

He that sweareth unto his neighbour, and disap |

pointeth him | not || though it | were to | his own | hindrance.

He that hath not given his money up | on - | usury || nor taken re | ward a | gainst the | innocent.

Whoso doeth | these - | things || shall | nev - | er - | fall.

PSALM xci.—*Qui habitat.*

WHOSO dwelleth under the defence of the | Most - | High || shall abide under the | shadow of | the Al | mighty.

I will say unto the LORD, Thou art my hope, and | my strong | hold || my God, in | him - | will I | trust.

For he shall deliver thee from the | snare of the | hunter || and | from the | noisome | pestilence.

He shall defend thee under his wings, and thou shalt be safe | under his | feathers || his faithfulness and truth shall | be thy | shield and | buckler.

Thou shalt not be afraid for any | terror by night || nor for the | arrow that | flieth by | day;

For the pestilence that | walketh in | darkness || nor for the sickness that de | stroyeth | in the | noonday.

A thousand shall fall beside thee, and ten thousand at | thy right | hand || but it shall | not come | nigh - | thee.

Yea, with thine eyes shalt | thou be | hold || and see the re | ward of | the un | godly.

For thou, Lord, | art my | hope ‖ thou hast set thine house of de | fence - | very | high.

There shall no evil happen | unto | thee ‖ neither shall any | plague come | nigh thy | dwelling.

For he shall give his angels charge | over | thee ‖ to | keep thee | in all thy | ways.

They shall bear thee | in their | hands ‖ that thou hurt not thy | foot a | gainst a | stone.

Thou shalt go upon the | lion and | adder ‖ the young lion and the dragon shalt thou | tread - | under thy | feet.

Because he hath set his love upon me, therefore will | I de | liver him ‖ I will set him up, be | cause he hath | known my | Name.

He shall call upon me, and | I will | hear him ‖ yea, I am with him in trouble; I will deliver him, and | bring - | him to | honor.

With long life will I | satis | fy him ‖ and | show him | my sal | vation.

Selection Sixth.

FROM PSALM xxxii.—*Beati, quorum.*

BLESSED is he whose unrighteousness | is for | given ‖ and | whose - | sin is | covered.

Blessed is the man unto whom the Lord im | puteth no | sin ‖ and in whose | spirit there | is no | guile.

I will acknowledge my sin | unto | thee ‖ and mine unrighteousness | have I | not - | hid.

I said, I will confess my sins un | to thee | Lord ‖ and so thou forgavest the | wickedness | of my | sin.

85

For this shall every one that is godly make his prayer unto thee, in a time when thou | mayest be | found || but in the great water-floods | they shall | not come | nigh him.

Thou art a place to hide me in; thou shalt preserve | me from | trouble || thou shalt compass me about with | songs - | of de | liverance.

I will inform thee, and teach thee in the way wherein | thou shalt | go || and I will | guide thee | with mine | eye.

Great plagues remain | for the un | godly || but whoso putteth his trust in the LORD, mercy embraceth | him on | every | side.

Be glad, O ye righteous, and re | joice in the | LORD || and be joyful, all | ye that are | true of | heart.

PSALM CXXX.—*De profundis.*

OUT of the deep have I called unto | thee, O | LORD || Lord, | hear - | my - | voice.

O let thine ears con | sider | well || the | voice of | my com | plaint.

If thou, LORD, wilt be extreme to mark what is | done a | miss || O Lord, | who - | may a | bide it?

For there is | mercy with | thee || therefore | shalt - | thou be | feared.

I look for the LORD; my soul doth | wait for | him || in his | word - | is my | trust.

My soul fleeth un | to the | Lord || before the morning watch; I say, be | fore the | morning | watch.

O Israel, trust in the Lord; for with the Lord | there is | mercy ‖ and with | him is | plenteous re | demption.

And he shall re | deem - | Israel ‖ from | all - | his | sins.

PSALM cxxi.—*Levavi oculos meos.*

I WILL lift up mine eyes un | to the | hills ‖ from | whence - | cometh my | help.

My help cometh even | from the | Lord ‖ who hath | made - | heaven and | earth.

He will not suffer thy foot | to be | moved ‖ and he that | keepeth thee | will not | sleep.

Behold, he that | keepeth | Israel ‖ shall | neither | slumber nor | sleep.

The Lord himself | is thy | keeper ‖ the Lord is thy defence up | on thy | right - | hand;

So that the sun shall not | burn thee by | day ‖ neither the | moon - | by - | night.

The Lord shall preserve thee | from all | evil ‖ yea, it is even | he that shall | keep thy | soul.

The Lord shall preserve thy going out, and thy | coming | in ‖ from this time | forth for | ever | more.

Selection Seventh.

PSALM xxiii.—*Dominus regit me.*

THE Lord | is my | shepherd ‖ therefore | can I | lack - | nothing.

He shall feed me in a | green - | pasture ‖ and lead me forth be | side the | waters of | comfort.

He shall con | vert my | soul ‖ and bring me

forth in the paths of righteousness | for his | Name's - | sake.

Yea, though I walk through the valley of the shadow of death, I will | fear no | evil || for thou art with me; thy rod and thy | staff - | comfort | me.

Thou shalt prepare a table before me against | them that | trouble me || thou hast anointed my head with oil | and my cup | shall be | full.

But thy loving-kindness and mercy shall follow me all the days | of my | life || and I will dwell in the house | of the | Lord for | ever.

Psalm xxxiv.—*Benedicam Domino.*

I WILL always give thanks un | to the | Lord || his praise shall | ever be | in my | mouth.

My soul shall make her boast | in the | Lord || the humble shall | hear there | of, and be | glad.

O praise the | Lord with | me || and let us magni | fy his | Name to | gether.

I sought the Lord | and he | heard me || yea, he delivered me | out of | all my | fear.

They had an eye unto him, | and were | lightened || and their | faces were | not a | shamed.

Lo, the poor crieth, and the Lord | heareth | him || yea, and saveth him | out of | all his | troubles.

The angel of the Lord tarrieth round about | them that | fear him || and de | liv - | ereth | them.

O taste, and see, how gracious the | Lord - | is || blessed is the | man that | trusteth in | him.

O fear the Lord, ye that | are his | saints || for they that | fear him | lack - | nothing.

The lions do lack, and | suffer | hunger ‖ but they who seek the Lord shall want no manner of | thing - | that is | good.

Come, ye children, and hearken | unto | me ‖ I will teach you the | fear - | of the | Lord.

What man is he that | lusteth to | live ‖ and would | fain see | good - | days?

Keep thy | tongue from | evil ‖ and thy | lips, that they | speak no | guile.

Eschew evil, | and do | good ‖ seek | peace, - | and en | sue it.

The eyes of the Lord are | over the | righteous ‖ and his ears are | open un | to their | prayers.

The countenance of the Lord is against them | that do | evil ‖ to root out the remembrance | of them | from the | earth.

The righteous cry, and the Lord | heareth | them ‖ and delivereth them | out of | all their | troubles.

The Lord is nigh unto them that are of a | contrite | heart ‖ and will save such as be | of an | humble | spirit.

Great are the troubles | of the | righteous ‖ but the Lord de | livereth him | out of | all.

He keepeth | all his | bones ‖ so that not | one of | them is | broken.

But misfortune shall | slay the un | godly ‖ and they that hate the | righteous | shall be | desolate.

The Lord delivereth the souls | of his | servants ‖ and all they that put their trust in | him shall | not be | destitute.

Psalm lxv.—*Te decet hymnus.*

THOU, O God, art | praised in | Sion || and unto thee shall the vow be per | formed | in Je | rusalem.

Thou that | hearest the | prayer || unto | thee shall | all flesh | come.

My misdeeds pre | vail a | gainst me || O be thou merciful | un - | to our | sins.

Blessed is the man whom thou choosest, and receivest | unto | thee || he shall dwell in thy court, and shall be satisfied with the pleasures of thy house, even | of thy | holy | temple.

Thou shalt show us wonderful things in thy righteousness, O God of | our sal | vation || thou that art the hope of all the ends of the earth, and of them that re | main in the | broad - | sea.

Who in his strength setteth | fast the | mountains || and is | girded a | bout with | power.

Who stilleth the raging | of the | sea || and the noise of his waves, and the | madness | of the | people.

They also that dwell in the uttermost parts of the earth shall be afraid | of thy | tokens || thou that makest the outgoings of the | morning and | evening to | praise thee.

Thou visitest the earth, and | blessest | it || thou | makest it | very | plenteous.

The river of God is | full of | water || thou preparest their corn, for so thou pro | videst | for the | earth.

Thou waterest her furrows; thou sendest rain into the little | valleys there | of || thou makest it soft with the drops of rain, and | blessest the | in-crease | of it.

Thou crownest the year | with thy | goodness ‖ and thy | clouds - | drop - | fatness.

They shall drop upon the dwellings | of the | wilderness ‖ and the little hills shall re | joice on | every | side.

The folds shall be | full of | sheep ‖ the valleys also shall stand so thick with corn, that | they shall | laugh and | sing.

Selection Eighth.

FROM PSALM lxxxiv.—*Quam dilecta.*

O HOW amiable | are thy | dwellings ‖ thou | Lord - | -of | hosts!

My soul hath a desire and longing to enter into the | courts of the | Lord ‖ my heart and my flesh re | joice in the | living | God.

Yea, the sparrow hath found her an house, and the swallow a nest, where she may | lay her | young ‖ even thy altars, O Lord of hosts, my | King - | and my | God.

Blessed are they that | dwell in thy | house ‖ they will be | alway | praising | thee.

Blessed is the man whose strength | is in | thee ‖ in whose | heart - | are thy | ways.

Who going through the vale of misery use it | for a | well ‖ and the | pools are | filled with | water.

They will go from | strength to | strength ‖ and unto the God of gods appeareth every | one of | them in | Sion.

O Lord God of hosts, | hear my | prayer | hearken, | O - | God of | Jacob.

For one day in | thy - | courts || is | better | than a | thousand.

I had rather be a door-keeper in the | house of my | God || than to dwell in the | tents - | of un | godliness.

For the Lord God is a light and defence; the Lord will give | grace and | worship || and no good thing shall he withhold from them that | live a | godly | life.

O Lord | God of | hosts || blessed is the man that | putteth his | trust in | thee.

PSALM lxxxv.—*Benedixisti, Domine.*

LORD, thou art become gracious un | to thy | land || thou hast turned away the cap | tivi | ty of | Jacob.

Thou hast forgiven the offence | of thy | people || and | covered | all their | sins.

Thou hast taken away all | thy dis | pleasure || and turned thyself from thy | wrathful | indig | nation.

Turn us, then, O | God, our | Saviour || and let thine | anger | cease from | us.

Wilt thou be displeased at | us for | ever || and wilt thou stretch out thy wrath from one gene | ration | to an | other?

Wilt thou not turn a | gain, and | quicken us | that thy people | may re | joice in | thee?

Show us thy | mercy, O - | Lord || and | grant us | thy sal | vation.

I will hearken what the Lord God will say

con | cerning | me ‖ for he shall speak peace unto his people, and to his saints, | that they | turn not a | gain.

For his salvation is nigh | them that | fear him ‖ that glory may | dwell - | in our | land.

Mercy and truth are | met to | gether ‖ righteousness and | peace have | kissed each | other.

Truth shall flourish out | of the | earth ‖ and righteousness hath | looked | down from | heaven.

Yea, the Lord shall show | loving | kindness ‖ and our | land shall | give her | increase.

Righteousness shall | go be | fore him ‖ and he shall direct his | going | in the | way.

Psalm xciii.—*Dominus regnavit.*

THE Lord is King, and hath put on | glorious ap | parel ‖ the Lord hath put on his apparel, and | girded him | self with | strength.

He hath made the round | world so | sure ‖ that it | can - | not be | moved.

Ever since the world began hath thy seat | been pre | pared ‖ thou | art from | ever | lasting.

The floods are risen, O Lord, the floods have lift | up their | voice ‖ the | floods lift | up their | waves.

The waves of the sea are mighty, and | rage - | horribly ‖ but yet the Lord, who | dwelleth on | high, is | mightier.

Thy testimonies, O Lord, are | very | sure ‖ holiness be | cometh thine | house for | ever.

Psalm xcvii.—*Dominus regnavit.*

THE Lord is King, the earth may be | glad there | of ‖ yea, the multitude of the isles | may be | glad there | of.

Clouds and darkness are | round a | bout him ‖ righteousness and judgment are the habi | ta- tion | of his | seat.

There shall go a | fire be | fore him ‖ and burn up his enemies | on - | every | side.

His lightnings gave shine un | to the | world ‖ the earth | saw it, and | was a | fraid.

The hills melted like wax at the presence | of the | Lord ‖ at the presence of the Lord | of the | whole - | earth.

The heavens have de | clared his | righteous- ness ‖ and all the | people have | seen his | glory.

Confounded be all they that worship carved images, and that delight in | vain - | gods ‖ wor- ship | him, - | all ye | gods.

Sion heard of it, | and re | joiced ‖ and the daughters of Judah were glad, because of thy | judgments, | O - | Lord.

For thou, Lord, art higher than all that are | in the | earth ‖ thou art exalted | far a | bove all | gods.

O ye that love the Lord, see that ye hate the thing | which is | evil ‖ the Lord preserveth the souls of his saints; he shall deliver them from the | hand of | the un | godly.

There is sprung up a | light | for the | right- eous ‖ and joyful gladness for | such as | are true | hearted.

Rejoice in the | Lord, ye | righteous ‖ and give thanks for a re | membrance | of his | holiness.

Selection Ninth.

Psalm viii.—*Domine, Dominus noster.*

O LORD, our Governor, how excellent is thy | Name in | all the | world ‖ thou that hast set thy | glory a | bove the | heavens!

Out of the mouth of very babes and sucklings, hast thou ordained strength, because | of thine | enemies ‖ that thou mightest still the enemy | and - | the a | venger.

For I will consider thy heavens, even the works | of thy | fingers ‖ the moon and the stars | which thou | hast or | dained.

What is man, that thou art | mindful of | him ‖ and the son of man, | that thou | visitest | him?

Thou madest him lower | than the | angels ‖ to crown him with | glo - | ry and | worship.

Thou makest him to have dominion of the works | of thy | hands ‖ and thou hast put all things in sub | jection | under his | feet;

All | sheep and | oxen ‖ yea, and the | beasts - | of the | field;

The fowls of the air, and the fishes | of the | sea ‖ and whatsoever walketh | through the | paths of the | seas.

O | Lord, our | Governor, how excellent is thy | Name in | all the | world!

From Psalm xxxiii.—*Exultate, justi.*

REJOICE in the Lord, | O ye | righteous ‖ for it becometh well the | just - | to be | thankful.

Praise the | Lord with | harp ‖ sing praises

unto him with the lute, and | instrument | of ten | strings.

Sing unto the Lord a | new - | song || sing praises unto him | with a | good - | courage.

For the word of the | Lord is | true || and | all his | works are | faithful.

He loveth righteousness | and - | judgment || the earth is full of the | goodness | of the | Lord.

By the word of the Lord were the | heavens | made || and all the hosts of them | by the breath of | his | mouth.

He gathereth the waters of the seas together, as it were up | on an | heap || and layeth up the deep, as | in a | treasure | house.

Let all the earth | fear the | Lord || stand in awe of him, all | ye that | dwell in the | world.

For he spake, and | it was | done || he commanded, | and - | it stood | fast.

From Psalm cxlvii.—*Laudate Dominum.*

O PRAISE the Lord, for it is a good thing to sing praises un | to our | God || yea, a joyful and pleasant | thing it | is to be | thankful.

The Lord doth build | up Je | rusalem || and gather together the | out - | casts of | Israel.

He healeth those that are | broken in | heart || and giveth medicine to | heal - | their - | sickness.

He telleth the number | of the | stars || and calleth them | all - | by their | names.

Great is our Lord, and | great is his | power | yea, and his | wisdom | is - | infinite.

The Lord setteth | up the | meek || and bringeth the ungodly | down - | to the | ground.

SELECTIONS OF PSALMS. [SEL. 9

O sing unto the | LORD with | thanksgiving ‖ sing praises upon the | harp un | to our | God;

Who covereth the heaven with clouds, and prepareth rain | for the | earth ‖ and maketh the grass to grow upon the mountains, and | herb for the | use of | men;

Who giveth fodder un | to the | cattle ‖ and feedeth the young | ravens that | call up | on him.

The LORD's delight is in | them that | fear him ‖ and put their | trust - | in his | mercy.

Praise the LORD, | O Je | rusalem ‖ praise thy | God, - | O - | Sion.

For he hath made fast the | bars of thy | gates ‖ and hath | blessed thy | children with | in thee.

He maketh peace | in thy | borders ‖ and filleth thee | with the | flour of | wheat.

He sendeth forth his commandment up | on - | earth ‖ and his word | runneth | very | swiftly.

He giveth | snow like | wool ‖ and scattereth the | hoar-frost | like - | ashes.

He casteth forth his | ice like | morsels ‖ who is able | to a | bide his | frost?

He sendeth out his word, and | melteth | them ‖ he bloweth with his wind, | and the | waters | flow.

He showeth his word | unto | Jacob ‖ his statutes and ordinances | unto | Isra | el.

He hath not dealt so with | any | nation ‖ neither have the heathen | knowledge | of his | laws.

From Psalm lvii.—*Miserere mei, Deus.*

SET up thyself, O God, a | bove the | heavens ‖ and thy | glory a | bove all the | earth.

My heart is fixed, O God, my | heart is | fixed ‖ I will | sing and | give - | praise.

Awake up, my glory; awake | lute and | harp ‖ I myself | will a | wake right | early.

I will give thanks unto thee, O Lord, a | mong the | people ‖ and I will sing unto | thee a | mong the | nations.

For the greatness of thy mercy reacheth | un- to the | heavens ‖ and thy | truth un | to the | clouds.

Set up thyself, O God, a | bove the | heavens ‖ and thy | glory a | bove all the | earth.

Selection Tenth

From Psalm xcvi.—*Cantate Domino.*

O SING unto the Lord a | new - | song ‖ sing unto the Lord, | all the | whole - | earth.

Sing unto the Lord, and | praise his | Name ‖ be telling of his sal | vation from | day to | day.

Declare his honour un | to the | heathen ‖ and his wonders | unto | all - | people.

For the Lord is great, and cannot worthily | be - | praised ‖ he is more to be | feared than | all - | gods.

Psalm cxlviii.—*Laudate Dominum.*

O PRAISE the | Lord of | heaven ‖ praise | - him | in the | height.

Praise him, all ye | angels of | his || praise | - him, | all his | hosts.

Praise him, | sun and | moon || praise him, | all ye | stars and | light.

Praise him, | all ye | heavens || and ye waters that | are a | bove the | heavens.

Let them praise the | Name of the | Lord || for he spake the word, and they were made; he commanded, | and they | were cre | ated.

He hath made them fast for | ever and | ever || he hath given them a law | which shall | not be | broken.

Praise the | Lord upon | earth || ye | dragons, | and all | deeps:

Fire and hail, | snow and | vapours || wind and | storm, ful | filling his | word:

Mountains | and all | hills || fruitful | trees and | all - | cedars.

Beasts | and all | cattle || worms | and - | feathered | fowls:

Kings of the earth | and all | people || princes and all | judges | of the | world:

Young men and maidens, old men and children, praise the | Name of the | Lord || for his Name only is excellent, and his praise a | bove - | heaven and | earth.

He shall exalt the horn of his people: all his | saints shall | praise him || even the children of Israel, even the | people that | serveth | him.

FROM PSALM cxlix.—*Cantate Domino.*

O SING unto the Lord a | new - | song || let the congre | gation of | saints - | praise him.

Let Israel rejoice in | him that | made him ‖ and let the children of Sion be | joyful | in their | King.

Let them praise his | Name in the | dance | let them sing praises unto | him with | tabret and | harp.

For the LORD hath pleasure | in his | people ‖ and | helpeth | the meek | hearted.

Psalm cl.—*Laudate Dominum.*

O PRAISE God | in his | holiness ‖ praise him in the | firmament | of his | power.

Praise him in his | noble | acts ‖ praise him according | to his | excellent | greatness.

Praise him in the | sound of the | trumpet ‖ praise him up | on the | lute and | harp.

Praise him in the | cymbals and | dances ‖ praise him up | on the | strings and | pipe.

Praise him upon the | well-tuned | cymbals ‖ praise him up | on the | loud - | cymbals.

Let every thing | that hath | breath ‖ praise | - - | -the | LORD.

SELECTIONS OF PSALMS

FOR HOLY DAYS, ETC.

Christmas=Day.

FROM PSALMS xlv. lxxxix. cx.

THY seat, O God, en | dureth for | ever ‖ the sceptre of thy kingdom | is a | right - | sceptre.

Thou hast loved righteousness, and | hated in | iquity ‖ wherefore God, even thy God, hath anointed thee with the oil of | gladness a | bove thy | fellows.

My song shall be alway of the loving-kindness | of the | LORD ‖ with my mouth will I ever be showing thy truth from one gener | ation | to an | other.

For I have said, Mercy shall be set | up for | ever ‖ thy truth shalt thou | stablish | in the | heavens.

The LORD is | our de | fence ‖ the Holy One of | Israel | is our | King.

Thou spakest sometime in visions unto thy | saints, and | saidst ‖ I have laid help upon One that is mighty, I have exalted One | chosen out | of the | people.

I will set his dominion | in the | sea ‖ and his | right hand | in the | floods.

And I will make | him my | First-born ‖ higher than the | kings - | of the | earth.

The LORD said un | to my | Lord ‖ Sit thou on my right hand until I make thine | enemies | thy - | footstool.

The LORD shall send the rod of thy power | out of | Sion ‖ be thou ruler, even in the | midst a | mong thine | enemies.

In the day of thy power shall the people offer thee free-will offerings with an | holy | worship | the dew of thy birth is | of the womb | of the | morning.

The LORD sware, and will | not re | pent ‖ Thou art a Priest for ever, after the | order | of Mel | chizedech.

Ash-Wednesday.

FROM PSALMS xxxii. xxxviii. cxxx.

BLESSED is he whose unrighteousness | is for | given ‖ and | whose - | sin is | covered.

Blessed is the man unto whom the LORD im | puteth no | sin ‖ and in whose | spirit there | is no | guile.

Put me not to rebuke, O LORD, | in thine | anger ‖ neither chasten me in thy | hea - | vy dis | pleasure:

For thine arrows stick | fast in | me ‖ and thy | hand - | presseth me | sore.

My wickednesses are gone | over my | head |

FOR HOLY DAYS.

and are like a sore burden, too | heavy for | me to | bear.

I will con | fess my | wickedness ‖ and be | sorry | for my | sin.

Haste | thee to | help me ‖ O Lord | God of | my sal | vation.

Out of the deep have I called unto | thee, O | Lord ‖ Lord, | hear - | my - | voice.

Let thine ears | be at | tentive ‖ to the voice | of my | suppli | cations.

If thou, Lord, shouldest be extreme to mark what is | done a | miss ‖ O | Lord, - | who shall | stand?

But there is for | giveness with | thee ‖ that | thou - | mayest be | feared.

Good Friday.
From Psalms xxii. lxix. xl.

MY God! my God! look upon me; why hast thou for | saken | me ‖ and art so far from my health, and from the | words of | my com | plaint?

But | thou art | holy ‖ O Thou that inhabitest the | praises of | Isra | el.

I am a worm, and | no - | man ‖ a reproach of men, and des | pised | of the | people.

All they that see me | laugh me to | scorn ‖ they shoot out the lip, they | shake the | head, - | saying,

He trusted in God, that he | would de | liver him ‖ let him deliver him, | if - | he will - | have him.

SELECTIONS OF PSALMS

The counsel of the wicked layeth | siege a | gainst me || they pierced my | hands - | and my | feet.

They part my | garments a | mong them || and cast | lots up | on my | vesture.

But be not thou far from | me. O | Lord || O my strength, | haste - | thee to | help me.

Thy rebuke hath broken my heart; I am | full of | heaviness || I looked for some to have pity on me, but there was no man, neither found I | any to | comfort | me.

They gave me | gall to | eat || and when I was thirsty they gave me | vinegar | to - | drink.

Sacrifice and meat-offering thou | wouldest | not || but mine | ears - | hast thou | opened.

Burnt-offerings and sacrifices for sin hast thou | not re | quired || then said I, | Lo, - | I - | come;

In the volume of the book it is written of me, that I should fulfil thy will, | O my | God || I am content to do it; yea, thy Law | is with | in my | heart.

Easter Day.

Instead of the "Venite, exultemus Domino."

CHRIST our Passover is | sacrificed | for us || therefore | let us | keep the | feast:

Not with the old leaven, neither with the leaven of | malice and | wickedness || but with the unleavened bread of sin | ceri | ty and | truth.

FOR HOLY DAYS.

CHRIST being raised from the dead, | dieth no | more || death hath no more do | minion | over | him.

For in that he died, he died unto | sin - | once || but in that he liveth, he | liveth | unto | God.

Likewise reckon ye also yourselves to be dead indeed | unto | sin || but alive unto God through | Jesus | Christ our | Lord.

CHRIST is risen | from the | dead || and become the first | fruits of | them that | slept.

For since by | man came | death || by man came also the resur | rection | of the | dead.

For as in Adam | all - | die || even so in Christ shall | all be | made a | live.

Glory be to the Father, | and to the | Son || and | to the | Holy | Ghost;

As it was in the beginning, is now, and | ever shall | be || world without | end. - | A - | men.

Ascension Day.

FROM PSALMS xxiv. xlvii.

LIFT up your heads, O ye gates; and be ye lift up, ye ever | lasting | doors || and the King of | glory | shall come | in.

Who is the | King of | glory || The LORD strong and mighty; even the | LORD - | mighty in | battle.

Lift up your heads, O ye gates; and be ye lift up, ye ever | lasting | doors || and the King of | glory | shall come | in.

Who is the | King of | glory || Even the Lord of hosts, | he is the | King of | glory.

O clap your hands together, | all ye | people || shout unto God | with the | voice of | triumph.

For the L rd most | high is | terrible || he is a great King | over | all the | earth.

God is gone up | with a | shout || the Lord | with the | sound of a | trumpet.

Sing praises to God, | sing - | praises || sing praises unto our | King, - | sing - | praises.

God reigneth | over the | heathen || God sitteth upon the | throne - | of his | holiness.

The princes of the people are gathered together, even the people of the | God of | Abraham || for the shields of the earth belong unto God : | he is | greatly ex | alted.

Whit=Sunday.

From Psalms ii. lxviii.

I WILL declare the decree : the Lord hath said | unto | me || Thou art my Son, this day have | I be | gotten | thee.

Desire of me, and I shall give thee the heathen for | thine in | heritance || and the utmost parts of the | earth for | thy pos | session.

Be wise now, therefore, | O ye | kings || be instructed, ye | judges | of the | earth.

Serve the | Lord with | fear || and re | joice - | with - | trembling.

Sing unto God, sing praises | to his | Name || extol him that rideth upon the heavens by his name JAH, | and re | joice be | fore him.

53

FOR HOLY DAYS.

Thou, O God, sentest a gracious rain upon | thine in | heritance ‖ and refreshedst it | when - | it was | weary.

The Lord | gave the | word ‖ great was the company | of - | those that | published it.

Though ye have lain among the pots, yet shall ye be as the wings | of a | dove ‖ covered with silver, and her | feathers with | yellow | gold.

Thou hast ascended on high; thou hast led captivity captive; thou hast received | gifts for | men ‖ yea, for the rebellious also, that the Lord | God might | dwell a | mong them.

Blessed be the Lord, who daily loadeth | us with | benefits ‖ even the | God of | our sal | vation.

Sing unto God, ye kingdoms | of the | earth ‖ O sing | praises | unto the | Lord:

To him that rideth upon the heaven of heavens, which | were of | old ‖ lo, he doth send out his voice, and | that a | mighty | voice.

Ascribe ye strength | unto | God ‖ his excellency is over Israel, and his | strength is | in the | clouds.

O God, thou art terrible out of thy | holy | places ‖ the God of Israel is he that giveth strength and power unto his people. | Bless - | ed be | God.

Thanksgiving Day.

PRAISE ye the Lord; for it is good to sing praises un | to our | God ‖ for it is pleasant, and | praise is | comely.

SELECTIONS OF PSALMS.

The Lord doth build | up Je | rusalem ‖ he gathereth together the | out - | casts of | Israel.

He healeth those that are | broken in | heart ‖ and | bindeth | up their | wounds.

He covereth the heaven with clouds, and prepareth rain | for the | earth ‖ he maketh the grass to | grow up | on the | mountains.

He giveth to the | beast his | food ‖ and to the | young - | ravens which | cry.

Praise the Lord, | O Je | rusalem ‖ praise thy God, - | O - | Sion.

For he hath strengthened the bars | of thy | gates ‖ he hath blessed thy | children | within | thee.

He maketh peace | in thy | borders ‖ and filleth thee | with the | finest | of the | wheat.

Glory be to the Father, | and to the | Son ‖ and | to the | Holy Ghost;

As it was in the beginning, is now, and | ever shall | be ‖ world without | end. - | A - | men.

Institution of Ministers.

Laudate nomen.

O PRAISE the Lord, laud ye the Name | of the | Lord ‖ praise it, O ye | servants | of the | Lord.

Ye that stand in the house | of the | Lord ‖ in the courts of the | house - | of our | God.

O praise the Lord, for the | Lord is gracious ‖ O sing praises unto his Name, | for - | it is | lovely.

FOR OCCASIONAL SERVICES.

The LORD is gracious and | merci | ful ‖ long-suffering, | and of | great - | goodness.

The LORD is loving unto | every | man ‖ and his mercy is | over | all his | works.

All thy works praise | thee, O | LORD ‖ and thy saints give | thanks - | unto | thee.

The LORD doth build | up Je | rusalem ‖ and gather together the | out - | casts of | Israel.

He healeth those that are | broken in | heart ‖ and giveth medicine | to - | heal their | sickness.

The LORD's delight is in | them that | fear him ‖ and put their | trust - | in his | mercy.

Praise the LORD, | O Je | rusalem ‖ praise thy | God, | O - | Sion.

For he hath made fast the bars | of thy | gates ‖ and hath | blessed thy | children with | in thee.

He maketh peace | in thy | borders ‖ and filleth thee | with the | flour of | wheat.

He is our God, even the God of whom | cometh sal | vation ‖ GOD is the Lord, by | whom we es | cape | death.

O God, wonderful art thou in thy | holy | places ‖ even the God of Israel, he will give strength and power unto his people. | Bless - | ed be | God.

Glory be to the Father, | and to the | Son ‖ and | to the | Holy Ghost;

As it was in the beginning, is now, and | ever shall | be ‖ world with | end. - | A - | men.

Burial of the Dead.

LORD, let me know my end, and the number | of my | days ‖ that I may be certified how | long I | have to | live.

Behold, thou hast made my days as it were a span long, and mine age is even as nothing in re | spect of | thee | and verily every man living is | alto | gether | vanity.

For man walketh in a vain shadow, and disquieteth him | self in | vain ‖ he heapeth up riches, and cannot | tell - | who shall | gather them.

And now, Lord, | what is my | hope ‖ Truly my | hope is | even in | thee.

Deliver me from all | mine of | fences ‖ and make me not a re | buke un | to the | foolish.

When thou with rebukes dost chasten man for sin, thou makest his beauty to consume away, like as it were a moth | fretting a | garment ‖ every man | therefore | is but | vanity.

Hear my prayer, O Lord, and with thine ears con | sider my | calling ‖ hold not thy | peace - | at my | tears:

For I am a | stranger | with thee ‖ and a sojourner as | all my | fathers | were.

O spare me a little, that I may re | cover my | strength ‖ before I go hence, | and be | no more | seen.

Lord, thou hast | been our | refuge ‖ from one gener | ation | to an | other.

Before the mountains were brought forth, or ever the earth and the | world were | made ‖ thou art God from everlasting, and | world with | out - | end.

FOR OCCASIONAL SERVICES.

Thou turnest man | to de | struction || again thou sayest, Come a | gain, ye | children of | men

For a thousand years in thy sight are | but as | yesterday || seeing that is past | as a | watch in the | night.

As soon as thou scatterest them they are even | as a | sleep || and fade away | suddenly | like the | grass.

In the morning it is green, and | groweth | up || but in the evening it is cut down, | dried - | up, and | withered.

For we consume away in | thy dis | pleasure || and are afraid at thy | wrathful | indig | nation.

Thou hast set our mis | deeds be | fore thee || and our secret sins in the | light - | of thy | countenance.

For when thou art angry, all our | days are | gone || we bring our years to an end, as it | were a | tale that is | told.

The days of our age are threescore years and ten; and though men be so strong that they come to fourscore years, yet is their strength then but | labour and | sorrow || so soon passeth it a | way, and | we are | gone.

So teach us to | number our | days || that we may apply our | hearts - | unto | wisdom.

Glory be to the Father, | and to the | Son || and | to the | Holy Ghost;

As it was in the beginning, is now, and | ever shall | be || world without | end. - | A - | men.

THE PSALTER, OR
PSALMS OF DAVID.

The First Day.

MORNING PRAYER.

PSALM i. *Beatus vir, qui non abiit.*

BLESSED is the man that hath not walked in the counsel of the ungodly, nor stood in the | way of | sinners || and hath not sat in the | seat - | of the | scornful.

2 But his delight is in the | law of the | LORD || and in his law will he exercise him | self - | day and | night.

3 And he shall be like a tree planted by the | water | side || that will bring forth his | fruit - | in due | season.

4 His leaf also | shall not | wither || and look, whatsoever he | doeth | it shall | prosper.

5 As for the ungodly, it is not | so with | them || but they are like the chaff, which the wind scattereth away | from the | face of the | earth.

6 Therefore the ungodly shall not be able to

stand | in the ' judgment || neither the sinners in the congre | gation | of the | righteous.

7 But the LORD knoweth the way | of the | righteous || and the way of the un | godly | shall - | perish.

PSALM ii. *Quare fremuerunt gentes?*

WHY do the heathen so furiously | rage to | gether || and why do the people im | agine a | vain - | thing?

2 The kings of the earth stand up, and the rulers take | counsel to | gether || against the LORD, and a | gainst - | his A | nointed.

3 Let us break their | bonds a | sunder || and cast a | way their | cords - | from us.

4 He that dwelleth in heaven shall | laugh them to | scorn || the LORD shall | have them | in de | rision.

5 Then shall he speak unto them | in his | wrath || and vex them | in his | sore dis | pleasure.

6 Yet have I | set my | King || upon my | holy | hill of | Sion.

7 I will preach the law, whereof the LORD hath said | unto | me || Thou art my son, this day have | I be | gotten | thee.

8 Desire of me, and I shall give thee the heathen for | thine in | heritance || and the utmost parts of the | earth for | thy pos | session.

9 Thou shalt bruise them with a | rod of | iron || and break them in pieces | like a | potter's | vessel.

10 Be wise now, therefore, | O ye | kings || be learned, ye that are | judges | of the | earth.

11 Serve the | Lord in | fear ‖ and re | joice | unto | him with | reverence.

12 Kiss the Son, lest he be angry, and so ye perish from the | right - | way ‖ if his wrath be kindled, yea but a little. Blessed are all they that | put their | trust in | him.

PSALM iii. *Domine, quid multiplicati?*

LORD, how are they in | creased that | trouble | me ‖ many are | they that | rise a | gainst me.

2 Many one there be that say | of my | soul ‖ There is no help | for him | in his | God.

3 But thou, O Lord, art | my de | fender ‖ thou art my worship, and the lifter | up - | of my | head.

4 I did call upon the Lord | with my | voice ‖ and he heard me out | of his | holy | hill.

5 I laid me down and slept, and rose | up a | gain ‖ for the | Lord sus | tained | me.

6 I will not be afraid for ten thousands | of the | people ‖ that have set themselves a | gainst me | round a | bout.

7 Up, Lord, and help me, | O my | God ‖ For thou smitest all mine enemies upon the cheekbone; thou hast broken the | teeth of | the ungodly.

8 Salvation belongeth un | to the | Lord ‖ and thy blessing | is up | on thy | people.

PSALM iv. *Cum invocarem.*

HEAR me, when I call, O God of my | right- eous | ness ‖ thou hast set me at liberty, when I was in trouble; have mercy upon me, and | hearken un | to my | prayer.

2 O ye sons of men, how long will ye blas | pheme mine | honour || and have such pleasure in vanity, and | seek - | after | falsehood?

3 Know this also, that the Lord hath chosen to himself the man | that is | godly || when I call upon the | Lord - | he will | hear me.

4 Stand in awe, and | sin - | not || commune with your own heart, and in your | chamber, | and be | still.

5 Offer the sacrifice of | righteous | ness || and put your | trust - | in the | Lord.

6 There be | many that | say || Who will | show us | any | good?

7 Lord, | lift thou | up || the light of thy | countenance | up - | on us.

8 Thou hast put gladness | in my | heart || since the time that their corn, and | wine, and | oil in | creased.

9 I will lay me down in peace, and | take my | rest || for it is thou, Lord, only that | makest me | dwell in | safety.

PSALM v.—*Verba mea auribus.*

PONDER my | word, O | Lord || con | sider my | medi | tation.

2 O hearken thou unto the voice of my calling, my King | and my | God || for unto thee | will I | make my | prayer.

3 My voice shalt thou hear be | times, O | Lord || early in the morning will I direct my prayer unto | thee, and | will look | up.

4 For thou art the God that hast no | pleasure in | wickedness ‖ neither shall any | evil | dwell with | thee.

5 Such as be foolish shall not stand | in thy | sight ‖ for thou hatest all | them that | work - | vanity.

6 Thou shalt destroy them | that speak | lies ‖ the LORD will abhor both the blood-thirsty | and de | ceitful | man.

7 But as for me, I will come into thine house, even upon the multitude | of thy | mercy ‖ and in thy fear will I worship to | ward thy | holy | temple.

8 Lead me, O LORD, in thy righteousness, because | of mine | enemies ‖ make thy way | plain be | fore my | face.

9 For there is no faithfulness | in his | mouth ‖ their inward | parts are | very | wickedness.

10 Their throat is an | open | sepulchre ‖ they | flatter | with their | tongue.

11 Destroy thou them, O God; let them perish through their own im | agi | nations ‖ cast them out in the multitude of their ungodliness; for they | have re | belled a | gainst thee.

12 And let all them that put their trust in | thee re | joice ‖ they shall ever be giving of thanks, because thou defendest them; they that love thy Name shall be | joy - | ful in | thee;

13 For thou, LORD, wilt give thy blessing un | to the | righteous ‖ and with thy favourable kind ness wilt thou defend | him, as | with a | shield.

EVENING PRAYER.

Psalm vi. *Domine, ne in furore.*

O LORD, rebuke me not in thine | indig | na-tion ‖ neither chasten | me in | thy dis-pleasure.

2 Have mercy upon me, O Lord, for | I am | weak ‖ O Lord, heal me, | for my | bones are | vexed.

3 My soul also is | sore - | troubled ‖ but, Lord, how long | wilt thou | punish | me?

4 Turn thee, O Lord, and de | liver my | soul ‖ O save me, | for thy | mercy's | sake.

5 For in death no man re | membereth | thee ‖ and who will give thee | thanks - | in the | pit?

6 I am weary of my groaning; every night wash | I my | bed ‖ and water my | couch - | with my | tears.

7 My beauty is gone for | very | trouble ‖ and worn away be | cause of | all mine | enemies.

8 Away from me all ye | that work | vanity ‖ for the Lord hath heard the | voice - | of my | weeping.

9 The Lord hath heard | my pe | tition ‖ the Lord | will re | ceive my | prayer.

10 All mine enemies shall be confounded, and | sore - | vexed ‖ they shall be turned back, and | put to | shame - | suddenly.

Psalm vii. *Domine, Deus meus.*

O LORD, my God, in thee have I | put my | trust ‖ save me from all them that persecute me, | and de | liver | me;

2 Lest he devour my soul like a lion, and | tear it in | pieces ‖ while | there is | none to | help.

3 O Lord my God, if I have done | any such | thing ‖ or if there be any | wickedness | in my | hands:
4 If I have rewarded evil unto him that dealt | friendly | with me ‖ yea, I have delivered him that without any | cause - | is mine | enemy:
5 Then let mine enemy persecute my | soul, and | take me ‖ yea, let him tread my life down upon the earth, and lay mine | honour | in the | dust.
6 Stand up, O Lord, in thy wrath, and lift up thyself, because of the indignation | of mine | enemies ‖ arise up for me in the judgment | that thou | hast com | manded.
7 And so shall the congregation of the people | come a | bout thee ‖ for their sakes therefore lift | up thy | self a | gain.
8 The Lord shall judge the people; give sentence with me, | O - | Lord ‖ according to my righteousness, and according to the innocency | that is | in - | me.
9 O let the wickedness of the ungodly | come to an | end ‖ but | guide - | thou the | just.
10 For the | righteous | God ‖ trieth the | very | hearts and | reins.
11 My help | cometh of | God ‖ who preserveth them | that are | true of | heart.
12 God is a righteous judge, | strong, and | patient ‖ and God is pro | voked | every | day.
13 If a man will not turn, he will | whet his | sword ‖ he hath bent his | bow, and | made it | ready.
14 He hath prepared for him the instruments |

of - | death ‖ he ordaineth his | arrows a | gainst the | persecutors.

15 Behold, he | travaileth with | mischief ‖ he hath conceived sorrow, and | brought - | forth un | godliness.

16 He hath graven and digged | up a | pit ‖ and is fallen himself into the destruction | that he | made for | other.

17 For his travail shall come upon his | own - | head | and his wickedness shall | fall on | his own | pate.

18 I will give thanks unto the LORD, according | to his righteous | ness ‖ and I will praise the Name | of the | LORD most | high.

PSALM viii. *Domine, Dominus noster.*

O LORD, our Governor, how excellent is thy Name in | all the | world ‖ thou that hast set thy | glory a | bove the | heavens!

2 Out of the mouth of very babes and sucklings, hast thou ordained strength, because | of thine | enemies ‖ that thou mightest still the enemy | and - | the a | venger.

3 For I will consider thy heavens, even the works | of thy | fingers ‖ the moon and the stars | which thou | hast or | dained.

4 What is man, that thou art | mindful of | him ‖ and the son of man, | that thou | visitest | him?

5 Thou madest him lower | than the | angels ‖ to crown him with | glo - | ry and | worship.

6 Thou makest him to have dominion of the works | of thy | hands ‖ and thou hast put all things in sub | jection | under his | feet:

7 All | sheep and | oxen ‖ yea, and the | beasts - | of the | field;

8 The fowls of the air, and the fishes | of the | sea ‖ and whatsoever walketh | through the | paths of the | seas.

9 O | Lord, our | Governor, how excellent is thy | Name in | all the | world!

The Second Day.
MORNING PRAYER.
PSALM ix. *Confitebor tibi.*

I WILL give thanks unto thee, O Lord, with my | whole - | heart ‖ I will speak of | all thy | marvellous | works.

2 I will be glad and re | joice in | thee ‖ yea, my songs will I make of thy | Name, O | thou, Most | Highest.

3 While mine enemies are | driven | back ‖ they shall fall and | perish | at thy | presence.

4 For thou hast maintained my right | and my | cause ‖ thou art set in the | throne that | judgest | right.

5 Thou hast rebuked the heathen, and de | stroyed the un | godly ‖ thou hast put out their | name for | ever and | ever.

6 O thou enemy, destructions are come to a per | petual | end ‖ even as the cities which thou hast destroyed, their me | morial is | perished | with them.

7 But the Lord shall en ‖ dure for | ever ‖ he hath also pre | pared his | seat for | judgment.

8 For he shall judge the | world in | righteous-

ness || and minister true | judgment | unto the | people.

9 The LORD also will be a defence | for the op | pressed || even a refuge in | due - | time of | trouble.

10 And they that know thy Name will put their | trust in | thee || for thou, LORD, hast never | failed | them that | seek thee.

11 O praise the LORD which | dwelleth in | Sion || show the | people | of his | doings.

12 For when he maketh inquisition for blood, he re | membereth | them || and forgetteth not the com | plaint - | of the | poor.

13 Have mercy upon me, O LORD; consider the trouble which I suffer of | them that | hate me || thou that liftest me up | from the | gates of | death;

14 That I may show all thy praises within the ports of the | daughter of | Sion || I will re | joice in | thy sal | vation.

15 The heathen are sunk down in the pit | that they | made || in the same net which they hid privily, | is their | foot - | taken.

16 The LORD is known to | execute | judgment || the ungodly is trapped in the | work of | his own | hands.

17 The wicked shall be turned | into | hell || and all the people | that for | get - | God.

18 For the poor shall not alway | be for | gotten || the patient abiding of the meek | shall not | perish for | ever.

19 Up, LORD, and let not man have the | upper | hand || let the heathen be | judged | in thy | sight.

20 Put them in | fear, O | Lord || that the heathen may know them | selves to | be but | men.

Psalm x. *Ut quid, Domine?*

WHY standest thou so far | off, O | Lord || and hidest thy face in the | needful | time of | trouble?

2 The ungodly, for his own lust, doth | persecute the | poor || let them be taken in the crafty wiliness | that they | have im | agined.

3 For the ungodly hath made boast of his own heart's de | sire || and speaketh good of the covetous, | whom - | God ab | horreth.

4 The ungodly is so proud, that he careth | not for | God || neither is | God in | all his | thoughts.

5 His ways are | alway | grievous || thy judgments are far above out of his sight, and therefore de | fieth he | all his | enemies.

6 For he hath said in his heart, Tush! I shall never | be cast | down || there shall no harm | happen | unto | me.

7 His mouth is full of cursing, de | ceit, and | fraud || under his tongue is un | godli | ness and | vanity.

8 He sitteth lurking in the thievish corners | of the | streets || and privily in his lurking dens doth he murder the innocent; his eyes are | set a | gainst the | poor.

9 For he lieth waiting secretly; even as a lion lurketh he | in his | den || that | he may | ravish the | poor.

10 He doth | ravish the | poor || when he getteth | him in | to his | net.

11 He falleth down, and | humbleth him | self ‖ that the congregation of the poor may fall into the | hands - | of his | captains.

12 He hath said in his heart, Tush! God | hath for | gotten ‖ he hideth away his face, and | he will | never | see it.

13 Arise, O Lord God, and lift | up thine | hand ‖ for | get - | not the | poor.

14 Wherefore should the wicked | blaspheme | God ‖ while he doth say in his heart, Tush! | thou God | carest not | for it.

15 Surely | thou hast | seen it ‖ for thou beholdest un | godli | ness and | wrong.

16 That thou mayest take the matter in | to thy | hand ‖ the poor committeth himself unto thee; for thou art the | helper | of the | friendless.

17 Break thou the power of the ungodly | and ma | licious ‖ take away his ungodliness, and | thou shalt | find - | none.

18 The Lord is King for | ever and | ever ‖ and the heathen are perished | out - | of the | land.

19 Lord, thou hast heard the desire | of the | poor ‖ thou preparest their heart, and thine | ear - | hearkeneth | thereto:

20 To help the fatherless and poor un | to their | right ‖ that the man of the earth be no | more ex | alted a | gainst them.

Psalm xi. *In Domino confido.*

IN the Lord put | I my | trust ‖ how say ye then to my soul, that she should flee as a | bird un | to the | hill.

2 For lo, the ungodly bend their bow, and make ready their arrows with | in the | quiver ‖ that they may privily shoot at them | which are | true of | heart.

3 For the foundations will | be cast | down | and what | hath the | righteous | done?

4 The Lord is in his | holy | temple ‖ the Lord's | seat - | is in | heaven.

5 His eyes con | sider the | poor ‖ and his eyelids | try the | children of | men.

6 The Lord al | loweth the | righteous ‖ but the ungodly, and him that delighteth in wickedness, | doth his | soul ab | hor.

7 Upon the ungodly he shall rain snares, fire and brimstone, storm and | tempest ‖ this shall | be their | portion to | drink.

8 For the righteous Lord | loveth | righteousness ‖ his countenance will be | hold the | thing that is | just.

EVENING PRAYER.

Psalm xii. *Salvum me fac.*

HELP me, Lord, for there is not one | godly man | left ‖ for the faithful are minished from a | mong the | children of | men.

2 They talk of vanity every one | with his | neighbour ‖ they do but flatter with their lips, and dissemble | in their | double | heart.

3 The Lord shall root out all de | ceitful | lips ‖ and the tongue that | speaketh | proud - | things:

4 Which have said, With our tongue will | we pre | vail || we are they that ought to speak: who is | lord - | over | us?

5 Now for the comfortless troubles' sake | of the | needy || and because of the deep | sighing | of the | poor.

6 I will up, | saith the | Lord || and will help every one from him that swelleth against him, | and will | set him at | rest.

7 The words of the Lord are | pure - | words || even as the silver which from the earth is tried, and purified | seven times | in the | fire.

8 Thou shalt keep them, | O - | Lord || thou shalt preserve him from this | gener | ation for | ever.

9 The ungodly walk on | every | side || when they are exalted, the children of | men are | put to re | buke.

Psalm xiii. *Usque quo, Domine?*

HOW long wilt thou forget me, O Lord; for - | ever || how long | wilt thou | hide thy | face - | from me?

2 How long shall I seek counsel in my soul, and be so vexed | in my | heart || how long shall mine | enemies | triumph | over me?

3 Consider, and hear me, O | Lord my | God || lighten my eyes, that I | sleep - | not in | death;

4 Lest mine enemy say, I have pre | vailed a | gainst him || for if I be cast down, they | that | trouble me | will re | joice at it.

5 But my trust is | in thy | mercy || and my heart is | joyful in | thy sal | vation.

[Evening.] THE PSALTER. [Day 2.

6 I will sing of the Lord, because he hath dealt so | lovingly | with me ‖ yea, I will praise the Name | of the | Lord most | highest.

Psalm xiv. *Dixit insipiens.*

THE fool hath said | in his | heart ‖ There | is - | no - | God.

2 They are corrupt, and become abominable | in their | doings ‖ there is none that doeth | good, - | no not | one.

3 The Lord looked down from heaven upon the | children of | men ‖ to see if there were any that would understand, and | seek - | after | God:

4 But they are all gone out of the way, they are altogether be | come a | bominable ‖ there is none that doeth | good, - | no not | one.

5 Their throat is an open sepulchre; with their tongues have | they de | ceived ‖ the poison of | asps is | under their | lips.

6 Their mouth is full of | cursing, and | bitterness ‖ their feet are | swift - | to shed | blood.

7 Destruction and unhappiness is in their ways, and the way of peace have they | not | known ‖ there is no fear of | God be | fore their | eyes.

8 Have they no knowledge, that they are all such | workers of | mischief ‖ eating up my people as it were bread, and call | not up | on the | Lord?

9 There were they brought in great fear, even where | no fear | was ‖ for God is in the gener | ation | of the | righteous.

10 As for you, ye have made a mock at the

counsel | of the | poor ‖ because he putteth his | trust - | in the Lord.

11 Who shall give salvation unto Israel out of Sion? When the Lord turneth the captivity | of his | people ‖ then shall Jacob rejoice, and | Israel | shall be | glad.

The Third Day.
MORNING PRAYER.

Psalm xv. *Domine, quis habitabit?*

LORD, who shall dwell | in thy | tabernacle ‖ or who shall rest up | on thy | holy | hill?

2 Even he that leadeth an | uncorrupt | life ‖ and doeth the thing which is right, and speaketh the | truth - | from his | heart.

3 He that hath used no deceit in his tongue, nor done evil | to his | neighbour ‖ and | hath not | slandered his | neighbour.

4 He that setteth not by himself, but is lowly in | his own | eyes ‖ and maketh much of | them that | fear the | Lord.

5 He that sweareth unto his neighbour, and disap | pointeth him | not ‖ though it | were to | his own | hindrance.

6 He that hath not given his money up | on - | usury ‖ nor taken re | ward a | gainst the | innocent.

7 Whoso doeth | these - | things ‖ shall | nev - | er - | fall.

Psalm xvi. *Conserva me, Domine.*

PRESERVE me, | O - | God ‖ for in | thee have I | put my | trust.

2 O my soul thou hast said un | to the | Lord ‖ Thou art my God; my goods are | nothing | unto | thee.

3 All my delight is upon the saints that are | in the | earth ‖ and upon such | as ex | cel in | virtue.

4 But they that run after an | other | god ‖ shall | have - | great - | trouble.

5 Their drink-offerings of blood | will I not | offer ‖ neither make mention of their | names with | in my | lips.

6 The Lord himself is the portion of mine inheritance, and | of my | cup ‖ thou shalt main | tain - | my - | lot.

7 The lot is fallen unto me in a | fair - | ground ‖ yea, I have a | goodly | herit | age.

8 I will thank the Lord for | giving me | warning ‖ my reins also chasten me | in the | night - | season.

9 I have set God | always be | fore me | for he is on my right hand, | therefore I | shall not | fall.

10 Wherefore my heart was glad, and my | glory re | joiced ‖ my flesh also | shall - | rest in | hope.

11 For why? thou shalt not leave my | soul in | hell ‖ neither shalt thou suffer thy | Holy One to | see cor | ruption.

12 Thou shalt show me the path of life: in thy presence is the | fulness of | joy ‖ and at thy right hand there is | pleasure for | ever | more.

Psalm xvii. *Exaudi, Domine.*

HEAR the right, O Lord, consider | my com | plaint ‖ and hearken unto my prayer that goeth not | out of | feigned | lips.

2 Let my sentence come forth | from thy | presence || and let thine eyes look up | on the | thing that is | equal.

3 Thou hast proved and visited mine heart in the night-season; thou hast tried me, and shalt find no | wickedness | in me || for I am utterly purposed that my | mouth shall | not of | fend.

4 Because of men's works that are done against the words | of thy | lips || I have kept me from the | ways of | the de | stroyer.

5 O hold thou up my goings | in thy | paths || that my | footsteps | slip - | not.

6 I have called upon thee, O God, for | thou shalt | hear me || incline thine ear to me, and | hearken un | to my | words.

7 Show thy marvellous loving-kindness, thou that art the Saviour of them which put their | trust in | thee || from such as re | sist thy | right - | hand.

8 Keep me as the apple | of an | eye || hide me under the | shadow | of thy | wings.

9 From the un | godly, that trouble | me || mine enemies encompass me around about, to | take a | way my | soul.

10 They are inclosed in | their own | fat || and their mouth | speaketh | proud - | things.

11 They lie waiting in our way on | every | side || turning their eyes | down - | to the | ground :

12 Like as a lion that is greedy | of his | prey || and as it were a lion's whelp | lurking in | se- cret | places.

13 Up, Lord, disappoint him, and cast him |

EVENING.] THE PSALTER. [DAY 3.

down || deliver my soul from the ungodly, which | is a | sword of | thine.

14 From the men of thy hand, O LORD, from the men, I say, and from the | evil | world || which have their portions in this life, whose bellies thou | fillest with | thy hid | treasure.

15 They have children at | their de | sire || and leave the rest of their | substance | for their | babes.

16 But as for me, I will behold thy | presence in | righteousness || and when I awake up after thy likeness, I | shall be | satisfied | with it.

EVENING PRAYER.

PSALM xviii. *Diligam te, Domine.*

I WILL love thee, O LORD, my strength. The LORD is my stony rock, and | my de | fence || my Saviour; my God, and my might, in whom I will trust; my buckler, the horn also of my sal | vation, | and my | refuge.

2 I will call upon the LORD, which is worthy | to be | praised || so shall I be | safe - | from mine | enemies.

3 The sorrows of death | compassed | me || and the overflowings of ungodliness | made - | me a | fraid.

4 The pains of hell | came a | bout me || the snares of | death - | over | took me.

5 In my trouble I will call up | on the | LORD || and com | plain un | to my | God:

6 So shall he hear my voice out of his | holy |

temple || and my complaint shall come before him; it shall enter | even | into his | ears.

7 The earth | trembled and | quaked || the very foundations also of the hills shook, and were re-moved, be | cause - | he was | wroth.

8 There went a smoke out | in his | presence || and a consuming fire out of his mouth, so that | coals were | kindled | at it.

9 He bowed the heavens also, | and came | down || and it was | dark - | under his | feet.

10 He rode upon the cherubim, | and did | fly || he came flying upon the | wings - | of the | wind.

11 He made darkness his | secret | place || his pavilion round about him with dark water, and thick | clouds to | cover | him.

12 At the brightness of his presence his | clouds re | moved || hailstones | and - | coals of | fire.

13 The Lord also thundered out of heaven, and the Highest | gave his | thunder || hailstones | and - | coals of | fire.

14 He sent out his | arrows, and | scattered them || he cast forth | lightnings, | and de | stroyed them.

15 The springs of waters were seen, and the foundations of the round world were discovered at thy | chiding, O | Lord || at the blasting of the | breath of | thy dis | pleasure.

16 He shall send down from on | high to | fetch me || and shall take me | out of | many | waters.

17 He shall deliver me from my strongest enemy, and from | them which | hate me || for they | are too | mighty | for me.

[EVENING.] THE PSALTER. [DAY 3.

18 They prevented me in the day | of my | trouble || but the | LORD was | my up | holder.
19 He brought me forth also into a | place of | liberty || he brought me forth, even because he had a | favour | unto | me.
20 The LORD shall reward me after my | right- eous | dealing || according to the cleanness of my hands | shall he | recom | pense me.
21 Because I have kept the ways | of the | LORD || and have not forsaken my God, | as the | wicked | doth.
22 For I have an eye unto | all his | laws || and will not cast out | his com | mandments | from me.
23 I was also uncor | rupt be | fore him || and es | chewed | my own | wickedness.
24 Therefore shall the LORD reward me after my | righteous | dealing || and according unto the cleanness of my | hands - | in his | eyesight.
25 With the holy thou | shalt be | holy || and with a perfect man | thou - | shalt be | perfect.
26 With the clean thou | shalt be | clean || and with the | froward thou | shalt learn | froward- ness.
27 For thou shalt save the people that are | in ad | versity || and shalt bring down the | high looks | of the | proud.
28 Thou also shalt | light my | candle || the LORD my God shalt make my | darkness | to be | light.
29 For in thee I shall discomfit an | host of | men || and with the help of my God I shall leap - | over the | wall.

30 The way of God is an unde | filed | way ‖ the word of the Lord also is tried in the fire : he is the defender of all them that | put their | trust in | him.

31 For who is God, | but the | Lord ‖ or who hath any | strength, ex | cept our | God?

32 It is God that girdeth me with | strength of | war ‖ and | maketh | my way | perfect.

33 He maketh my | feet like | hart's feet ‖ and | setteth me | upon | high.

34 He teacheth mine | hands to | fight ‖ and mine arms shall break | even a | bow of | steel.

35 Thou hast given me the defence of | thy sal | vation ‖ thy right hand also shall hold me up, and thy loving cor | rection shall | make me | great.

36 Thou shalt make room enough under me | for to | go ‖ that my | footsteps | shall not | slide.

37 I will follow upon mine enemies, and | over | take them ‖ neither will I turn again | till I | have de | stroyed them.

38 I will smite them, that they shall not be | able to | stand ‖ but | fall - | under my | feet.

39 Thou hast girded me with strength un | to the | battle ‖ thou shalt throw down mine | enemies | under | me.

40 Thou hast made mine enemies also to turn their | backs up | on me ‖ and I shall de | stroy - | them that | hate me.

41 They shall cry, but there shall be | none to | help them ‖ yea, even unto the Lord shall they cry, | but he | shall not | hear them.

42 I will beat them as small as the dust be |

fore the | wind || I will cast them out as the | clay - | in the | streets.

43 Thou shalt deliver me from the strivings of the | people || and thou shalt make me the | head - | of the | heathen.

44 A people whom I | have not | known || shall | serve - | - - | me.

45 As soon as they hear of me, they | shall o | bey me || but the strange children | shall dis | semble | with me.

46 The strange | children shall | fail || and be a | fraid out | of their | prisons.

47 The Lord liveth, and blessed be | my strong | helper || and praised be the | God of | my sal | vation :

48 Even the God that seeth that I | be a | venged || and subdueth the | people | unto | me.

49 It is he that delivereth me from my cruel enemies, and setteth me up a | bove mine | adversaries || thou shalt rid me | from the | wicked | man.

50 For this cause will I give thanks unto thee, O Lord, a | mong the | Gentiles || and sing | praises | unto thy | Name.

51 Great prosperity giveth he un | to his | King || and showeth loving-kindness unto David, his Anointed, and unto his | seed for | ever | more.

The Fourth Day.
MORNING PRAYER.
Psalm xix. *Cœli enarrant.*

THE heavens declare the | glory of | God || and the firmament | showeth his | handy | work.

2 One day | telleth an | other ‖ and one night | certi | fieth an | other.

3 There is neither | speech nor | language ‖ but their | voices are | heard a | mong them.

4 Their sound is gone out into | all - | lands ‖ and their words into the | ends - | of the | world.

5 In them hath he set a tabernacle | for the | sun ‖ which cometh forth as a bridegroom out of his chamber, and rejoiceth as a | giant to | run his | course.

6 It goeth forth from the uttermost parts of the heaven, and runneth about unto the end of | it a | gain ‖ and there is nothing | hid from the | heat there | of.

7 The law of the LORD is an undefiled law, con | verting the | soul ‖ the testimony of the Lord is sure, and giveth | wisdom | unto the | simple.

8 The statutes of the LORD are right, and re | joice the | heart ‖ the commandment of the LORD is pure, and giveth | light un | to the | eyes.

9 The fear of the LORD is clean, and en | dureth for | ever ‖ the judgments of the LORD are true, and | righteous | alto | gether.

10 More to be desired are they than gold, yea, than | much fine | gold ‖ sweeter also than honey, | and the | honey | comb.

11 Moreover, by them is thy | servant | taught ‖ and in keeping of them | there is | great re | ward.

12 Who can tell how | oft he of | fendeth ‖ O cleanse thou me | from my | secret | faults.

13 Keep thy servant also from presumptuous sins, lest they get the dominion | over | me ‖ so

shall I be undefiled, and innocent | from the | great of | fence.

14 Let the words of my mouth, and the meditation | of my | heart ‖ be always ac | ceptable | in thy | sight.

15 O | -- | Lord ‖ my | strength and | my re | deemer.

PSALM XX. *Exaudiat te, Dominus.*

THE Lord hear thee in the | day of | trouble ‖ the Name of the | God of | Jacob de | fend thee:

2 Send thee help | from the | sanctuary ‖ and strengthen thee | out of | Sion:

3 Remember | all thy | offerings ‖ and ac | cept thy | burnt - | sacrifice:

4 Grant thee thy | heart's de | sire ‖ and ful | fil - | all thy | mind.

5 We will rejoice in thy salvation, and triumph in the Name of the | Lord our | God ‖ the Lord per | form all | thy pe | titions.

6 Now know I that the Lord helpeth his Anointed, and will hear him from his | holy | heaven ‖ even with the wholesome | strength of | his right | hand.

7 Some put their trust in chariots, and | some in | horses ‖ but we will remember the | Name of the | Lord our | God.

8 They are brought | down and | fallen ‖ but we are | risen, and | stand - | upright.

9 Save, Lord; and hear us, O | King of heaven ‖ when we | call up | on - | thee.

PSALM xxi. *Domine, in virtute tua.*

THE King shall rejoice in thy | strength, O | Lord ‖ exceeding glad shall he | be of | thy sal | vation.

2 Thou hast given him his | heart's de | sire ‖ and hast not denied him the re | quest - | of his | lips.

3 For thou shalt prevent him with the | blessings of | goodness ‖ and shalt set a crown of pure | gold up | on his | head.

4 He asked life of thee, and thou gavest him a | long - | life ‖ even | for - | ever and | ever.

5 His honour is great in | thy sal | vation ‖ glory and great worship | shalt thou | lay up | on him.

6 For thou shalt give him ever | lasting fe | licity ‖ and make him glad with the | joy - | of thy | countenance.

7 And why? because the King putteth his trust | in the | Lord ‖ and in the mercy of the Most Highest | he shall | not mis | carry.

8 All thine enemies shall | feel thy | hand ‖ thy right hand shall | find out | them that | hate thee.

9 Thou shalt make them like a fiery oven in time | of thy | wrath ‖ the Lord shall destroy them in his displeasure, and the | fire - | shall con | sume them.

10 Their fruit shalt thou root out | of the | earth ‖ and their seed from a | mong the | children of | men.

11 For they intended | mischief a | gainst

[EVENING.]   THE PSALTER.   [DAY 4.

thee ǁ and imagined such a device as they are not | able | to per | form.

12 Therefore shalt thou put | them to | flight ǁ and the strings of thy bow shalt thou make ready a | gainst the | face of | them.

13 Be thou exalted, LORD, in | thine own strength ǁ so will we | sing, and | praise thy | power.

EVENING PRAYER.

PSALM xxii. *Deus, Deus meus!*

MY God! my God! look upon me; why hast thou for | saken | me ǁ and art so far from my health, and from the | words of | my com | plaint?

2 O my God, I cry in the day-time: but thou | hearest | not ǁ and in the night-season also I | take - | no - | rest.

3 And thou con | tinuest | holy ǁ O thou | Worship of | Isra | el.

4 Our fathers | hoped in | thee ǁ they trusted in thee, and thou | didst de | liver | them.

5 They called upon thee, | and were | holpen ǁ they put their trust in thee, | and were | not con- founded.

6 But as for me, I am a worm, and | no - | man ǁ a very scorn of men, and the | outcast | of the | people.

7 All they that see me | laugh me to | scorn ǁ they shoot out their lips, and | shake their | heads, - | saying,

8 He trusted in GOD, that he would de | liver |

him || let him deliver him, | if he | will - | have him.

9 But thou art he that took me out of my | mother's | womb || thou wast my hope, when I hanged yet up | on my | mother's | breasts.

10 I have been left unto thee ever | since I was | born || thou art my God even | from my | mother's | womb.

11 O go not from me ; for trouble is | hard at | hand || and | there is | none to | help me.

12 Many oxen are | come a | bout me || fat bulls of Basan close me | in on | every | side.

13 They gape upon me | with their | mouths || as it were a ramping | and a | roaring | lion.

14 I am poured out like water, and all my bones are | out of | joint || my heart also in the midst of my body is | even like | melting | wax.

15 My strength is dried up like a potsherd, and my tongue cleaveth | to my | gums || and thou shalt bring me in | to the | dust of | death.

16 For many dogs are | come a | bout me || and the counsel of the wicked | layeth | siege a | gainst me.

17 They pierced my hands and my feet; I may tell | all my | bones || they stand | staring and | looking up | on me.

18 They part my | garments a | mong them || and cast | lots up | on my | vesture.

19 But be not thou far from me, | O - | Lord || thou art my succour, | haste | thee to | help me.

20 Deliver my | soul from the | sword || my darling from the | power | of the | dog.

21 Save me from the | lion's | mouth || thou

EVENING.] THE PSALTER. [DAY 4.

hast heard me also from a | mong the | horns of the | unicorns.

22 I will declare thy Name un | to my | brethren ‖ in the midst of the congregation | will I | praise - | thee.

23 O praise the LORD | ye that | fear him ‖ magnify him, all ye of the seed of Jacob, and fear him | all ye | seed of | Israel.

24 For he hath not despised nor abhorred the low estate | of the | poor ‖ he hath not hid his face from him; but when he called | unto | him he | heard him.

25 My praise is of thee in the great | congregation ‖ my vows will I perform in the | sight of | them that | fear him.

26 The poor shall eat, | and be | satisfied ‖ they that seek after the LORD, shall praise him; your | heart shall | live for | ever.

27 All the ends of the world shall remember themselves, and be turned un | to the | LORD ‖ and all the kindreds of the nations shall | worship be | fore - | him.

28 For the kingdom | is the | LORD's ‖ and he is the | Governor a | mong the | people.

29 All such as be fat up | on - | earth ‖ have eaten, and | worship | ped.

30 All they that go down into the dust shall | kneel be | fore him ‖ and no man hath | quickened | his own | soul.

31 My | seed shall | serve him ‖ they shall be counted unto the | LORD for a | gener | ation.

32 They shall come, and the heavens shall de |

clare his | righteousness ‖ unto a people that shall be born, | whom the | Lord hath | made.

Psalm xxiii. *Dominus regit me.*

THE Lord | is | my | shepherd ‖ therefore | can I | lack - | nothing.

2 He shall feed me in a | green - | pasture ‖ and lead me forth be | side the | waters of | comfort.

3 He shall con | vert my | soul ‖ and bring me forth in the paths of righteousness | for his | Name's - | sake.

4 Yea, though I walk through the valley of the shadow of death, I will | fear no | evil ‖ for thou art with me; thy rod and thy | staff - | comfort | me.

5 Thou shalt prepare a table before me against | them that | trouble me ‖ thou hast anointed my head with oil, | and my | cup shall be | full.

6 But thy loving-kindness and mercy shall follow me all the days | of my | life ‖ and I will dwell in the house | of the | Lord for | ever.

The Fifth Day.
MORNING PRAYER.

Psalm xxiv. *Domini est terra.*

THE earth is the Lord's, and all that | therein | is ‖ the compass of the world, and | they that | dwell there | in.

2 For he hath founded it up | on the | seas ‖ and prepared | it up | on the | floods.

3 Who shall ascend into the hill | of the |

Lord || or who shall rise up | in his | holy | place?

4 Even he that hath clean hands, and a | pure - | heart || and that hath not lift up his mind unto vanity, nor | sworn to de | ceive his | neighbour.

5 He shall receive the blessing | from the | Lord || and righteousness from the | God of | his sal | vation.

6 This is the generation of | them that | seek him || even of them that | seek thy | face, O | Jacob.

7 Lift up your heads, O ye gates; and be ye lift up, ye ever | lasting | doors || and the King of | glory | shall come | in.

8 Who is the | King of | glory? || It is the Lord strong and mighty, even the | Lord - | mighty in | battle.

9 Lift up your heads, O ye gates; and be ye lift up, ye ever | lasting | doors || and the King of | glory | shall come | in.

10 Who is the | King of | glory? || Even the Lord of hosts, | he is the | King of | glory.

PSALM xxv. *Ad te, Domine, levavi.*

UNTO thee, O Lord, will I lift up my soul; my God, I have put my | trust in | thee || O let me not be confounded, neither let mine enemies | triumph | over | me.

2 For all they that hope in thee shall not | be a | shamed || but such as transgress without a cause | shall be | put to con | fusion.

3 Show me thy | ways, O | Lord || and | teach - | me thy | paths.

4 Lead me forth in thy | truth, and | learn me || for thou art the God of my salvation; in thee hath been my | hope - | all the day | long.

5 Call to remembrance, O Lord, thy | tender | mercies || and thy loving-kindnesses, which | have been | ever of | old.

6 O remember not the sins and offences | of my | youth || but according to thy mercy think thou upon me, O | Lord, - | for thy | goodness.

7 Gracious and righteous | is the | Lord || therefore will he teach | sinners | in the | way.

8 Them that are meek shall he | guide in | judgment || and such as are gentle, | them shall he | learn his | way.

9 All the paths of the Lord are | mercy and | truth || unto such as keep his | covenant | and his | testimonies.

10 For thy Name's sake, | O - | Lord || be merciful unto my | sin, for | it is | great.

11 What man is he that | feareth the | Lord || him shall he teach in the | way that | he shall | choose.

12 His soul shall | dwell at | ease || and his | seed shall in | herit the | land.

13 The secret of the Lord is among | them that | fear him || and he will | shew - | them his | covenant.

14 Mine eyes are ever looking up | to the | Lord || for he shall pluck my | feet out | of the | net.

15 Turn thee unto me, and have | mercy up | on me || for I am | desolate | and in | misery.

[MORNING.]   THE PSALTER.   [DAY 5.

16 The sorrows of my heart | are en | larged ‖
O bring thou me | out - | of my | troubles.

17 Look upon my adversity | and - | misery ‖
and for | give me | all my | sin.

18 Consider mine enemies, how | many they |
are ‖ and they bear a | tyrannous | hate a | gainst
me.

19 O keep my soul | and de | liver me ‖ let me
not be confounded, for I have | put my | trust in |
thee.

20 Let perfectness and righteous dealing |
wait up | on me ‖ for my | hope hath | been in |
thee.

21 Deliver Israel, | O - | God ‖ out of | all - |
his - | troubles.

PSALM XXVI. *Judica me, Domine.*

BE thou my judge, O LORD, for I have | walk-
ed | innocently ‖ my trust hath been also in
the LORD, | therefore | shall I not | fall.

2 Examine me, O | LORD, and | prove me ‖ try
out my | reins - | and my | heart.

3 For thy loving-kindness is ever be | fore
mine | eyes ‖ and I will | walk - | in thy | truth.

4 I have not dwelt with | vain - | persons ‖
neither will I have | fellowship | with the de |
ceitful.

5 I have hated the congregation | of the |
wicked ‖ and will not | sit a | mong the un |
godly.

6 I will wash my hands in innocency, | O - |
LORD ‖ and so will I | go - | to thine | altar;

7 That I may show the voice of | thanks - | giving || and tell of | all thy | wondrous | works.

8 Lord, I have loved the habitation | of thy | house || and the place | where thine | honour | dwelleth.

9 O shut not up my soul | with the | sinners || nor my life | with the | blood - | thirsty;

10 In whose | hands is | wickedness || and their right | hand is | full of | gifts.

11 But as for me, I will | walk - | innocently || O deliver me, and be | merciful | unto | me.

12 My foot | standeth | right || I will praise the | Lord in the | congre | gations.

EVENING PRAYER.

Psalm xxvii. *Dominus illuminatio.*

THE Lord is my light and my salvation; whom then | shall I | fear || the Lord is the strength of my life; of whom then | shall I | be a | fraid?

2 When the wicked, even mine enemies and my foes, came upon me to eat | up my | flesh || they | stum - | bled and | fell.

3 Though a host of men were laid against me, yet shall not my | heart be a | fraid || and though there rose up war against me, yet will I | put my | trust in | him.

4 One thing have I desired of the Lord, which I | will re | quire || even that I may dwell in the house of the Lord all the days of my life, to behold the fair beauty of the Lord, | and to | visit his | temple.

5 For in the time of trouble he shall hide me | in his | tabernacle ‖ yea, in the secret place of his dwelling shall he hide me, and set me up up | on a | rock of | stone.

6 And now shall he lift | up mine | head ‖ above mine | enemies | round a | bout me.

7 Therefore will I offer in his dwelling an oblation, | with great | gladness ‖ I will sing and speak | praises | unto the | Lord.

8 Hearken unto my voice, O Lord, when I | cry unto | thee | have mercy up | on me, | and - | hear me.

9 My heart hath talked of thee, | Seek ye my | face ‖ Thy face, | Lord - | will I | seek.

10 O hide not thou thy | face from | me ‖ nor cast thy servant a | way - | in dis | pleasure.

11 Thou hast | been my | succour ‖ leave me not, neither forsake me, O | God of | my sal | vation.

12 When my father and my | mother for | sake me, ‖ the Lord - | taketh me | up.

13 Teach me thy | way, O | Lord ‖ and lead me in the right way, be | cause - | of mine | enemies.

14 Deliver me not over into the will | of mine | adversaries ‖ for there are false witnesses risen up against me, and | such - | as speak | wrong.

15 I should | utterly have | fainted ‖ but that I believe verily to see the goodness of the Lord | in the | land of the | living.

16 O tarry thou the | Lord's - | leisure ‖ be strong, and he shall comfort thine heart; and put | thou thy | trust in the | Lord.

Psalm xxviii. *Ad te, Domine.*

UNTO thee will I cry, O | Lord, my | strength ‖ think no scorn of me; lest, if thou make as though thou hearest not, I become like them that go | down in | to the | pit.

2 Hear the voice of my humble petitions, when I | cry unto | thee ‖ when I hold up my hands towards the mercy-seat | of thy | holy | temple.

3 O pluck me not away, neither destroy me with the ungodly and | wicked | doers ‖ which speak friendly to their neighbours, but imagine | mischief | in their | hearts.

4 Reward them according | to their | deeds ‖ and according to the wickedness | of their | own in | ventions.

5 Recompense them after the work | of their | hands ‖ pay them | that they | have de | served.

6 For they regard not in their mind the works of the Lord, nor the operation | of his | hands ‖ therefore shall he break them down, and | not - | build them | up.

7 Praised | be the | Lord ‖ for he hath heard the voice | of my | humble pe | titions.

8 The Lord is my strength, and my shield; my heart hath trusted in him, and | I am | helped ‖ therefore my heart danceth for joy, and in my | song - | will I | praise him.

9 The Lord | is my | strength ‖ and he is the wholesome de | fence of | his A | nointed.

10 O save thy people, and give thy blessing unto | thine in | heritance ‖ feed them, and | set them | up for | ever.

PSALM xxix. *Afferte Domino.*

BRING unto the Lord, O ye mighty, bring young rams un | to the | Lord || ascribe unto the | Lord - | worship and | strength.

2 Give the Lord the honour due un | to his | Name || worship the | Lord with | holy | worship.

3 It is the Lord that com | mandeth the | waters || it is the glorious | God that | maketh the | thunder.

4 It is the Lord that ruleth the sea; the voice of the Lord is mighty in | oper | ation || the voice of the Lord | is a | glorious | voice.

5 The voice of the Lord breaketh the | cedar | trees || yea, the Lord | breaketh the | cedars of | Libanus.

6 He maketh them also to | skip like a | calf || Libanus also, and Sirion | like a | young - | unicorn.

7 The voice of the Lord divideth the flames of fire; the voice of the Lord | shaketh the | wilderness || yea, the Lord shaketh the | wilderness of | Cades.

8 The voice of the Lord maketh the hinds to bring forth young, and discovereth | the thick | bushes || in his temple doth every man | speak - | of his | honour.

9 The Lord sitteth above the | water | flood || and the Lord re | maineth a | King for | ever.

10 The Lord shall give strength un | to his | people || the Lord shall give his | people the | blessing of | peace.

The Sixth Day.

MORNING PRAYER.

Psalm xxx. *Exaltabo te, Domine.*

I WILL magnify thee, O Lord; for thou hast | set me | up || and not made my | foes to | triumph | over me.

2 O Lord, my God, I cried | unto | thee || and | thou hast | healed | me.

3 Thou, Lord, hast brought my soul | out of | hell || thou hast kept my life from them that go | down - | to the | pit.

4 Sing praises unto the Lord, O ye | saints of | his || and give thanks unto him, for a re | membrance | of his | holiness.

5 For his wrath endureth but the twinkling of an eye, and in his | pleasure is | life || heaviness may endure for a night, but joy | cometh | in the | morning.

6 And in my prosperity I said, I shall never | be re | moved || thou, Lord, of thy goodness, hast | made my | hill so | strong.

7 Thou didst turn thy | face from | me || and | I was | trou - | bled.

8 Then cried I unto | thee, O | Lord || and gat me | to my | Lord right | humbly.

9 What profit is there | in my | blood || when I go | down - | to the | pit?

10 Shall the dust give thanks | unto | thee || or shall | it de | clare thy | truth?

11 Hear, O Lord, and have | mercy up | on me || Lord, | be - | thou my | helper.

12 Thou hast turned my heaviness | into |

joy, || thou hast put off my sackcloth, and | girded | me with | gladness.

13 Therefore shall every good man sing of thy praise | without | ceasing || O my God, I will give thanks | unto | thee for | ever.

PSALM xxxi. *In te, Domine, speravi.*

IN thee, O LORD, have I | put my | trust || let me never be put to confusion; de | liver me | in thy | righteousness.

2 Bow down thine | ear to | me || make | haste - | to de | liver me.

3 And be thou my strong rock, and house | of de | fence || that | thou - | mayest | save me.

4 For thou art my strong rock, | and my | castle || be thou also my guide, and lead me | for thy | Name's - | sake.

5 Draw me out of the net that they have laid | privily | for me || for | thou - | art my | strength.

6 Into thy hands I com | mend my | spirit || for thou hast redeemed me, O | LORD, thou | God of | truth.

7 I have hated them that hold of super | stitious | vanities || and my | trust hath | been in the | LORD.

8 I will be glad, and rejoice | in thy | mercy || for thou hast considered my trouble, and hast known my | soul - | in ad | versities.

9 Thou hast not shut me up into the hand | of the | enemy || but hast set my feet | in a | large - | room.

10 Have mercy upon me, O LORD, for | I am in | trouble || and mine eye is consumed for very heaviness; yea, my | soul - | and my | body.

11 For my life is waxen | old with | heaviness ǁ and my | years - | with - | mourning.
12 My strength faileth me, because of | mine in | iquity ǁ and my | bones - | are con | sumed.
13 I became a reproof among all mine enemies, but especially a | mong my | neighbours ǁ and they of mine acquaintance were afraid of me; and they that did see me without, con | veyed them | selves - | from me.
14 I am clean forgotten as a dead man | out of | mind ǁ I am become | like a | broken | vessel.
15 For I have heard the blasphemy | of the | multitude ǁ and fear is on every side; while they conspire together against me, and take their counsel to | take a | way my | life.
16 But my hope hath been in | thee, O | Lord ǁ I have said | Thou - | art my | God.
17 My time is in thy hand; deliver me from the hand | of mine | enemies ǁ and from | them that | persecute | me.
18 Show thy servant the light | of thy | countenance ǁ and save me | for thy | mercy's | sake.
19 Let me not be confounded, O Lord, for I have | called up | on thee ǁ let the ungodly be put to confusion, and be put to | silence | in the | grave.
20 Let the lying lips be | put to | silence ǁ which cruelly, disdainfully, and despitefully | speak a | gainst the | righteous.
21 O how plentiful is thy goodness, which thou hast laid up for | them that | fear thee ǁ and that thou hast prepared for them that put their trust in thee, even be | fore the | sons of | men!

22 Thou shalt hide them privily by thine own presence from the pro | voking of | all men || thou shalt keep them secretly in thy tabernacle | from the | strife of | tongues.

23 Thanks | be to the | Lord || for he hath showed me marvellous great kindness | in a | strong - | city.

24 And when I made | haste, I | said || I am cast out of the | sight - | of thine | eyes.

25 Nevertheless, thou heardest the voice | of my | prayer || when I | cried - | unto | thee.

26 O love the Lord, all | ye his | saints || for the Lord preserveth them that are faithful, and plenteously re | wardeth the | proud - | doer.

27 Be strong, and he shall es | tablish your | heart || all ye that put your | trust - | in the | Lord.

EVENING PRAYER.

Psalm xxxii. *Beati, quorum.*

BLESSED is he whose unrighteousness | is for | given || and | whose - | sin is | covered.

2 Blessed is the man unto whom the Lord im | puteth no | sin || and in whose | spirit there | is no | guile.

3 For whilst I | held my | tongue || my bones consumed away | through my | daily com | plaining.

4 For thy hand is heavy upon me | day and | night || and my moisture is | like the | drought in | summer.

5 I will acknowledge my sin | unto | thee || and mine unrighteousness | have I | not - | hid.

6 I said, I will confess my sins un | to the | Lord || and so thou forgavest the | wickedness | of my | sin.

7 For this shall every one that is godly make his prayer unto thee, in a time when thou | mayest be | found || but in the great water-floods | they shall | not come | nigh him.

8 Thou art a place to hide me in; thou shalt preserve | me from | trouble || thou shalt compass me about with | songs - | of de | liverance.

9 I will inform thee, and teach thee in the way wherein | thou shalt | go || and I will | guide thee | with mine | eye.

10 Be ye not like to horse and mule, which have | no under | standing || whose mouths must be held with bit and bridle, | lest they | fall up | on thee.

11 Great plagues remain | for the un | godly | but whoso putteth his trust in the Lord, mercy embraceth | him on | every | side.

12 Be glad, O ye righteous, and re | joice in the | Lord || and be joyful, all | ye that are | true of | heart.

Psalm xxxiii. *Exultate, justi.*

REJOICE in the Lord, | O ye | righteous || for it becometh well the | just - | to be | thankful.

2 Praise the | Lord with | harp || sing praises unto him with the lute, and | instrument | of ten | strings.

3 Sing unto the Lord a | new - | song ‖ sing praises lustily unto him | with a | good - | courage.

4 For the word of the | Lord is | true ‖ and | all his | works are | faithful.

5 He loveth righteousness | and - | judgment ‖ the earth is full of the | goodness | of | the | Lord.

6 By the word of the Lord were the | heavens - | made ‖ and all the hosts of them | by the | breath of his | mouth.

7 He gathereth the waters of the sea together as it were up | on an | heap ‖ and layeth up the deep, as | in a | treasure | house.

8 Let all the earth | fear the | Lord ‖ stand in awe of him, all | ye that | dwell in the | world.

9 For he spake, and | it was | done ‖ he com | manded | and it stood | fast.

10 The Lord bringeth the counsel of the | heathen to | nought ‖ and maketh the devices of the people to be of none effect, and casteth | out the | counsels of | princes.

11 The counsel of the Lord shall en | dure for | ever ‖ and the thoughts of his heart from gener | ation to | gener | ation.

12 Blessed are the people whose God is the | Lord Je | hovah ‖ and blessed are the folk that he hath chosen to | him to | be his in | heritance.

13 The Lord looked down from heaven, and beheld all the | children of | men ‖ from the habitation of his dwelling he considereth all | them that | dwell on the | earth.

14 He fashioneth all the | hearts of | them ‖ and under | standeth | all their | works.

15 There is no king that can be saved by the multitude | of an | host ‖ neither is any mighty man de | livered | by much | strength.

16 A horse is counted but a vain thing to | save a | man ‖ neither shall he deliver any man | by his | great - | strength.

17 Behold, the eye of the LORD is upon | them that | fear him ‖ and upon them that put their | trust - | in his | mercy;

18 To deliver their | soul from | death ‖ and to feed them | in the | time of | dearth.

19 Our soul hath patiently tarried | for the | LORD ‖ for he is our | help - | and our | shield.

20 For our heart shall re | joice in | him ‖ because we have hoped | in his | holy | Name.

21 Let thy merciful kindness, O LORD, | be up | on us ‖ like as we do | put our | trust in | thee.

PSALM xxxiv. *Benedicam Domino.*

I WILL alway give thanks un | to the | LORD ‖ his praise shall | ever be | in my | mouth.

2 My soul shall make her boast | in the | LORD ‖ the humble shall | hear there | of and be | glad.

3 O praise the | LORD with | me ‖ and let us magni | fy his | Name to | gether.

4 I sought the LORD, | and he | heard me ‖ yea, he delivered me | out of | all my | fear.

5 They had an eye unto him, | and were | lightened ‖ and their | faces were | not a | shamed.

6 Lo, the poor crieth, and the LORD | heareth | him ‖ yea, and saveth him | out of | all his | troubles.

7 The angel of the Lord tarrieth round about | them that | fear him ‖ and de | liv - | ereth | them.

8 O taste, and see, how gracious the | Lord - | is ‖ blessed is the | man that | trusteth in | him.

9 O fear the Lord, ye that | are his | saints ‖ for they that | fear him | lack - | nothing.

10 The lions do lack, and | suffer | hunger ‖ but they who seek the Lord shall want no manner of | thing - | that is | good.

11 Come, ye children, and hearken | unto | me ‖ I will teach you the | fear - | of the | Lord.

12 What man is he that | lusteth to | live ‖ and would | fain see | good - | days?

13 Keep thy | tongue from | evil ‖ and thy | lips, that they | speak no | guile.

14 Eschew evil, | and do | good ‖ seek | peace, - | and en | sue it.

15 The eyes of the Lord are | over the | righteous ‖ and his ears are | open un | to their | prayers.

16 The countenance of the Lord is against them | that do | evil ‖ to root out the remembrance | of them | from the | earth.

17 The righteous cry, and the Lord | heareth | them ‖ and delivereth them | out of | all their | troubles.

18 The Lord is nigh unto them that are of a | contrite | heart ‖ and will save such as be | of an | humble | spirit.

19 Great are the troubles | of the | righteous ‖ but the Lord de | livereth him | out of | all.

20 He keepeth | all his | bones ‖ so that not one of | them is | broken.

21 But misfortune shall | slay the un | godly ‖ and they that hate the | righteous | shall be | desolate.

22 The Lord delivereth the souls | of his | servants ‖ and all they that put their trust in | him shall | not be | destitute.

The Seventh Day.

MORNING PRAYER.

Psalm xxxv. *Judica me, Domine.*

PLEAD thou my cause, O Lord, with them that | strive with | me ‖ and fight thou against | them that | fight against | me.

2 Lay hand upon the | shield and | buckler ‖ and | stand - | up to | help me.

3 Bring forth the spear, and stop the way against them that | persecute | me ‖ say unto my soul | I am | thy sal | vation.

4 Let them be confounded, and put to shame, that seek | after my | soul ‖ let them be turned back, and brought to confusion, that im | agine | mischief | for me.

5 Let them be as the dust be | fore the | wind ‖ and the angel of the | Lord - | scattering | them.

6 Let their way be | dark and | slippery ‖ and let the angel of the | Lord - | persecute | them.

7 For they have privily laid their net to destroy me with | out a | cause ‖ yea, even without a cause have they | made a | pit for my | soul.

8 Let a sudden destruction come upon him unawares, and his net that he hath laid privily |

[Morning.] THE PSALTER. [Day 7

catch him | self ‖ that he may fall | into | his own | mischief.

9 And, my soul, be joyful | in the | Lord ‖ it shall re | joice in | his sal | vation.

10 All my bones shall say, Lord, who is like unto thee, who deliverest the poor from him that | is too | strong for him ‖ yea, the poor, and him that is in misery, | from - | him that | spoileth him?

11 False witnesses | did rise | up ‖ they laid to my charge | things that | I knew | not.

12 They rewarded me | evil for | good ‖ to the great dis | comfort | of my | soul.

13 Nevertheless, when they were sick, I put on sackcloth, and humbled my | soul with | fasting ‖ and my prayer shall turn | into | mine own | bosom.

14 I behaved myself as though it had been my friend | or my | brother ‖ I went heavily, as one that | mourneth | for his | mother.

15 But in mine adversity they rejoiced, and gathered them | selves to | gether ‖ yea, the very abjects came together against me unawares, making mouths | at me, and | ceased | not.

16 With the flatterers were | busy | mockers ‖ who gnashed up | on me | with their | teeth.

17 Lord, how long wilt thou | look upon | this ‖ O deliver my soul from the calamities which they bring on me, and my | darling | from the | lions.

18 So will I give thee thanks in the great | congre | gation ‖ I will praise | thee a | mong much | people.

19 O let not them that are mine enemies tri-

umph over | me un | godly ‖ neither let them wink with their eyes, that | hate me with | out a | cause.

20 And why? their communing is | not for | peace ‖ but they imagine deceitful words against them that are | quiet | in the | land.

21 They gaped upon me with their | mouths, and | said ‖ Fie on thee! fie on thee! we | saw it | with our | eyes.

22 This thou hast | seen, O | Lord ‖ hold not thy tongue then; go not | far from | me, O | Lord.

23 Awake, and stand up to | judge my | quarrel ‖ avenge thou my cause, my | God - | and my | Lord.

24 Judge me, O Lord my God, according | to thy | righteousness ‖ and let them not | triumph | over | me.

25 Let them not say in their hearts, There! there! so | would we | have it ‖ neither let them | say, We | have de | voured him.

26 Let them be put to confusion and shame together, that rejoice | at my | trouble ‖ let them be clothed with rebuke and dishonour, that | boast them | selves a | gainst me.

27 Let them be glad and rejoice, that favour my | righteous | dealing ‖ yea, let them say alway, Blessed be the Lord, who hath pleasure in the pros | perity | of his | servant.

28 And as for my tongue, it shall be talking | of thy | righteousness ‖ and of thy | praise, - | all the day | long.

[MORNING.] THE PSALTER. [DAY 7

Psalm xxxvi. *Dixit injustus.*

MY heart showeth me the wickedness of | the un | godly ‖ that there is no fear of | God be | fore his | eyes.

2 For he flattereth himself in | his own | sight ‖ until his abominable | sin be | found - | out.

3 The words of his mouth are unrighteous and | full of de | ceit ‖ he hath left off to behave himself | wisely, | and to do | good.

4 He imagineth mischief upon his bed, and hath set himself in | no good | way ‖ neither doth he abhor | any thing | that is | evil.

5 Thy mercy, O Lord, reacheth un | to the | heavens ‖ and thy faithfulness | un - | to the | clouds.

6 Thy righteousness standeth like the | strong - | mountains ‖ thy judgments are | like the | great - | deep.

7 Thou, Lord, shalt save both man and beast; how excellent is thy | mercy, O | God ‖ and the children of men shall put their trust under the | shadow | of thy | wings.

8 They shall be satisfied with the plenteous-ness | of thy | house ‖ and thou shalt give them drink of thy pleasures, as | out - | of the | river.

9 For with thee is the | well of | life ‖ and in thy | light shall | we see | light.

10 O continue forth thy loving-kindness unto | them that | know thee ‖ and thy righteousness unto | them that are | true of | heart.

11 O let not the foot of pride | come a | gainst me ‖ and let not the hand of the un | godly | cast me | down.

12 There are they fallen, all | that work | wickedness ‖ they are cast down, and shall | **not** be | able to | stand.

EVENING PRAYER.

Psalm xxxvii. *Noli æmulari.*

FRET not thyself because of | the un | godly ‖ neither be thou envious a | gainst the | evil | doers.

2 For they shall soon be cut down | like the | grass ‖ and be withered | even | as the green | herb.

3 Put thou thy trust in the Lord, and be | doing | good ‖ dwell in the land, and verily | thou - | shalt be | fed.

4 Delight thou | in the | Lord ‖ and he shall | give thee thy | heart's de | sire.

5 Commit thy way unto the Lord, and **put** thy | trust in | him ‖ and | he shall | bring it to | pass.

6 He shall make thy righteousness as clear | as the | light ‖ and thy just | dealing | as the | noon-day.

7 Hold thee still in the Lord, and abide | patiently up | on him ‖ but grieve not thyself at him whose way doth prosper, against the man that doeth | after | evil | counsels.

8 Leave off from wrath, and let | go dis | pleasure ‖ fret not thyself, else shalt thou be | moved | to do | evil.

9 Wicked doers shall be | rooted | out ‖ **and**

they that patiently abide the LORD, | those shall in | herit the | land.

10 Yet a little while, and the ungodly shall be | clean - | gone ‖ thou shalt look after his place, and | he shall | be a | way.

11 But the meek-spirited shall pos | sess the | earth ‖ and shall be refreshed in the | multi | tude of | peace.

12 The ungodly seeketh counsel a | gainst the | just ‖ and gnasheth up | on him | with his | teeth.

13 The LORD shall | laugh him to | scorn ‖ for he hath | seen that his | day is | coming.

14 The ungodly have drawn out the sword, and have | bent their | bow ‖ to cast down the poor and needy, and to slay such as are of a | right - | conver | sation.

15 Their sword shall go through their | own - | heart ‖ and their | bow - | shall be | broken.

16 A small thing that the | righteous | hath ‖ is better than great | riches of | the un | godly.

17 For the arms of the ungodly | shall be | broken ‖ and the | LORD up | holdeth the | rightous.

18 The LORD knoweth the days | of the | godly ‖ and their inheritance | shall en | dure for | ever.

19 They shall not be confounded in the | perilous | time ‖ and in the days of dearth | they shall | have e | nough.

20 As for the ungodly, they shall perish, and the enemies of the LORD shall consume as the |

fat of | lambs ‖ yea, even as the smoke shall | they con | sume a | way.

21 The ungodly borroweth, and payeth | not a | gain ‖ but the righteous is | merci | ful and | liberal.

22 Such as are blessed of God, shall pos | sess the | land ‖ and they that are cursed of him, | shall be | rooted | out.

23 The LORD ordereth a | good man's | going ‖ and maketh his way ac | ceptable | to him | self.

24 Though he fall, he shall not be | cast a | way ‖ for the LORD up | holdeth him | with his | hand.

25 I have been young, and | now am | old ‖ and yet saw I never the righteous forsaken, nor his | seed - | begging their | bread.

26 The righteous is ever merciful, | and - | lendeth ‖ and | his . | seed is | blessed.

27 Flee from evil, and do the thing | that is | good ‖ and | dwell for | ever | more.

28 For the LORD loveth the thing | that is | right ‖ he forsaketh not his that be godly, but they | are pre | served for | ever.

29 The unrighteous | shall be | punished ‖ as for the seed of the ungodly, it | shall be | rooted | out.

30 The righteous shall in | herit the | land ‖ and | dwell there | in for | ever.

31 The mouth of the righteous is exercised | in - | wisdom ‖ and his tongue | will be | talking of | judgment.

32 The law of his God is | in his | heart ‖ and his | goings | shall not | slide.

33 The ungodly | seeth the | righteous ‖ and | seeketh oc | casion to | slay him.

34 The Lord will not leave him | in his | hand ‖ nor con | demn him | when he is | judged.

35 Hope thou in the Lord, and keep his way, and he shall promote thee, that thou shalt pos | sess the | land ‖ when the ungodly shall | perish, | thou shalt | see it.

36 I myself have seen the ungodly in | great - | power ‖ and flourishing | like a | green bay | tree.

37 I went by, and | lo, he was | gone ‖ I sought him, but his place could | no - | where be | found.

38 Keep innocency, and take heed unto the thing | that is | right ‖ for that shall bring a man | peace - | at the | last.

39 As for the transgressors, they shall | perish to | gether ‖ and the end of the ungodly is, they shall be | rooted | out at the | last.

40 But the salvation of the righteous cometh | of the | Lord ‖ who is also their strength | in the | time of | trouble.

41 And the Lord shall stand | by them and | save them ‖ he shall deliver them from the ungodly, and shall save them, because they | put their | trust in | him.

The Eighth Day.
MORNING PRAYER.
Psalm xxxviii. *Domine, ne in furore.*

PUT me not to rebuke, O Lord, | in thine | anger ‖ neither chasten me | in thy | heavy dis | pleasure

2 For thine arrows stick | fast in | me ‖ and thy | hand - | presseth me | sore.

3 There is no health in my flesh, because of | thy dis | pleasure ‖ neither is there any rest in my bones, by | reason | of my | sin.

4 For my wickednesses are gone | over my | head ‖ and are like a sore burden, too | heavy for | me to | bear.

5 My wounds stink, and | are cor | rupt ‖ through my | fool - | ish - | ness.

6 I am brought into so great trouble | and - | misery ‖ that I go | mourning | all the day | long.

7 For my loins are filled with a | sore dis | ease ‖ and there is no | whole part | in my | body.

8 I am feeble and | sore - | smitten ‖ I have roared for the very dis | quietness | of my | heart.

9 Lord, thou knowest all | my de | sire ‖ and my groaning | is not | hid from | thee.

10 My heart panteth, my | strength hath | failed me ‖ and the sight of mine | eyes is | gone - | from me.

11 My lovers and my neighbours did stand looking up | on my | trouble ‖ and my | kinsmen | stood afar | off.

12 They also that sought after my life laid | snares for | me ‖ and they that went about to do me evil talked of wickedness, and imagined de | ceit all the | day - | long.

13 As for me, I was like a | deaf man, and | heard not ‖ and as one that is dumb, who | doth not | open his | mouth.

14 I became even as a man that | heareth | not ‖ and in whose | mouth are | no re | proofs.

15 For in thee, O Lord, have I | put my | trust ‖ thou shalt answer for me, | O - | Lord my | God.

16 I have required that they, even mine enemies, should not triumph | over | me ‖ for when my foot slipt, they re | joiced | greatly a | gainst me.

17 And I truly am set | in the | plague ‖ and my heaviness is | ever | in my | sight.

18 For I will con | fess my | wickedness ‖ and be | sorry | for my | sin.

19 But mine enemies live, | and are | mighty ‖ and they that hate me wrongfully | are - | many in | number.

20 They also that reward evil for good | are a | gainst me ‖ because I follow the | thing that | good - | is.

21 Forsake me not, O | Lord, my | God ‖ be not | thou - | far - | from me.

22 Haste | thee to | help me ‖ O Lord | God of | my sal | vation.

Psalm xxxix. *Dixi, custodiam.*

I SAID, I will take heed | to my | ways ‖ that I of | fend not | in my | tongue.

2 I will keep my mouth as it were | with a | bridle ‖ while the un | godly is | in my | sight.

3 I held my tongue, and | spake - | nothing ‖ I kept silence, yea, even from good words; but it was | pain and | grief to | me.

4 My heart was hot within me; and while I

was thus musing the | fire - | kindled ‖ and at the last I | spake - | with my | tongue ;

5 Lord, let me know my end, and the number | of my | days ‖ that I may be certified how | long I | have to | live.

6 Behold, thou hast made my days as it were a | span - | long ‖ and mine age is even as nothing in respect of thee, and verily every man living is | alto | gether | vanity.

7 For man walketh in a vain shadow, and disquieteth him | self in | vain ‖ he heapeth up riches, and cannot | tell - | who shall | gather them.

8 And now, Lord, | what is my | hope ‖ Truly my | hope is | even in | thee.

9 Deliver me from all | mine offences ‖ and make me not a re | buke un | to the | foolish.

10 I became dumb, and opened | not my | mouth ‖ for | it was | thy - | doing.

11 Take thy plague a | way from | me ‖ I am even consumed by the means | of thy | heavy | hand.

12 When thou with rebukes dost chasten man for sin, thou makest his beauty to consume away, like as it were a moth | fretting a | garment ‖ every man | therefore | is but | vanity.

13 Hear my prayer, O Lord, and with thine ears con | sider my | calling ‖ hold not thy | peace - | at my | tears.

14 For I am a | stranger | with thee ‖ and a sojourner, as | all my | fathers | were.

15 O spare me a little, that I may re | cover

my | strength ‖ before I go hence, | and be | no more | seen.

PSALM xl. *Expectans expectavi.*

I WAITED patiently | for the | LORD ‖ and he inclined unto me, | and - | heard my | calling.

2 He brought me also out of the horrible pit, out of the | mire and | clay ‖ and set my feet upon the | rock, and | ordered my | goings.

3 And he hath put a new song | in my | mouth ‖ even a thanks | giving un | to our | God.

4 Many shall | see it, and | fear ‖ and shall put their | trust - | in the | LORD.

5 Blessed is the man that hath set his·hope | in the | LORD ‖ and turned not unto the proud, and to such as | go a | bout with | lies.

6 O LORD my God, great are the wondrous works which thou hast done, like as be also thy thoughts, which | are to | us-ward ‖ and yet there is no man that | ordereth them | unto | thee.

7 If I should declare them, and | speak of | them ‖ they should be more than I am | able | to ex | press.

8 Sacrifice and meat-offering thou | wouldest | not ‖ but mine | ears - | hast thou | opened.

9 Burnt-offerings and sacrifice for sin hast thou | not re | quired ‖ then said I, | Lo, - , I - | come;

10 In the volume of the book it is written of me, that I should fulfil thy will, | O my | God ‖ I am content to do it; yea, thy law | is with | in my | heart.

11 I have declared thy righteousness in the great | congre | gation ‖ lo, I will not refrain my lips, O | Lord, and | that thou | knowest.

12 I have not hid thy righteousness with | in my | heart ‖ my talk hath been of thy truth, | and of | thy sal | vation.

13 I have not kept back thy loving | mercy and | truth ‖ from the | great - | congre | gation.

14 Withdraw not thou thy mercy from me, | O - | Lord ‖ let thy loving-kindness and thy | truth al | way pre | serve me.

15 For innumerable troubles are come about me; my sins have taken such hold upon me, that I am not able | to look | up ‖ yea, they are more in number than the hairs of my head, and my | heart hath | failed | me.

16 O Lord, let it be thy pleasure to de | liver | me ‖ make | haste, O | Lord, to | help me.

17 Let them be ashamed, and confounded together, that seek after my soul | to de | stroy it ‖ let them be driven backward, and put to re | buke, that | wish me | evil.

18 Let them be desolate, and re | warded with | shame ‖ that say unto me, Fie up | on thee! fie up | on thee!

19 Let all those that seek thee, be joyful and | glad in | thee ‖ and let such as love thy salvation, say | alway, The | Lord be | praised!

20 As for me, I am | poor and | needy ‖ but the | Lord - | careth | for me.

21 Thou art my helper | and re | deemer ǀ make no long | tarrying, | O my | God.

EVENING PRAYER.

PSALM xli. *Beatus qui intelligit.*

BLESSED is he that considereth the | poor and | needy ‖ the LORD shall deliver him | in the | time of | trouble.

2 The LORD preserve him, and keep him alive, that he may be blessed up | on - | earth ‖ and deliver not thou him into the | will - | of his | enemies.

3 The LORD comfort him when he lieth sick up | on his | bed ‖ make thou all his | bed- | in his | sickness.

4 I said, LORD, be merciful | unto | me ‖ heal my soul, for | I have | sinned a | gainst thee.

5 Mine enemies speak | evil of | me ‖ When shall he die, | and his | name - | perish?

6 And if he come to see me, he | speaketh | vanity ‖ and his heart conceiveth falsehood within himself; and when he | cometh | forth, he | telleth it.

7 All mine enemies whisper to | gether a | gainst me ‖ even against me | do they im | agine this | evil.

8 Let the sentence of guiltiness pro | ceed a | gainst him ‖ and now that he lieth, let him | rise - | up no | more.

9 Yea, even mine own familiar friend | whom I | trusted ‖ who did also eat of my bread, hath | laid great | wait - | for me.

10 But be thou merciful unto | me, O | LORD ‖ raise thou me up again, | and I | shall re | ward them.

11 By this I know thou | favorest | me ‖ that mine enemy | doth not | triumph a | gainst me.

12 And when I am in my health, thou up | holdest | me ‖ and shalt set me be | fore thy | face for | ever.

13 Blessed be the Lord | God of | Israel ‖ world without | end - | A - | men.

Psalm xlii. *Quemadmodum.*

LIKE as the hart desireth the | water | brooks ‖ so longeth my soul | after | thee, O | God.

2 My soul is athirst for God, yea, even for the | living | God ‖ when shall I come to appear be | fore the | presence of | God?

3 My tears have been my meat | day and | night ‖ while they daily say unto me, | Where is | now thy | God?

4 Now when I think thereupon, I pour out my heart | by my | self ‖ for I went with the multitude, and brought them forth in | to the | house of | God;

5 In the voice of | praise and | thanksgiving ‖ among such as | keep - | holy | day.

6 Why art thou so full of heaviness, | O my | soul ‖ and why art thou so dis | quieted | with | in me?

7 Put thy | trust in | God ‖ for I will yet give him thanks for the | help - | of his | countenance

8 My God, my soul is | vexed with | in me ‖ therefore will I remember thee concernig the land of Jordan, and the | little | hill of | Hermon.

9 One deep calleth another, because of the

noise | of the | water-pipes ‖ all thy waves and storms are | gone - | over | me.

10 The Lord hath granted his loving-kindness | in the | day-time ‖ and in the night-season did I sing of him, and made my prayer un | to the | God of my | life.

11 I will say unto the God of my strength, Why hast thou for | gotten | me ‖ why go I thus heavily, while the | enemy op | presseth | me?

12 My bones are smitten asunder as | with a | sword ‖ while mine enemies that trouble me | cast me | in the | teeth;

13 Namely, while they say daily | unto | me ‖ Where | - is | now thy | God?

14 Why art thou so vexed, | O my | soul ‖ and why art thou so dis | quieted | within | me?

15 O put thy | trust in | God ‖ for I will yet thank him, which is the help of my | counten-ance, | and my | God.

Psalm xliii. *Judica me, Deus.*

GIVE sentence with me, O God, and defend my cause against the un | godly | people ‖ O deliver me from the de | ceitful and | wicked | man.

2 For thou art the God of my strength, why hast thou | put me | from thee ‖ and why go I so heavily, while the | enemy op | presseth | me?

3 O send out thy light and thy truth, that | they may | lead me ‖ and bring me unto thy holy hill, | and - | to thy | dwelling.

4 And that I may go unto the altar of God, even unto the God of my | joy and | gladness ‖

and upon the harp will I give thanks unto | thee, O | God, my | God.

5 Why art thou so heavy, | O my | soul ‖ and why art thou so dis | quieted | within | me ?

6 O put thy | trust in | God ‖ for I will yet give him thanks, which is the help of my | countenance, | and my | God.

The Ninth Day.

MORNING PRAYER.

PSALM xliv.   *Deus, auribus.*

WE have heard with our ears, O God, our | fathers have | told us ‖ what thou hast done in | their - | time of | old ;

2 How thou hast driven out the heathen with thy hand, and | planted them | in ‖ how thou hast destroyed the | nations, and | cast them | out.

3 For they gat not the land in possession through | their own | sword ‖ neither was it | their own | arm that | helped them :

4 But thy right hand, and thine arm, and the light | of thy | countenance ‖ because thou hadst a | favour | unto | them.

5 Thou art my | King, O | God ‖ send | help - | unto | Jacob.

6 Through thee will we over | throw our | enemies ‖ and in thy Name will we tread them under that | rise - | up a | gainst us.

7 For I will not | trust in my | bow ‖ it is not my | sword - | that shall | help me ;

8 But it is thou that savest us | from our |

enemies ‖ and puttest them | to con | fusion that | hate us

9 We make our boast of God | all day | long ‖ and will | praise thy | Name for | ever.

10 But now thou art far off, and puttest us | to con | fusion ‖ and goest not | forth - | with our | armies.

11 Thou makest us to turn our backs up | on our | enemies ‖ so that they which | hate us | spoil our | goods.

12 Thou lettest us be eaten | up like | sheep ‖ and hast scattered | us a | mong the | heathen.

13 Thou sellest thy | people for | nought ‖ and takest | no - | money | for them.

14 Thou makest us to be rebuked | of our | neighbours ‖ to be laughed to scorn, and had in derision of them | that are | round a | bout us.

15 Thou makest us to be a by-word a | mong the | heathen ‖ and that the people | shake their | heads - | at us.

16 My confusion is | daily be | fore me ‖ and the shame of my | face hath | covered | me ;

17 For the voice of the slanderer | and blas | phemer ‖ for the | enemy | and a | venger.

18 And though all this be come upon us, yet do we | not for | get thee ‖ nor behave ourselves | frowardly | in thy | covenant.

19 Our heart is not | turned | back ‖ neither our steps gone | out - | of thy | way ;

20 No, not when thou hast smitten us into the | place of | dragons ‖ and covered us | with the | shadow of | death.

21 If we have forgotten the Name of our God,

and holden up our hands to any | strange - | god ‖ shall not God search it out? for he knoweth the very | secrets | of the | heart.

22 For thy sake also are we killed | all the day | long ‖ and are counted as sheep ap | point- ed | to be | slain.

23 Up, Lord, why | sleepest | thou ‖ awake, and be not | absent from | us for | ever.

24 Wherefore hidest | thou thy | face ‖ and for- gettest our | misery | and - | trouble?

25 For our soul is brought low, even un | to the | dust ‖ our belly | cleaveth | unto the | ground.

26 A | rise, and | help us ‖ and deliver us, | for thy | mercy's | sake.

PSALM xlv. *Eructavit cor meum.*

MY heart is inditing of a | good - | matter ‖ I speak of the things which I have | made un | to the | King.

2 My tongue | is the | pen ‖ of | - a | ready | writer.

3 Thou art fairer than the | children of | men ‖ full of grace are thy lips, because God hath | blessed | thee for | ever.

4 Gird thee with thy sword upon thy thigh, O | thou Most | Mighty ‖ according to thy | wor- ship | and re | nown.

5 Good luck have thou | with thine | honour ‖ ride on, because of the word of truth, of meek- ness, and righteousness; and thy right hand shall | teach thee | terrible | things.

6 Thy arrows are very sharp, and the people

shall be subdued | unto | thee ‖ even in the midst a | mong the | King's - | enemies.

7 Thy seat, O God, en | dureth for | ever ‖ the sceptre of thy kingdom | is a | right - | sceptre.

8 Thou hast loved righteousness, and | hated in | iquity ‖ wherefore God, even thy God, hath anointed thee with the oil of | gladness a | bove thy | fellows.

9 All thy garments smell of myrrh, | aloes, and | cassia ‖ out of the ivory palaces, whereby | they have | made thee | glad.

10 Kings' daughters were among thy | honourable | women ‖ upon thy right hand did stand the queen in a vesture of gold, wrought a | bout with | divers | colours.

11 Hearken, O daughter, and consider; in | cline thine | ear ‖ forget also thine own people, | and thy | father's | house.

12 So shall the King have pleasure | in thy | beauty ‖ for he is thy Lord God, and | worship | thou - | him.

13 And the daughter of Tyre shall be there | with a | gift ‖ like as the rich also among the people shall make their | suppli | cation be | fore thee.

14 The King's daughter is all | glorious with | in ‖ her clothing | is of | wrought - | gold.

15 She shall be brought unto the King in raiment of | needle | work ‖ the virgins that be her fellows shall bear her company, and shall be | brought - | unto | thee.

16 With joy and gladness shall | they be | brought ‖ and shall enter in | to the | King's - | palace.

17 Instead of thy fathers, thou | shalt have | children ‖ whom thou mayest make | princes | in all | lands.

18 I will remember thy Name from one genera‐tion | to an | other ‖ therefore shall the people give thanks unto thee, | world with | out ‐ | end.

PSALM xlvi. *Deus noster refugium.*

GOD is our | hope and | strength ‖ a very | pres‐ent | help in | trouble.

2 Therefore will we not fear, though the | earth be | moved ‖ and though the hills be car‐ried into the | midst ‐ | of the | sea.

3 Though the waters thereof | rage and | swell ‖ and though the mountains shake at the | tem‐pest | of the | same.

4 The rivers of the flood thereof shall make glad the | city of | God ‖ the holy place of the tabernacle | of the | Most ‐ | Highest.

5 God is in the midst of her, therefore shall she | not be re | moved ‖ God shall | help her, and | that right | early.

6 The heathen make much ado, and the | king‐doms are | moved ‖ but God hath showed his voice, and the | earth shall | melt a | way.

7 The LORD of | hosts is | with us ‖ the God of | Jacob | is our | refuge.

8 O come hither, and behold the works | of the | LORD ‖ what destruction he hath | brought up | on the | earth.

9 He maketh wars to cease in | all the | world ‖ he breaketh the bow, and knappeth the spear in sunder, and burneth the | chariots | in the | fire.

10 Be still then, and know that | I am | God ‖ I will be exalted among the heathen, and I will be ex | alted | in the | earth.

11 The LORD of | hosts is | with us ‖ the God of | Jacob | is our | refuge.

EVENING PRAYER.

PSALM xlvii. *Omnes gentes, plaudite.*

O CLAP your hands together, | all ye | people ‖ O sing unto God | with the | voice of | melody.

2 For the LORD is high, and | to be | feared ‖ he is the great | King upon | all the | earth.

3 He shall subdue the people | under | us ‖ and the | nations | under our | feet.

4 He shall choose out an | heritage | for us ‖ even the worship of | Jacob, | whom he | loved.

5 God is gone up with a | merry | noise ‖ and the LORD | with the | sound of the | trump.

6 O sing praises, sing praises | unto our | God ‖ O sing praises, sing | praises | unto our | King.

7 For God is the King of | all the | earth ‖ sing ye | praises with | under | standing.

8 God reigneth | over the | heathen ‖ God sitteth up | on his | holy | seat.

9 The princes of the people are joined unto the people of the | God of | Abraham ‖ for God, which is very high exalted, doth defend the earth, | as 't | were with a | shield.

PSALM xlviii. *Magnus Dominus.*

GREAT is the Lord, and highly | to be | praised ‖ in the city of our God, even up | on his | holy | hill.

2 The hill of Sion is a fair place, and the joy of the | whole - | earth ‖ upon the north side lieth the city of the great King; God is well known in her palaces | as a | sure - | refuge.

3 For lo, the kings | of the | earth ‖ are gathered, and | gone - | by to | gether.

4 They marvelled to | see such | things ‖ they were astonished, and | suddenly | cast - | down.

5 Fear came there upon them; | and - | sorrow ‖ as upon a | woman | in her | travail.

6 Thou shalt break the | ships of the | sea ‖ thr | ough the | east - | wind.

7 Like as we have heard, so have we seen in the city of the Lord of hosts, in the city | of our | God ‖ God up | holdeth the | same for | ever.

8 We wait for thy loving-kindness, | O - | God ‖ in the | midst - | of thy | temple.

9 O God, according to thy Name, so is thy praise unto the | world's - | end ‖ thy right hand is | full of | righteous | ness.

10 Let the Mount Sion rejoice, and the daughter of | Judah be | glad ‖ be | cause of | thy - | judgments.

11 Walk about Sion, and go | round a | bout her ‖ and | tell the | towers there | of.

12 Mark well her bulwarks, set | up her | houses ‖ that ye may tell | them - | that come | after.

13 For this God is our God for | ever and | ever ‖ he shall be our | guide - | unto | death.

[Evening.] THE PSALTER. [Day 9.

PSALM xlix. *Audite hæc, omnes.*

O HEAR ye this, | all ye | people ‖ ponder it with your ears, all | ye that | dwell in the | world;

2 High and low, | rich and | poor ‖ one | with - | an · | other.

3 My mouth shall | speak of | wisdom ‖ and my heart shall | muse of | under | standing.

4 I will incline mine ear | to the | parable ‖ and show my dark | speech up | on the | harp.

5 Wherefore should I fear in the | days of | wickedness ‖ and when the wickedness of my heels | compasseth me | round a | bout?

6 There be some that put their trust | in their | goods ‖ and boast themselves in the | multitude | of their | riches.

7 But no man may de | liver his | brother ‖ nor make agreement | unto | God for | him;

8 For it cost more to re | deem their | souls ‖ so that he must let | that a | lone for | ever;

9 Yea, though he | live - | long ‖ and | see - | not the | grave.

10 For he seeth that wise men also die and | perish to | gether ‖ as well as the ignorant and foolish, and | leave their | riches for | other.

11 And yet they think that their houses shall con | tinue for | ever ‖ and that their dwelling-places shall endure from one generation to another; and call the lands | after | their own | names.

12 Nevertheless, man will not a | bide in | honor ‖ seeing he may be compared unto the beasts that perish; this | is the | way of | them.

13 This is their | foolish | ness ‖ and their pos | terity | praise their | saying.

14 They lie in the hell like sheep; death gnaweth upon them, and the righteous shall have dominion over them | in the | morning ‖ their beauty shall consume in the sepulchre | out - | of their | dwelling.

15 But God hath delivered my soul from the | place of | hell ‖ for | he - | shall re | ceive me.

16 Be not thou afraid, though one | be made | rich ‖ or if the glory of his | house - | be in | creased;

17 For he shall carry nothing away with him | when he | dieth ‖ neither shall his | pomp - | follow | him.

18 For while he lived, he counted himself an | happy | man ‖ and so long as thou doest well unto thyself, men will | speak - | good of | thee.

19 He shall follow the generation | of his | fathers ‖ and shall | never | see - | light.

20 Man being in honour hath no | under | standing ‖ but is compared un | to the | beasts that | perish.

The Tenth Day.
MORNING PRAYER.

Psalm l. *Deus deorum.*

THE Lord, even the most mighty | God, hath | spoken ‖ and called the world, from the rising up of the sun unto the | going | down there | of.

2 Out of Sion hath | God ap | peared ‖ in | perfect | beau - | ty.

3 Our God shall come, and shall | not keep | silence ‖ there shall go before him a consuming

fire, and a mighty tempest shall be | stirred up | round a | bout him.

4 He shall call the heaven | from a | bove ‖ and the earth, that | he may | judge his | people.

5 Gather my saints together | unto | me ‖ those that have made a covenant | with me | with - | sacrifice.

6 And the heavens shall de | clare his | right-eousness ‖ for | God is | Judge him | self.

7 Hear, O my people, and | I will | speak ‖ I myself will testify against thee, O Israel; for I am God, | even | thy - | God.

8 I will not reprove thee because of thy sacrifices, or for thy | burnt - | offerings ‖ because they | were not | alway be | fore me.

9 I will take no bullock out | of thine | house ‖ nor | he-goat | out of thy | folds.

10 For all the beasts of the | forest are | mine ‖ and so are the cattle up | on a | thousand | hills.

11 I know all the fowls up | on the | mountains ‖ and the wild beasts of the | field are | in my | sight.

12 If I be hungry, I | will not | tell thee ‖ for the whole world is mine, and | all that | is there | in.

13 Thinkest thou that I will | eat bulls' | flesh ‖ and | drink the | blood of | goats?

14 Offer unto | God thanks | giving ‖ and pay thy vows un | to the | Most - | Highest.

15 And call upon me in the | time of | trouble ‖ so will I hear thee, and | thou shalt | praise - | me.

16 But unto the un | godly said | God ‖ Why dost thou preach my laws, and takest my | covenant | in thy | mouth;

17 Whereas thou hatest to | be re | formed ‖ and hast | cast my | words be | hind thee?

18 When thou sawest a thief, thou consentedst | unto | him ‖ and hast been par | taker | with the a | dulterers.

19 Thou hast let thy mouth speak | wicked | ness ‖ and with thy tongue thou | hast set | forth de | ceit.

20 Thou sattest, and spakest a | gainst thy | brother ‖ yea, and hast slandered | thine own | mother's | son.

21 These things hast thou done, and I held my tongue, and thou thoughtest wickedly, that I am even such a one | as thy | self ‖ but I will reprove thee, and set before thee the | things that | thou hast | done.

22 O consider this, ye that for | get - | God ‖ lest I pluck you away, and there be | none to de | liver | you.

23 Whoso offereth me thanks and praise, he | honoureth | me ‖ and to him that ordereth his conversation right, will I | show the sal | vation of | God.

PSALM li. *Miserere mei, Deus.*

HAVE mercy upon me, O God, after thy | great - | goodness ‖ according to the multitude of thy mercies do a | way - | mine of | fences.

2 Wash me throughly | from my | wickedness ‖ and | cleanse me | from my | sin.

3 For I ac | knowledge my | faults ‖ and my | sin is | ever be | fore me.

4 Against thee only have I sinned, and done this evil | in thy | sight ‖ that thou mightest be justified in thy saying, and | clear when | thou art | judged.

5 Behold, I was | shapen in | wickedness ‖ and in sin hath my | mother con | ceived | me.

6 But lo, thou requirest truth in the | inward | parts ‖ and shalt make me to understand | wisdom | secret | ly.

7 Thou shalt purge me with hyssop, and I | shall be | clean ‖ thou shalt wash me, and I shall be | whi - | ter than | snow.

8 Thou shalt make me hear of | joy and | gladness ‖ that the bones which thou hast | broken | may re | joice.

9 Turn thy face | from my | sins ‖ and put out | all - | my mis | deeds.

10 Make me a clean | heart, O | God ‖ and renew a | right - | spirit with | in me.

11 Cast me not away | from thy | presence ‖ and take not thy | Holy | Spirit | from me.

12 O give me the comfort of thy | help a | gain ‖ and stablish me | with thy | free - | Spirit.

13 Then shall I teach thy ways un | to the | wicked ‖ and sinners shall be con | verted | unto | thee.

14 Deliver me from blood-guiltiness, O God, thou that art the God | of my | health ‖ and my tongue shall | sing - | of thy | righteousness.

15 Thou shalt open my | lips, O | Lord ‖ and my | mouth shall | show thy | praise.

16 For thou desirest no sacrifice, else would I | give it | thee ‖ but thou delightest | not - | in burnt | offerings.

17 The sacrifice of God is a | troubled | spirit ‖ a broken and contrite heart, O God, | shalt thou | not de | spise.

18 O be favourable and gracious | unto | Sion ‖ build thou the | walls - | of Je | rusalem.

19 Then shalt thou be pleased with the sacrifice of righteousness, with the burnt-offerings | and ob | lations ‖ then shall they offer young | bullocks up | on thine | altar.

Psalm lii. *Quid gloriaris?*

WHY boastest thou thy | self, thou | tyrant ‖ that | thou canst | do - | mischief;

2 Whereas the | goodness of | God ‖ en | dur - | eth yet | daily?

3 Thy tongue im | agineth | wickedness ‖ and with lies thou cuttest | like a | sharp - | razor.

4 Thou hast loved unrighteousness | more than | goodness ‖ and to talk of | lies - | more than | righteousness.

5 Thou hast loved to speak all words that | may do | hurt ‖ O | thou - | false - | tongue.

6 Therefore shall God destroy | thee for | ever ‖ he shall take thee, and pluck thee out of thy dwelling, and root thee out of the | land - | of the | living.

7 The righteous also shall see | this, and | fear ‖ and shall | laugh - | him to | scorn;

8 Lo, this is the man that took not God | for his | strength ‖ but trusted unto the multitude of

his riches, and strengthened him | self - | in his | wickedness.

9 As for me, I am like a green olive-tree in the | house of | God ‖ my trust is in the tender mercy of | God for | ever and | ever.

10 I will always give thanks unto thee for that | thou hast | done ‖ and I will hope in thy Name, for thy | saints - | like it | well.

EVENING PRAYER.

PSALM liii. *Dixit insipiens.*

THE foolish body hath said | in his | heart ‖ There | is - | no - | God.

2 Corrupt are they, and become abominable | in their | wickedness ‖ there is | none that | doeth | good.

3 God looked down from heaven upon the | children of | men ‖ to see if there were any that would understand, and | seek - | after | God.

4 But they are all gone out of the way, they are altogether be | come a | bominable ‖ there is also none that doeth | good, - | no not | one.

5 Are not they without understanding that work | wicked | ness ‖ eating up my people as if they would eat bread? they | have not | called upon | God.

6 They were afraid where | no fear | was ‖ for God hath broken the bones of him that besieged thee; thou hast put them to confusion, be | cause - | God hath de | spised them.

7 Oh, that the salvation were given unto Is-

rael | out of | Sion ‖ Oh, that the Lord would deliver his | people | out of cap | tivity!

8 Then should | Jacob re | joice ‖ and Israel | should be | right - | glad.

Psalm liv. *Deus, in nomine.*

SAVE me, O God, for thy | Name's - | sake ‖ and a | venge me | in thy | strength.

2 Hear my | prayer, O | God ‖ and hearken unto the | words - | of my | mouth.

3 For strangers are risen | up a | gainst me ‖ and tyrants, which have not God before their eyes, | seek - | after my | soul.

4 Behold, God | is my | helper ‖ the Lord is with | them that up | hold my | soul.

5 He shall reward evil un | to mine | enemies ‖ destroy thou | them - | in thy | truth.

6 An offering of a free heart will I give thee, and praise thy | Name, O | Lord ‖ be | cause it | is so | comfortable.

7 For he hath delivered me out of | all my | trouble ‖ and mine eye hath seen his de | sire up | on mine | enemies.

Psalm lv. *Exaudi, Deus.*

HEAR my | prayer, O | God ‖ and hide not thy | self from | my pe | tition.

2 Take heed unto me, and | hear - | me ‖ how I mourn in my | prayer - | and am | vexed.

3 The enemy crieth so, and the ungodly cometh | on so | fast ‖ for they are minded to do me some mischief, so maliciously | are they | set a | gainst me.

4 My heart is disquieted with | in - | me ‖ and the fear of | death is | fallen up | on me.

5 Fearfulness and trembling are | come up | on me ! and an horrible dread hath | over | whelmed | me.

6 And I said, Oh that I had wings | like a | dove ‖ for then would I flee a | way, and | be at | rest.

7 Lo, then would I get me a | way, far | off ‖ and remain | in the | wilder | ness.

8 I would make | haste to es | cape ‖ because of the | stormy | wind and | tempest.

9 Destroy their tongues, O Lord, | and di | vide them ‖ for I have spied unrighteousness and | strife - | in the | city.

10 Day and night they go about within the | walls there | of ‖ mischief also and | sorrow are | in the | midst of it.

11 Wickedness | is there | in ‖ deceit and guile go not | out - | of their | streets.

12 For it is not an open enemy that hath done me | this dis | honour ‖ for | then I | could have | borne it :

13 Neither was it mine adversary that did magnify him | self a | gainst me ‖ for then peradventure I would have | hid my | self - | from him :

14 But it was even thou, | my com | panion ‖ my guide, and mine | own fa | miliar | friend.

15 We took sweet | counsel to | gether ‖ and walked in the | house of | God as | friends.

16 Let death come hastily upon them, and let them go down quick | into | hell ‖ for wickedness is in their | dwellings, | and a | mong them.

17 As for me, I will | call upon | God ‖ and the | Lord shall | save - | me.

18 In the evening, and morning, and at noon-day will I pray, | and that | instantly ‖ and | he shall | hear my | voice.

19 It is he that hath delivered my soul in peace from the battle that | was a | gainst me ‖ for there | were - | many | with me.

20 Yea, even God, that endureth forever, shall hear me, and | bring them | down ‖ for they will not | turn, nor | fear - | God.

21 He laid his hands upon such as be at | peace with | him ‖ and he | brake his | cove | nant.

22 The words of his mouth were softer than butter, having | war in his | heart ‖ his words were smoother than oil, and | yet they be | very | swords.

23 O cast thy burden upon the Lord, and | he shall | nourish thee ‖ and shall not suffer the | righteous to | fall for | ever.

24 And | as for | them ‖ thou, O God, shalt bring them into the | pit - | of de | struction.

25 The blood-thirsty and deceitful men shall not live out | half their | days ‖ nevertheless, my trust shall | be in | thee, O | Lord.

The Eleventh Day.
MORNING PRAYER.

Psalm lvi. *Miserere mei, Deus.*

BE merciful unto me, O God, for man goeth about | to de | vour me ‖ he is daily | fighting | and troubling | me.

2 Mine enemies are daily in hand to | swallow

me | up ‖ for they be many that fight against me, O | thou - | Most - | Highest.

3 Nevertheless, though I am | sometimes a | fraid ‖ yet put | I my | trust in | thee.

4 I will praise God, because | of his | word ‖ I have put my trust in God, and will not fear what | flesh can | do unto | me.

5 They daily mis | take my | words ‖ all that they imagine | is to | do me | evil.

6 They hold all together, and keep them | selves - | close ‖ and mark my steps, when they lay | wait - | for my | soul.

7 Shall they escape | for their | wickedness ‖ thou, O God, in thy dis | pleasure shalt | cast them | down.

8 Thou tellest my wanderings: put my tears in | to thy | bottle ‖ are not these things | noted | in thy | book?

9 Whensoever I call upon thee, then shall mine enemies be | put to | flight ‖ this I know; for | God is | on my | side.

10 In God's word will | I re | joice ‖ in the LORD's word | will I | comfort | me.

11 Yea, in God have I | put my | trust ‖ I will not be afraid what | man can | do unto | me.

12 Unto thee, O God, will I | pay my | vows ‖ unto | thee will | I give | thanks.

13 For thou hast delivered my soul from death, and my | feet from | falling ‖ that I may walk before God in the | light - | of the | living.

PSALM lvii. *Miserere mei, Deus.*

BE merciful unto me, O God, be merciful unto me; for my soul | trusteth in | thee ‖ and

under the shadow of thy wings shall be my ref-
uge, until this | tyranny be | over | past.

2 I will call unto the most | high - | God ¶
even unto the God that shall perform the cause |
which I | have in | hand.

3 He shall | send from | heaven ‖ and save me
from the reproof of him | that would | eat me |
up.

4 God shall send forth his | mercy and | truth ‖
my soul | is a | mong - | lions.

5 And I lie even among the children of men,
that are | set on | fire ‖ whose teeth are spears
and arrows, and their | tongue a | sharp - | sword.

6 Set up thyself, O God, a | bove the | heavens ‖
and thy | glory a | bove all the | earth.

7 They have laid a net for my feet, and pres-
sed | down my | soul ‖ they have digged a pit be-
fore me, and are fallen into the | midst of | it
them | selves.

8 My heart is fixed, O God, my | heart is |
fixed ‖ I will | sing - | and give | praise.

9 Awake up, my glory; awake, | lute and |
harp ‖ I myself | will a | wake right | early.

10 I will give thanks unto thee, O Lord, a |
mong the | people ‖ and I will sing unto | thee
a | mong the | nations.

11 For the greatness of thy mercy reacheth
un | to the | heavens ‖ and thy | truth un | to
the | clouds.

12 Set up thyself, O God, a | bove the |
heavens ‖ and thy | glory a | bove all the |
earth.

PSALM lviii. *Si vere utique.*

ARE your minds set upon righteousness, O ye | congre | gation ‖ and do ye judge the thing that is right, | O ye | sons of | men?

2 Yea, ye imagine mischief in your heart up | on the | earth ‖ and your | hands - | deal with | wickedness.

3 The ungodly are froward, even from their | mother's | womb ‖ as soon as they are born, they go a | stray, - | and speak | lies.

4 They are as venomous as the poison | of a | serpent ‖ even like the deaf | adder, that | stoppeth her | ears;

5 Which refuses to hear the | voice of the | charmer ‖ cha | rm he | never so | wisely.

6 Break their teeth, O God, in their mouths; smite the jaw-bones of the | lions, O | LORD ‖ let them fall away like water that runneth apace : and when they shoot their arrows let | them be | rooted | out.

7 Let them consume away like a snail, and be like the untimely fruit | of a | woman ‖ and let them | not - | see the | sun.

8 Or ever your pots be made | hot with | thorns ‖ so let indignation vex him, even as a | thing - | that is | raw.

9 The righteous shall rejoice when he | seeth the | vengeance ‖ he shall wash his footsteps in the | blood of | the un | godly.

10 So that a man shall say, Verily there is a reward | for the | righteous ‖ doubtless there is a | God that | judgeth the | earth.

EVENING PRAYER.

Psalm lix. *Eripe me de inimicis.*

DELIVER me from mine | enemies, O | God ‖ defend me from them | that rise | up a | gainst me.

2 O deliver me from the | wicked | doers ‖ and save me | from the | blood-thirsty | men.

3 For lo, they lie waiting | for my | soul ‖ the mighty men are gathered against me, without any offence or | fault of | me, O | Lord.

4 They run and prepare themselves with | out my | fault ‖ arise thou therefore to | help me, | and be | bold.

5 Stand up, O Lord God of hosts, thou God of Israel, to visit | all the | heathen ‖ and be not merciful unto them that offend | of ma | licious | wickedness.

6 They go to and fro | in the | evening ‖ they grin like a dog, and | run a | bout through the | city.

7 Behold, they speak with their mouth, and swords are | in their | lips ‖ for | who - | doth - | hear?

8 But thou, O Lord, shalt have them | in de | rision ‖ and thou shalt laugh | all the | heathen to | scorn.

9 My strength will I ascribe | unto | thee ‖ for thou art the | God - | of my | refuge.

10 God showeth me his goodness | plenteous | ly ‖ and God shall let me see my de | sire up | on mine | enemies.

11 Slay them not, lest my | people for | get it ‖

but scatter them abroad among the people, and put them down, O | Lord - | our de | fence.

12 For the sin of their | mouth, and for the words of their lips, they shall be taken | in their | pride ‖ and why? their preaching | is of | cursing and | lies.

13 Consume them in thy wrath, consume them, that | they may | perish ‖ and know that it is God that ruleth in Jacob, and unto the | ends - | of the | world.

14 And in the evening they | will re | turn ‖ grin like a dog, and will | go a | bout the | city.

15 They will run here and | there for | meat ‖ and grudge if they | be not | satis | fied.

16 As for me, I will sing of thy power, and will praise thy mercy be | times in the | morning ‖ for thou hast been my defence and my refuge in the | day - | of my | trouble.

17 Unto thee, O my strength, | will I | sing ‖ for thou, O God, art my refuge, | and my | merciful | God.

PSALM lx. *Deus, repulisti nos.*

O GOD, thou hast cast us out, and scattered | us a | broad ‖ thou hast also been displeased: O turn thee | unto | us a | gain.

2 Thou hast moved the land, and di | vided | it ‖ heal the sores there | of, - | for it | shaketh.

3 Thou hast showed thy people | heavy | things ‖ thou hast given us a | drink of | deadly | wine.

4 Thou hast given a token for | such as | fear thee ‖ that they may triumph be | cause - | of the | truth.

5 Therefore were thy be | loved de | livered ‖ help me with | thy right | hand, and | hear me.

6 God hath spoken in his holiness, I will rejoice, and di | vide - | Sichem ‖ and mete | out the | valley of | Succoth.

7 Gilead is mine, and Ma | nasses is | mine ‖ Ephraim also is the strength of my head; | Judah | is my | lawgiver;

8 Moab is my wash-pot; over Edom will I cast | out my | shoe ‖ Philistia, | be thou | glad of | me.

9 Who will lead me into the | strong - | city ‖ who will | bring me | into | Edom?

10 Hast not thou cast us | out, O | God ‖ wilt not thou, O God, | go out | with our | hosts?

11 O be thou our | help in | trouble ‖ for | vain is the | help of | man.

12 Through God will we | do great | acts ‖ for it is he that | shall tread | down our | enemies.

Psalm lxi. *Exaudi, Deus.*

HEAR my | crying, O | God ‖ give | ear un | to my | prayer.

2 From the ends of the earth will I | call up | on thee ‖ when my | heart - | is in | heaviness.

3 O set me up upon the rock that is | higher than | I ‖ for thou hast been my hope, and a strong tower | for me a | gainst the | enemy.

4 I will dwell in thy tabernacle | for - | ever ‖ and my trust shall be under the | covering | of thy | wings.

5 For thou, O Lord, hast | heard my de | sires ‖ and hast given an heritage unto | those that | fear thy | Name.

MORNING.] THE PSALTER. [DAY 12.

6 Thou shalt grant the King a | long - | life ‖ that his years may endure through | out all | gener | ations.

7 He shall dwell before | God for | ever ‖ O prepare thy loving mercy and faithfulness, | that they | may pre | serve him.

8 So will I always sing praise un | to thy | Name ‖ that I may | daily per | form my | vows.

The Twelfth Day.
MORNING PRAYER.
PSALM lxii. *Nonne Deo?*

MY soul truly waiteth | still upon | God ‖ for of him | cometh | my sal | vation.

2 He verily is my strength and | my sal | vation ‖ he is my defence, so that I | shall not | greatly | fall.

3 How long will ye imagine mischief against | every | man ‖ Ye shall be slain all the sort of you; yea, as a tottering wall shall ye be, and | like a | broken | hedge.

4 Their device is only how to put him out whom | God will ex | alt ‖ their delight is in lies; they give good words with their mouth, but | curse - | with their | heart.

5 Nevertheless, my soul, wait thou | still upon | God ‖ for my | hope - | is in | him.

6 He truly is my strength and | my sal | vation ‖ he is my defence, so | that I | shall not | fall.

7 In God is my health | and my | glory ‖ the rock of my might, and in | God - | is my | trust

8 O put your trust in him | alway, ye | people || pour out your hearts before him, for | God - | is our | hope.

9 As for the children of men, they | are but | vanity || the children of men are deceitful upon the weights; they are altogether lighter than | vani | ty it | self.

10 O trust not in wrong and robbery · give not yourselves | unto | vanity || if riches inc.ease, set | j .t your | heart up | on them.

11 God spake once, and twice I have also | heard the | same || that power be | longeth | unto | God;

12 And that thou, | Lord, art | merciful || for thou rewardest every man ac | cording | to his | work.

Psalm lxiii. *Deus, Deus meus.*

O GOD, thou | art my | God || early | will I | seek - | thee.

2 My soul thirsteth for thee; my flesh also longeth | after | thee || in a barren and dry land | where no | water | is.

3 Thus have I looked for thee in | ho.i | ness || that I might be | hold thy | power and | glory.

4 For thy loving-kindness is better than the | life it | self || my | lips shall | praise - | thee.

5 As long as I live will I magnify thee | in this | manner || and lift up my | hands - | in thy | Name.

6 My soul shall be satisfied, even as it were with | marrow and | fatness || when my mouth praiseth | thee with | joyful | lips.

7 Have I not remembered thee | in my | bed ⁞ and thought upon | thee when | I was | waking?

8 Because thou hast | been my | helper ‖ therefore under the shadow of thy | wings will | I re | joice.

9 My soul | hangeth up | on thee ‖ thy right hand | hath up | holden | me.

10 These also that seek the hurt | of my | soul ‖ they | shall go | under the | earth.

11 Let them fall upon the edge | of the | sword ‖ that they may | be a | portion for | foxes.

12 But the King shall rejoice in God; all they also that swear by him shall | be com | mended ‖ for the mouth of them that speak | lies - | shall be | stopped.

PSALM lxiv. *Exaudi, Deus.*

HEAR my voice, O God, | in my | prayer ‖ preserve my life from | fear - | of the | enemy.

2 Hide me from the gathering together | of the | froward ‖ and from the insur | rection of | wicked | doers;

3 Who have whet their tongue | like a | sword | and shoot out their arrows, | even | bitter | words;

4 That they may privily shoot at him | that is | perfect ‖ suddenly do they | hit him, and | fear - | not.

5 They encourage them | selves in | mischief ‖ and commune among themselves, how they may lay snares; and say, that | no - | man shall | see them.

6 They imagine wickedness, and | practise | it ‖ that they keep secret among themselves, every man in the | deep - | of his | heart.

7 But God shall suddenly shoot at them with a | swift - | arrow ‖ that | they - | shall be | wounded.

8 Yea, their own tongues shall | make them | fall ‖ insomuch that whoso seeth them shall | laugh - | them to | scorn.

9 And all men that see it shall say, This hath | God - | done ‖ for they shall perceive | that it | is his | work.

10 The righteous shall rejoice in the Lord, and put his | trust in | him ‖ and all they that are true of | heart - | shall be | glad.

EVENING PRAYER.

Psalm lxv. *Te decet hymnus.*

THOU, O God, art | praised in | Sion ‖ and unto thee shall the vow be per | formed | in Je | rusalem.

2 Thou that | hearest the | prayer ‖ unto | thee shall | all flesh | come.

3 My misdeeds pre | vail a | gainst me ‖ O be thou merciful | un - | to our | sins.

4 Blessed is the man whom thou choosest, and receivest | unto | thee ‖ he shall dwell in thy court, and shall be satisfied with the pleasures of thy house, even | of thy | holy | temple.

5 Thou shalt show us wonderful things in thy righteousness, O God of | our sal | vation ‖ thou that art the hope of all the ends of the earth, and of them that re | main in the | broad - | sea.

6 Who in his strength setteth | fast the | mountains ‖ and is | girded a | bout with | power

7 Who stilleth the raging | of the | sea ‖ and the noise of his waves, and the | madness | of the | people.

8 They also that dwell in the uttermost parts of the earth shall be afraid | at thy | tokens ‖ thou that makest the outgoings of the | morning and | evening to | praise thee.

9 Thou visitest the earth, and | blessest | it ‖ thou | makest it | very | plenteous.

10 The river of God is | full of | water ‖ thou preparest their corn, for so thou pro | videst | for the | earth.

11 Thou waterest her furrows; thou sendest rain into the little | valleys there | of ‖ thou makest it soft with the drops of rain, and | bless-est the | increase | of it.

12 Thou crownest the year | with thy | good-ness ‖ and thy | clouds - | drop - | fatness.

13 They shall drop upon the dwellings | of the | wilderness ‖ and the little hills shall re | joice on | every | side.

14 The folds shall be | full of | sheep ‖ the val-leys also shall stand so thick with corn, | that they shall | laugh and | sing.

PSALM lxvi. *Jubilate Deo.*

O BE joyful in God, | all ye | lands ‖ sing praises unto the honour of his Name; make his | praise - | to be | glorious.

2 Say unto God, O how wonderful art thou | in thy | works ‖ through the greatness of thy power shall thine enemies be found | liars | unto | thee.

3 For all the world shall | worship | thee ‖ sing of thee, and | praise - | thy - | Name.

4 O come hither, and behold the | works of | God ‖ how wonderful he is in his doing to | ward the | children of | men.

5 He turned the sea into | dry - | land ‖ so that they went through the water on foot; there did | we re | joice there | of.

6 He ruleth with his power for ever; his eyes be | hold the | people ‖ and such as will not believe shall not be able | to ex | alt them | selves.

7 O praise our | God, ye | people ‖ and make the voice of his | praise - | to be | heard ;

8 Who holdeth our | soul in | life ‖ and suffereth | not our | feet to | slip.

9 For thou, O God, hast | proved | us ‖ thou also hast tried us, | like as | silver is | tried.

10 Thou broughtest us in | to the | snare ‖ and laidest | trouble up | on our | loins.

11 Thou sufferedst men to ride | over our | heads ‖ we went through fire and water, and thou broughtest us out in | to a | wealthy | place.

12 I will go into thine house with | burnt - | offerings ‖ and will pay thee my vows, which I promised with my lips, and spake with my mouth, | when I | was in | trouble.

13 I will offer unto thee fat burnt-sacrifices, with the | incense of | rams ‖ I will | offer | bullocks and | goats.

14 O come hither, and hearken, all ye that | fear - | God ‖ and I will tell you what he hath | done for my | soul.

[MORNING.] THE PSALTER. [DAY 13

15 I called unto him | with my | mouth ‖ and gave him | praises | with my | tongue.

16 If I incline unto wickedness | with mine | heart ‖ the | Lord - | will not | hear me.

17 But | God hath | heard me ‖ and considered the | voice - | of my | prayer.

18 Praised be God, who hath not cast | out my | prayer ‖ nor | turned his | mercy | from me.

PSALM lxvii. *Deus misereatur.*

GOD be merciful unto us, | and - | bless us ‖ and show us the light of his countenance, and be | merciful | unto | us;

2 That thy way may be | known upon | earth ‖ thy saving | health a | mong all | nations.

3 Let the people praise | thee, O | God ‖ yea, let | all the | people | praise thee.

4 O let the nations rejoice | and be | glad ‖ for thou shalt judge the folk righteously, and govern the | nations | upon | earth.

5 Let the people praise | thee, O | God ‖ yea, let | all the | people | praise thee.

6 Then shall the earth bring | forth her | increase ‖ and God, even our own God, shall | give | - us his | blessing.

7 God | - shall | bless us ‖ and all the ends | of the | world shall | fear him.

The Thirteenth Day.

MORNING PRAYER.

PSALM lxviii. *Exurgat Deus.*

LET God arise, and let his enemies | be - | scattered ‖ let them also that | hate him | flee be | fore him.

2 Like as the smoke vanisheth, so shalt thou | drive them a | way ‖ and like as wax melteth at the fire, so let the ungodly perish | at the | presence of | God.

3 But let the righteous be glad, and re | joice before | God ‖ let them | also be | merry and | joyful.

4 O sing unto God, and sing praises un | to his | Name ‖ magnify him that rideth upon the heavens, as it were upon an horse; praise him in his Name JAH, | and re | joice be | fore him.

5 He is a Father of the fatherless, and defendeth the cause | of the | widows ‖ even God in his | holy | habi | tation.

6 He is the God that maketh men to be of one mind in an house, and bringeth the prisoners out | of cap | tivity ‖ but letteth the runagates con | tinue | in - | scarceness.

7 O God, when thou wentest forth be | fore the | people ‖ when thou | wentest | through the | wilderness,

8 The earth shook, and the heavens dropped at the | presence of | God ‖ even as Sinai also was moved at the presence of God, who | is the | God of | Israel.

9 Thou, O God, sentest a gracious rain upon | thine in | heritance ‖ and refreshedst it | when - | it was | weary.

10 Thy congregation shall | dwell there | in ‖ for thou, O God, hast of thy goodness pre | pared | for the | poor.

11 The Lord | gave the | word ‖ great was the | company | of the | preachers.

12 Kings with their armies did flee, and | were dis | comfited ‖ and they of the | household di | vided the | spoil.

13 Though ye have lain among the pots, yet shall ye be as the wings | of a | dove ‖ that is covered with silver wings, | and her | feathers like | gold.

14 When the Almighty scattered kings for | their - | sake ‖ then were they as | white as | snow in | Salmon.

15 As the hill of Basan, so is | God's - | hill ‖ even an high hill, | as the | hill of | Basan.

16 Why hop ye so, ye high hills? this is God's hill, in the which it pleaseth | him to | dwell ‖ yea, the LORD will a | bide in | it for | ever.

17 The chariots of God are twenty thousand, even | thousands of | angels ‖ and the Lord is among them as in the | holy | place of | Sinai.

18 Thou art gone up on high, thou hast led captivity captive, and received | gifts for | men ‖ yea, even for thine enemies, that the LORD | God might | dwell a | mong them.

19 Praised be the | Lord - | daily ‖ even the God who helpeth us, and poureth his | bene | fits up | on us.

20 He is our God, even the God of whom | cometh sal | vation ‖ GOD is the Lord, by | whom we es | cape - | death.

21 God shall wound the head | of his | enemies ‖ and the hairy scalp of such a one as goeth on | still in his | wicked | ness.

22 The Lord hath said, I will bring my people again, as I | did from | Basan ‖ mine own will I

bring again, as I did sometime | from the | deep of the | sea.

23 That thy foot may be dipped in the blood | of thine | enemies ‖ and that the tongue of thy dogs may be | red - | through the | same.

24 It is well seen, O God, | how thou | goest ‖ how thou, my God and King, | goest | in the | sanctuary.

25 The singers go before, the minstrels | follow | after ‖ in the midst are the damsels | playing | with the | timbrels.

26 Give thanks, O Israel, unto God the Lord in the | congre | gations ‖ from the | ground - | of the | heart.

27 There is little Benjamin their ruler, and the princes of | Judah their | council ‖ the princes of Zebulon, | and the | princes of | Nephthali.

28 Thy God hath sent forth | strength for | thee ‖ stablish the thing, O God, that | thou hast | wrought in | us,

29 For thy temple's sake | at Je | rusalem ‖ so shall kings bring | presents | unto | thee.

30 When the company of the spearmen, and multitude of the mighty are scattered abroad among the beasts of the people, so that they humbly bring | pieces of | silver ‖ and when he hath scattered the people | that de | light in | war;

31 Then shall the princes come | out of | Egypt ‖ the Morians' land shall soon stretch | out her | hands unto | God.

32 Sing unto God, O ye kingdoms | of the | earth ‖ O sing | praises un | to the | Lord;

[EVENING.] THE PSALTER. [DAY 13

33 Who sitteth in the heavens over all, from | the begin | ning ‖ lo, he doth send out his voice ; yea, and | that a | mighty | voice.

34 Ascribe ye the power to God | over | Israel ‖ his worship and | strength is | in the | clouds.

35 O God, wonderful art thou in thy | holy | places ‖ even the God of Israel, he will give strength and power unto his people. | Bless - | ed be | God.

EVENING PRAYER.

PSALM lxix.   *Salvum me fac.*

SAVE me, | O - | God ‖ for the waters are come in, | even | unto my | soul.

2 I stick fast in the deep mire, where | no ground | is ‖ I am come into deep waters, so that the | floods run | over | me.

3 I am weary of crying ; my | throat is | dry ‖ my sight faileth me for waiting so | long up | on my | God.

4 They that hate me without a cause are more than the hairs | of my | head ‖ they that are mine enemies, and would de | stroy me | guiltless, are | mighty.

5 I paid them the things that I | never | took ‖ God, thou knowest my simpleness, and my faults | are not | hid from | thee.

6 Let not them that trust in thee, O Lord God of hosts, be ashamed | for my | cause ‖ let not those that seek thee be confounded through me, O | Lord - | God of | Israel.

7 And why ? for thy sake have I | suffered re | proof ‖ shame | hath - | covered my | face.

8 I am become a stranger un | to my | brethren ‖ even an alien un | to my | mother's | children.

9 For the zeal of thine house hath even | eaten | me ‖ and the rebukes of them that rebuked | thee are | fallen upon | me.

10 I wept, and chastened my | self with | fasting ‖ and that was | turned to | my re | proof.

11 I put on | sackcloth | also ‖ and | they - | jested up | on me.

12 They that sit in the gate | speak a | gainst me ‖ and the drunkards | make - | songs up | on me.

13 But, Lord, I make my prayer | unto | thee ‖ in | an ac | ceptable | time.

14 Hear me, O God, in the multitude | of thy | mercy ‖ even in the | truth of | thy sal | vation.

15 Take me out of the mire, that I | sink - | not ‖ O let me be delivered from them that hate me, and | out of | the deep | waters.

16 Let not the water-flood drown me, neither let the deep | swallow me | up ‖ and let not the pit | shut her | mouth up | on me.

17 Hear me, O Lord, for thy loving-kindness is | comfort | able ‖ turn thee unto me according to the | multitude | of thy | mercies :

18 And hide not thy face from thy servant; for I | am in | trouble ‖ O | haste - | thee, and | hear me.

19 Draw nigh unto my | soul, and | save it ‖ O deliver me, be | cause - | of mine | enemies.

20 Thou hast known my reproof, my shame, and | my dis | honour ‖ mine adversaries are | all - | in thy | sight.

21 Thy rebuke hath broken my heart; I am | full of | heaviness ‖ I looked for some to have pity on me, but there was no man, neither found I | any to | comfort | me.

22 They gave me | gall to | eat ‖ and when I was thirsty they | gave me | vinegar to | drink.

23 Let their table be made a snare to take them | selves with | al ‖ and let the things that should have been for their wealth be unto them | an oc | casion of | falling.

24 Let their eyes be blinded, | that they | see not ‖ and ever | bow thou | down their | backs.

25 Pour out thine indig | nation up | on them ‖ and let thy wrathful dis | pleasure take | hold of | them.

26 Let their habi | tation be | void ‖ and no man to | dwell - | in their | tents.

27 For they persecute him whom | thou hast | smitten ‖ and they talk how they may vex | them whom thou hast | wounded.

28 Let them fall from one wickedness | to an | other ‖ and not | come in | to thy | righteousness.

29 Let them be wiped out of the book | of the | living ‖ and not be | written a | mong the | right-eous.

30 As for me, when I am poor | and in | heavi-ness ‖ thy help, O | God, shall | lift me | up.

31 I will praise the Name of God | with a | song ‖ and magni | fy it | with thanks | giving.

32 This also shall | please the | Lord ‖ better than a bullock | that hath | horns and | hoofs.

33 The humble shall consider this, | and be | glad ‖ seek ye after God, | and your | soul shall | live.

34 For the Lord | heareth the | poor ‖ and de | spiseth | not his | prisoners.

35 Let heaven and | earth - | praise him ‖ the sea, and | all that | moveth there | in.

36 For God will save Sion, and build the | cities of | Judah ‖ that men may dwell there, and | have it | in pos | session.

37 The posterity also of his servants | shall in | herit it ‖ and they that love his | Name shall | dwell there | in.

Psalm lxx. *Deus, in adjutorium.*

HASTE thee, O God, | to de | liver me ‖ make haste to | help - | me, O | Lord.

2 Let them be ashamed and confounded that seek | after my | soul ‖ let them be turned backward and put to confusion | that - | wish me | evil.

3 Let them for their reward be soon | brought to | shame ‖ that cry | over | me, There! | there!

4 But let all those that seek thee be joyful and | glad in | thee ‖ and let all such as delight in thy salvation say alway, The | Lord - | be - | praised.

5 As for me, I am poor | and in | misery ‖ haste thee | unto | me, O | God.

6 Thou art my helper, and | my re | deemer ‖ O Lord, | make - | no long | tarrying.

The Fourteenth Day.

MORNING PRAYER.

Psalm lxxi. *In te, Domine, speravi.*

IN thee, O Lord, have I put my trust; let me never be put | to con | fusion ‖ but rid me, and deliver me, in thy righteousness; incline thine ear | unto | me, and | save me.

2 Be thou my stronghold, whereunto I may | alway re | sort ‖ thou hast promised to help me, for thou art my house of de | fence, - | and my | castle.

3 Deliver me, O my God, out of the hand of | the un | godly ‖ out of the hand of the un | righteous and | cruel | man.

4 For thou, O Lord God, art the thing | that I | long for ‖ thou art my hope, | even | from my | youth.

5 Through thee have I been holden up ever since | I was | born ‖ thou art he that took me out of my mother's womb; my praise | shall be | always of | thee.

6 I am become as it were a monster | unto | many ‖ but my sure | trust - | is in | thee.

7 O let my mouth be filled | with thy | praise ‖ that I may sing of thy glory and | honour | all the day | long.

8 Cast me not away in the | time of | age ‖ forsake me not | when my | strength - | faileth me.

9 For mine enemies speak against me; and they that lay wait for my soul take their counsel to | gether, | saying ‖ God hath forsaken him;

persecute him, and take him, for there is | none - | to de | liver him.

10 Go not far from me, | O - | God ‖ my God, | haste - | thee to | help me.

11 Let them be confounded and perish that are a | gainst my | soul ‖ let them be covered with shame and dishonour that | seek to | do me | evil.

12 As for me, I will patiently a | bide - | alway ‖ and will | praise thee | more and | more.

13 My mouth shall daily speak of thy righteousness | and sal | vation ‖ for I | know no | end there | of.

14 I will go forth in the strength of the | Lord - | God ‖ and will make mention | of thy | righteousness | only.

15 Thou, O God, hast taught me from my youth up | until | now ‖ therefore will I tell | of thy | wondrous | works.

16 Forsake me not, O God, in mine old age, when | I am gray | headed ‖ until I have showed thy strength unto this generation, and thy power to all them | that are | yet for to | come.

17 Thy righteousness, O God, is | very | high ‖ and great things are they that thou hast done; O God, | who is | like unto | thee!

18 O what great troubles and adversities hast thou showed me! and yet didst thou | turn and re | fresh me ‖ yea, and broughtest me from the | deep of the | earth a | gain.

19 Thou hast brought me to | great - | honour ‖ and comforted | me on | every | side:

20 Therefore will I praise thee, and thy faith-

fulness, O God, playing upon an | instrument of | music ‖ unto thee will I sing upon the harp, O thou | Holy | One of | Israel.

21 My lips will be fain when I sing | unto | thee ‖ and so will my soul | whom thou | hast de | livered.

22 My tongue also shall talk of thy righteousness | all the day | long ‖ for they are confounded and brought unto shame that | seek to | do me | evil.

PSALM lxxii. *Deus, judicium.*

GIVE the King thy judgments, | O - | God ¶ and thy righteousness un | to the | King's - | son.

2 Then shall he judge thy people according | unto | right ‖ and de | fend - | the - | poor.

3 The mountains also | shall bring | peace ₰ and the little hills | righteousness | unto the | people.

4 He shall keep the simple folk | by their | right ‖ defend the children of the poor, and | punish the | wrong - | doer.

5 They shall fear thee, as long as the sun and | moon en | dureth ‖ from one gener | ation | to an | other.

6 He shall come down like the rain into a | fleece of | wool ‖ even as the | drops that | water the | earth.

7 In his time shall the | righteous ! flourish ⁋ yea, and abundance of peace, so long | as the | moon en | dureth.

8 His dominion shall be also from the one sea |

to the | other ‖ and from the flood un | to the | world's - | end.

9 They that dwell in the wilderness shall | kneel be | fore him ‖ his enemies | shall - | lick the | dust.

10 The kings of Tharsis and of the isles | shall give | presents ‖ the kings of Arabia and | Saba | shall bring | gifts.

11 All kings shall fall | down be | fore him ‖ all | nations shall | do him | service.

12 For he shall deliver the poor | when he | crieth ‖ the needy also, and | him that | hath no | helper.

13 He shall be favourable to the | simple and | needy ‖ and shall preserve the | souls - | of the | poor.

14 He shall deliver their souls from | false- hood and | wrong ‖ and dear shall their | blood be | in his | sight.

15 He shall live, and unto him shall be given of the | gold of A | rabia ‖ prayer shall be made ever unto him, and | daily | shall he be | praised.

16 There shall be an heap of corn in the earth, high up | on the | hills ‖ his fruit shall shake like Libanus, and shall be green in the city like | grass up | on the | earth.

17 His Name shall endure for ever; his Name shall remain under the sun amongst | the pos | terities ‖ which shall be blessed through him; and | all the | heathen shall | praise him.

18 Blessed be the LORD God, even the | God of | Israel ‖ which only | doeth | wondrous | things;

19 And blessed be the Name of his Majesty | for - | ever ‖ and all the earth shall be filled with his Majesty. | Amen, | A - | men.

EVENING PRAYER.

PSALM lxxiii. *Quam bonus Israel!*

TRULY God is loving | unto | Israel ‖ even unto such as are | of a | clean - | heart.

2 Nevertheless, my feet were | almost | gone ‖ my | treadings had | well-nigh | slipt.

3 And why? I was grieved | at the | wicked ‖ I do also see the un | godly in | such pros | perity.

4 For they are in no | peril of | death ‖ but are | lust - | y and | strong.

5 They come in no misfortune like | other | folk ‖ neither are they | plagued like | other | men.

6 And this is the cause that they are so | bolder with | pride ‖ and | over | whelmed with | cruelty.

7 Their eyes | swell with | fatness ‖ and they do | even | what they | lust.

8 They corrupt other, and speak of | wicked | blasphemy ‖ their talking is a | gainst the | Most - | High.

9 For they stretch forth their mouth un | to the | heaven ‖ and their tongue | goeth | through the | world.

10 Therefore fall the people | unto | them ‖ and thereout suck they | no - | small ad | vantage

11 Tush, say they, how should | God per ceive it ‖ is there | knowledge in | the Most | High ?

12 Lo, these are the ungodly, these prosper in the world, and these have riches | in pos | session ‖ and I said, Then have I cleansed my heart in vain, and | washed mine | hands in | innocency.

13 All the day long have | I been | punished ‖ and | chastened | every | morning.

14 Yea, and I had almost said | even as | they ‖ but lo, then I should have condemned the gener | ation | of thy | children.

15 Then thought I to under | stand - | this ‖ but it | was too | hard - | for me,

16 Until I went into the sanctu | ary of | God ‖ then understood I the | end - | of these | men ;

17 Namely, how thou dost set them in | slippery | places ‖ and casteth them down, | and de | stroyest | them.

18 O how suddenly do | they con | sume ‖ perish, and | come to a | fearful | end !

19 Yea, even like as a dream when | one a | waketh ‖ so shalt thou make their image to | vanish | out of the | city.

20 Thus my | heart was | grieved ‖ and it went | even | through my | reins.

21 So foolish | was I, and | ignorant ‖ even as it | were a | beast be | fore thee.

22 Nevertheless, I am | alway by | thee ‖ for thou hast holden me | by my | right - | hand.

23 Thou shalt guide me | with thy | counsel ‖ and after that re | ceive - | me with | glory.

Evening.] THE PSALTER. [Day 14

24 Whom have I in | heaven but | thee ‖ and there is none upon earth that I desire in com | pari | son of | thee.

25 My flesh and my | heart - | faileth ‖ but God is the strength of my heart, | and my | portion for | ever.

26 For lo, they that forsake | thee shall | perish ‖ thou hast destroyed all them that commit | forni | cation a | gainst thee.

27 But it is good for me to hold me fast by God to put my trust in the | Lord - | God ‖ and to speak of all thy works in the | gates of the | daughter of | Sion.

Psalm lxxiv. *Ut quid, Deus?*

O GOD, wherefore art thou absent | from us so | long ‖ why is thy wrath so hot against the | sheep - | of thy | pasture?

2 O think upon thy | congre | gation ‖ whom thou hast purchased, | and re | deemed of | old.

3 Think upon the tribe of | thine in | heritance ‖ and Mount Sion, | wherein | thou hast | dwelt.

4 Lift up thy feet, that thou mayest utterly destroy | every | enemy ‖ which hath done | evil | in thy | sanctuary.

5 Thine adversaries roar in the midst of thy | congre | gations ‖ and set | up their | banners for | tokens.

6 He that hewed timber afore out of the | thick - | trees ‖ was known to bring it | to an | excellent | work.

7 But now they break down all the carved | work there | of ‖ with | axes | and - | hammers.

8 They have set fire upon thy | holy | places ‖ and have defiled the dwelling-place of thy Name, | even | unto the | ground.

9 Yea, they said in their hearts, Let us make havoc of them | alto | gether ‖ thus have they burnt up all the houses of | God - | in the | land.

10 We see not our tokens; there is not one | prophet | more ‖ no, not one is there among us. that under | standeth | any | more.

11 O God, how long shall the adversary | do this dis | honour ‖ how long shall the enemy blas | pheme thy | Name? for | ever?

12 Why withdrawest | thou thy | hand ‖ why pluckest thou not thy right hand out of thy bosom | to con | sume the | enemy?

13 For God is my | King of | old ‖ the help that is done upon earth, he | doeth | it him | self.

14 Thou didst divide the sea | through thy | power ‖ thou breakest the heads of the | dragons | in the | waters.

15 Thou smotest the heads of Leviathan | in - | pieces ‖ and gavest him to be meat for the | people | in the | wilderness.

16 Thou broughtest out fountains and waters out of the | hard - | rocks ‖ thou | driedst up | mighty | waters.

17 The day is thine, and the | night is | thine ‖ thou hast prepared the | light - | and the | sun.

18 Thou hast set all the borders | of the | earth ‖ thou hast | made - | summer and | winter.

19 Remember this, O Lord, how the enemy |

hath re | buked ‖ and how the foolish people | hath blas | phemed thy | Name.

20 O deliver not the soul of thy turtle-dove unto the multitude | of the | enemies ‖ and forget not the congregation | of the | poor for | ever.

21 Look up | on the | covenant ‖ for all the earth is full of darkness, and | cruel | habi | tations.

22 O let not the simple go a | way a | shamed ‖ but let the poor and needy give | praise un | to thy | Name.

23 Arise, O God, maintain | thine own | cause ‖ remember how the foolish | man blas | phemeth thee | daily.

24 Forget not the voice | of thine | enemies ‖ the presumption of them that hate thee increaseth | ever | more and | more.

The Fifteenth Day.
MORNING PRAYER.

PSALM lxxv. *Confitebimur tibi.*

UNTO thee, O God, | do we give | thanks ‖ yea, unto | thee - | do we give | thanks.

2 Thy Name also | is so | nigh ‖ and that do thy | wondrous | works de | clare.

3 When I receive the | congre | gation ‖ I shall judge ac | cording | unto | right.

4 The earth is weak, and all the inhabiters | there - | of ‖ I bear | up the | pillars | of it.

5 I said unto the fools, Deal | not so | madly ‖ and to the ungodly, | Set not | up your | horn.

6 Set not up your | horn on | high ‖ and | speak not | with a stiff | neck.

7 For promotion cometh neither from the east, nor | from the | west ‖ nor | yet - | from the | south.

8 And why? | God is the | Judge ‖ he putteth down one, and | setteth | up an | other.

9 For in the hand of the LORD there is a cup, and the | wine is | red ‖ it is full mixt, and he | poureth | out of the | same.

10 As for the | dregs there | of ‖ all the ungodly of the earth shall | drink them and | suck them | out.

11 But I will talk of the | God of | Jacob ‖ and | praise - | him for | ever.

12 All the horns of the ungodly also | will I | break ‖ and the horns of the | righteous shall | be ex | alted.

PSALM lxxvi. *Notus in Judæa.*

IN Jewry is | God - | known ‖ his | Name is | great in | Israel.

2 At Salem | is his | tabernacle ‖ and his | dwell - | ing in | Sion.

3 There brake he the arrows | of the | bow ‖ the shield, the | sword, - | and the | battle.

4 Thou art of more | honour and | might ‖ than the | hills - | of the | robbers.

5 The proud are robbed, they have | slept their | sleep ‖ and all the men whose hands were | mighty | have found | nothing.

6 At thy rebuke, O | God of | Jacob ‖ both the | chariot and | horse are | fallen.

7 Thou, even thou art | to be | feared ‖ and who may stand in thy | sight when | thou art | angry?

8 Thou didst cause thy judgment to be | heard from | heaven ‖ the earth | trembled, | and was | still,

9 When God a | rose to | judgment ‖ and to help | all the | meek upon | earth.

10 The fierceness of man shall turn | to thy | praise ‖ and the fierceness of them | shalt - | thou re | frain.

11 Promise unto the LORD your God, and keep it, all ye that are | round a | bout him ‖ bring presents unto him that | ought - | to be | feared.

12 He shall refrain the | spirit of | princes ‖ and is wonderful among the | kings - | of the | earth.

PSALM lxxvii. *Voce mea ad Dominum.*

I WILL cry unto God | with my | voice ‖ even unto God will I cry with my voice, and he shall | hearken | unto | me.

2 In the time of my trouble I | sought the | Lord ‖ my sore ran, and ceased not in the night-season; my | soul re | fused | comfort.

3 When I am in heaviness, I will | think upon | God ‖ when my heart is | vexed, I | will com | plain.

4 Thou holdest mine | eyes - | waking ‖ I am so feeble | that I | cannot | speak.

5 I have considered the | days of | old ‖ and the | years - | that are | past.

6 I call to re | membrance my | song ‖ and in the night I commune with mine own heart, and | search - | out my | spirit.

7 Will the Lord absent him | self for | ever ‖ and will he be | no - | more in | treated?

8 Is his mercy clean | gone for | ever ‖ and is his promise come utterly to an | end for | ever | more?

9 Hath God forgotten | to be | gracious ‖ and will he shut up his loving | kindness | in dis | pleasure?

10 And I said, It is mine | own in | firmity ‖ but I will remember the years of the right hand | of the | Most - | Highest.

11 I will remember the works | of the | Lord ‖ and call to mind thy | wonders | of old | time.

12 I will think also of | all thy | works ‖ and my talking | shall be | of thy | doings.

13 Thy way, O | God, is | holy ‖ who is so great a | God as | our - | God?

14 Thou art the God that | doest | wonders ‖ and hast declared thy | power a | mong the | people.

15 Thou hast mightily de | livered thy | people ‖ even the | sons of | Jacob and | Joseph.

16 The waters saw thee, O God, the waters saw thee, and | were a | fraid ‖ the | depths - | also were | troubled.

17 The clouds poured out water, the | air - | thundered ‖ and thine | arrows | went a | broad.

18 The voice of thy thunder was heard | round a | bout ‖ the lightnings shone upon the ground; the earth was | moved, and | shook with | al.

19 Thy way is in the sea, and thy paths in the | great - | waters ‖ and thy | footsteps | are not | known.
20 Thou leddest thy | people like | sheep ‖ by the | hand of | Moses and | Aaron.

EVENING PRAYER.

PSALM lxxviii. *Attendite, popule.*

HEAR my law, | O my | people ‖ incline your ears unto the | words - | of my | mouth.
2 I will open my mouth | in a | parable ‖ I will de | clare hard | sentences of | old ;
3 Which we have | heard and | known ‖ and such as our | fa - | thers have | told us ;
4 That we should not hide them from the children of the gener | ations to | come ‖ but to show the honour of the LORD, his mighty and wonderful | works that | he hath | done.
5 He made a covenant with Jacob, and gave | Israel a | law ‖ which he commanded our fore | fathers to | teach their | children ;
6 That their posterity | might know | it ‖ and the children | which were | yet un | born ;
7 To the intent that when | they came | up ‖ they might show | their - | children the | same ;
8 That they might put their | trust in | God ‖ and not to forget the works of God, but to | keep - | his com | mandments ;
9 And not to be as their forefathers, a faithless and stubborn | gener | ation ‖ a generation that set not their heart aright, and whose spirit cleaveth not | steadfastly | unto | God ;

10 Like as the | children of | Ephraim ‖ who being harnessed, and carrying bows, turned themselves back | in the | day of | battle.

11 They kept not the | covenant of | God ‖ and | would not | walk in his | Law;

12 But forgat what | he had | done ‖ and the wonderful works that | he had | showed | for them.

13 Marvellous things did he in the sight of our forefathers, in the | land of | Egypt ‖ even | in the | field of | Zoan.

14 He divided the sea, and | let them go | through ‖ he made the waters to | stand - | on an | heap.

15 In the day-time also he led them | with a | cloud ‖ and all the night through | with a | light of | fire.

16 He clave the hard rocks | in the | wilderness ‖ and gave them drink thereof, as it had been | out of | the great | depth.

17 He brought waters out of the | stony | rock ‖ so that it | gushed out | like the | rivers.

18 Yet for all this they sinned | more a | gainst him ‖ and provoked the | Most Highest | in the | wilderness.

19 They tempted God | in their | hearts ‖ and required | meat - | for their | lust.

20 They spake against God | also, | saying ‖ Shall God prepare a | table | in the | wilderness?

21 He smote the stony rock indeed, that the water gushed out, and the streams | flowed with | al ‖ but can he give bread also, or provide | flesh - | for his | people?

22 When the Lord heard this, | he was | wroth ‖ so the fire was kindled in Jacob, and there came up heavy dis | pleasure a | gainst - | Israel ;

23 Because they believed | not in | God ‖ and put | not their | trust in his | help.

24 So he commanded the | clouds a | bove] and | opened the | doors of | heaven.

25 He rained down manna also upon them | for to | eat ‖ and | gave them | food from | heaven.

26 So man did eat | angels' | food ‖ for he | sent them | meat e | nough.

27 He caused the east wind to blow | under | .eaven ‖ and through his power he brought | in the | south-west | wind.

28 He rained flesh upon them as | thick as | dust ‖ and feathered fowls | like as the | sand of the | sea.

29 He let it fall a | mong their | tents ‖ even round a | bout their | habi | tation.

30 So they did eat, and were well filled ; for he gave them their | own de | sire ‖ they were not disap | pointed | of their | lust.

31 But while the meat was yet in their mouths, the heavy wrath of God came upon them, and slew the | wealthiest | of them ‖ yea, and smote down the chosen | men that | were in | Israel.

32 But for all this they | sinned yet | more ‖ and believed | not his | wondrous | works.

33 Therefore their days did he con | sume in | vanity ‖ and their | years - | in - | trouble

34 When he slew them, they | sought - | him ‖

and turned them early, and in | quired | after | God.

35 And they remembered that God | was their | strength ‖ and that the high | God was | their re | deemer.

36 Nevertheless, they did but flatter him | with their | mouth ‖ and dissembled | with him | in their | tongue.

37 For their heart was not | whole with | him ‖ neither continued they | steadfast | in his | covenant.

38 But he was so merciful, that he forgave | their mis | deeds ‖ and de | stroyed | them - | not.

39 Yea, many a time turned he his | wrath a | way ‖ and would not suffer his whole dis | pleasure | to a | rise.

40 For he considered that they | were but | flesh ‖ and that they were even a wind that passeth away, and | cometh | not a | gain.

41 Many a time did they provoke him | in the | wilderness ‖ and | grieved him | in the | desert.

42 They turned back, and | tempted | God ‖ and moved the | Holy | One in | Israel.

43 They thought not | of his | hand ‖ and of the day when he delivered them from the | hand - | of the | enemy ;

44 How he had wrought his miracles | in - | Egypt ‖ and his wonders | in the | field of | Zoan

45 He turned their waters | into | blood ‖ so that they might not | drink - | of the | rivers.

46 He sent lice among them, and de | voured them | up ‖ and | frogs - | to de | stroy them.

47 He gave their fruit un | to the | caterpillar ‖ and their | labour un | to the | grasshopper.

48 He destroyed their | vines with | hailstones ‖ and their | mulberry | trees with the | frost.

49 He smote their cattle | also with | hailstones ‖ and their | flocks - | with hot | thunderbolts.

50 He cast upon them the furiousness of his wrath, anger, dis | pleasure, and | trouble ‖ and sent | evil | angels a | mong them.

51 He made a way to his indignation, and spared not their | soul from | death ‖ but gave their life | over | to the | pestilence.

52 And smote all the | first-born in | Egypt ‖ the most principal and mightiest | in the | dwellings of | Ham.

53 But as for his own people he led them | forth like | sheep ‖ and carried them in the | wilderness | like a | flock.

54 He brought them out safely, that they | should not | fear ‖ and overwhelmed their | enemies | with the | sea.

55 And brought them within the borders | of his | sanctuary ‖ even to his mountain, which he purchased | with his | right - | hand.

56 He cast out the heathen | also be | fore them ‖ caused their land to be divided among them for an heritage, and made the tribes of Israel to | dwell - | in their | tents.

57 So they tempted, and displeased the most | high - | God ‖ and kept | not his | testi | monies.

58 But turned their backs, and fell away | like

their | forefathers ‖ starting a | side like a | broken | bow.

59 For they grieved him with | their hill | altars ǁ and provoked him to dis | pleasure | with their | images.

60 When God heard this, | he was | wroth ǁ and took | sore dis | pleasure at | Israel ;

61 So that he forsook the tebernacle | in - | Silo ‖ even the tent that he had | pitched a | mong - | men.

62 He delivered their power in | to cap | tivity ‖ and their beauty in | to the | enemy's | hand.

63 He gave his people over also un | to the | sword ‖ and was | wroth with | his in | heritance.

64 The fire consumed | their young | men ‖ and their maidens | were not | given to | marriage.

65 Their priests were slain | with the | sword ‖ and there were no widows to | make - | lamen | tation.

66 So the Lord awaked as | one out of | sleep ‖ and like a | giant re | freshed with | wine.

67 He smote his enemies in the hinder | parts ‖ and put them | to a per | petual | shame.

68 He refused the tabernacle | of - | Joseph ‖ and chose | not the | tribe of | Ephraim ;

69 But chose the | tribe of | Judah ‖ even the hill of | Sion | which he | loved.

70 And there he built his | temple on | high ‖ and laid the foundation of it like the ground which | he hath | made con | tinually.

71 He chose David | also his | servant ‖ and took him a | way - | from the | sheep-folds.

72 As he was following the ewes great with young ones | he - | took him ‖ that he might feed Jacob his people, and | Israel | his in | heritance

73 So he fed them with a faithful and | true - | heart ‖ and ruled them prudently | with - | all his | power.

The Sixteenth Day.
MORNING PRAYER.

PSALM lxxix. *Deus, venerunt.*

O GOD, the heathen are come into | thine in | heritance ‖ thy holy temple have they defiled, and made Je | rusalem an | heap of | stones.

2 The dead bodies of thy servants have they given to be meat unto the fowls | of the | air ‖ and the flesh of thy saints unto the | beasts - | of the | land.

3 Their blood have they shed like water on every side | of Je | rusalem ‖ and there was | no man to | bury | them.

4 We are become an open shame | to our | enemies ‖ a very scorn and derision unto them | that are | round a | bout | us.

5 LORD, how long wilt | thou be | angry ‖ shall thy jealousy | burn like | fire for | ever?

6 Pour out thine indignation upon the heathen that | have not | known thee ‖ and upon the kingdoms that have not | called up | on thy | Name.

7 For they have de | voured | Jacob ‖ and laid | waste his | dwelling | place.

8 O remember not our old sins, but have mercy upon us, and | that - | soon ‖ for we are | come to | great - | misery.

9 Help us, O God of our salvation, for the glory | of thy | Name ‖ O deliver us, and be merciful unto our sins, | for thy | Name's - | sake.

10 Wherefore do the | heathen | say ‖ Where | - is | now their | God ?

11 O let the vengeance of thy servants' | blood that is | shed ‖ be openly showed upon the | heathen, | in our | sight.

12 O let the sorrowful sighing of the prisoners | come be | fore thee ‖ according to the greatness of thy power, preserve thou those that | are ap | pointed to | die.

13 And for the blasphemy wherewith our neighbours have blas | phemed | thee ‖ reward thou them, O Lord, | seven-fold | into their | bosom.

14 So we, that are thy people, and sheep of thy pasture, shall give thee | thanks for | ever ‖ and will alway be showing forth thy praise from gener | ation to | gener | ation.

Psalm lxxx. *Qui regis Israel.*

HEAR, O thou Shepherd of Israel, thou that leadest Joseph | like a | sheep ‖ show thyself also, thou that sittest up | on the | Cheru | bim.

2 Before Ephraim, Benjamin, | and Ma | nasses ‖ stir up thy | strength, and | come, and | help us.

3 Turn us again, | O - | God ‖ show the light of thy countenance, | and we | shall be | whole.

4 O Lord | God of | hosts ‖ how long wilt thou be angry | with thy | people that | prayeth?

5 Thou feedest them with the | bread of | tears ‖ and givest them plenteousness | of - | tears to | drink.

6 Thou hast made us a very strife un | to our | neighbours ‖ and our enemies | laugh - | us to | scorn.

7 Turn us again, thou | God of | hosts ‖ show the light of thy countenance, | and we | shall be | whole.

8 Thou hast brought a vine | out of | Egypt ‖ thou hast cast out the | heathen, and | planted | it.

9 Thou madest | room - | for it ‖ and when it had taken | root, it | filled the | land.

10 The hills were covered with the | shadow | of it ‖ and the boughs thereof were like the | goodly | cedar | trees.

11 She stretched out her branches un | to the | sea ‖ and her | boughs un | to the | river.

12 Why hast thou then broken | down her | hedge ‖ that all they that go | by pluck | off her | grapes?

13 The wild boar out of the wood doth | root it | up ‖ and the wild beasts | of the | field de | vour it.

14 Turn thee again, thou God of hosts, look | down from | heaven ‖ be | hold, and | visit this | vine:

15 And the place of the vineyard that thy right | hand hath | planted ‖ and the branch that thou madest so | strong - | for thy | self.

16 It is burnt with fire, | and cut | down ‖ and they shall perish at the re | buke - | of thy | countenance.

17 Let thy hand be upon the man of | thy right | hand ‖ and upon the son of man, whom thou madest so | strong for | thine own | self.

18 And so will not we go | back from | thee ‖ O let us live, and we shall | call up | on thy | Name.

19 Turn us again, O Lord | God of | hosts ‖ show the light of thy countenance, | and - | we shall be | whole.

Psalm lxxxi. *Exultate Deo.*

SING we merrily unto | God our | strength ‖ make a cheerful noise un | to the | God of | Jacob.

2 Take the psalm, bring | hither the | tabret ‖ the merry | harp - | with the | lute.

3 Blow up the trumpet in the | new - | moon ‖ even in the time appointed, and up | on our | solemn | feast-day.

4 For this was made a | statute for | Israel ‖ and a | law of the | God of | Jacob.

5 This he ordained in Joseph | for a | testimony ‖ when he came out of the land of Egypt, and had | heard a | strange - | language.

6 I eased his shoulder | from the | burden ‖ and his hands were delivered | from - | making the | pots.

7 Thou calledst upon me in troubles, and I de | livered | thee ‖ and heard thee what time as the | storm - | fell up | on thee.

[Evening.] THE PSALTER. [Day 16]

8 I | proved thee | also ‖ at the | wa - | ters of | strife.

9 Hear, O my people; and I will assure | thee, O | Israel ‖ if thou wilt | hearken | unto | me,

10 There shall no strange god | be in | thee ‖ neither shalt thou worship | any | other | god.

11 I am the LORD thy God, who brought thee out of the | land of | Egypt ‖ open thy mouth | wide, and | I shall | fill it.

12 But my people would not | hear my voice ‖ and Israel | would - | not o | bey me:

13 So I gave them up unto their | own hearts' | lusts ‖ and let them follow their | own im | agin | ations.

14 Oh that my people would have hearkened | unto | me ‖ for if Israel had | walked | in my | ways,

15 I should soon have put | down their | enemies ‖ and turned my hand a | gainst their | adver | saries.

16 The haters of the LORD should have been | found - | liars ‖ but their time should | have en | dured for | ever.

17 He should have fed them also with the | finest wheat | flour ‖ and with honey out of the stony rock should | I have | satis | fied thee.

EVENING PRAYER.

PSALM lxxxii. *Deus steti..*

GOD standeth in the congre | gation of | princes ‖ he is a | Judge a | mong - | gods.

2 How long will ye give | wrong - | judgment ‖ and accept the | persons of | the un | godly?

3 Defend the | poor and | fatherless ‖ see that such as are in need | and ne | cessity have | right.

4 Deliver the | out-cast and | poor ‖ save them from the | hand of | the un | godly.

5 They will not be learned, nor understand, but walk on | still in | darkness ‖ all the foundations of the | earth are | out of | course.

6 I have said, | Ye are | gods ‖ and ye are all the children | of the | Most - | Highest.

7 But ye shall | die like | men ‖ and | fall like | one of the | princes.

8 Arise, O God, and judge | thou the | earth ‖ for thou shalt take all | heathen to | thine in | heritance.

Psalm lxxxiii.   *Deus, quis similis?*

HOLD not thy tongue, O God, keep | not still | silence ‖ refrain | not thy | self, O | God.

2 For lo, thine enemies | make a | murmuring ‖ and they that hate thee have | lift - | up their | head.

3 They have imagined craftily a | gainst thy | people ‖ and taken counsel a | gainst thy | secret | ones.

4 They have said, Come, and let us root them out, that they be no | more a | people ‖ and that the name of Israel may be | no more | in re | membrance.

5 For they have cast their heads together with | one con | sent ‖ and are con | federate a | gainst - | thee;

6 The tabernacles of the Edomites, | and the | Ishmaelites ‖ the Moabites, | and - | Hagar | enes;

7 Gebal, and | Ammon, and | Amalek ‖ the Philistines, with | them that | dwell at | Tyre.

8 Assur also is | joined with | them ‖ and have | holpen the | children of | Lot.

9 But do thou to them as un | to the | Midianites ‖ unto Sisera, and unto Jabin | at the | brook of | Kison;

10 Who | perished at | Endor ‖ and became | as the dung | of the | earth.

11 Make them and their princes like | Oreb and | Zeb ‖ yea, make all their princes like as | Zeba | and Sal | mana;

12 Who say, Let us take | to our | selves ‖ the houses of | God - | in pos | session.

13 O my God, make them like un | to a | wheel ‖ and as the | stubble be | fore the | wind;

14 Like as the fire that burneth | up the | wood ‖ and as the flame | that con | sumeth the | mountains.

15 Persecute them even so | with thy | tempest ‖ and make them a | fraid - | with thy | storm.

16 Make their faces ashamed, | O - | Lord ‖ that | they may | seek thy | Name.

17 Let them be confounded and vexed ever | more and | more ‖ let them be | put to | shame, and | perish.

18 And they shall know that thou, whose Name is Je | ho - | vah ‖ art only the Most Highest | over | all the | earth.

Psalm lxxxiv. *Quam dilecta.*

O HOW amiable | are thy | dwellings ‖ thou | Lord - | - of | hosts!

2 My soul hath a desire and longing to enter into the | courts of the | Lord ‖ my heart and my flesh re | joice in the | living | God.

3 Yea, the sparrow hath found her an house, and the swallow a nest, where she may | lay her | young ‖ even thy altars, O Lord of hosts, my | King - | and my | God.

4 Blessed are they that | dwell in thy | house ‖ they will be | alway | praising | thee.

5 Blessed is the man whose strength | is in | thee ‖ in whose | heart - | are thy | ways.

6 Who going through the vale of misery use it | for a | well ‖ and the | pools are | filled with | water.

7 They will go from | strength to | strength ‖ and unto the God of gods appeareth every | one of | them in | Sion.

8 O Lord God of hosts, | hear my | prayer ‖ hearken, | O - | God of | Jacob.

9 Behold, O God | our de | fender ‖ and look upon the | face of | thine A | nointed.

10 For one day in | thy - | courts ‖ is | better | than a | thousand.

11 I had rather be a door-keeper in the house | of my | God ‖ than to dwell in the | tents - | of un | godliness.

12 For the Lord God is a light and defence; the Lord will give | grace and | worship ‖ and no good thing shall he withhold from them that | live a | godly | life.

13 O Lord | God of | hosts ‖ blessed is the man that | putteth his | trust in | thee.

PSALM lxxxv. *Benedixisti, Domine.*

LORD, thou art become gracious un | to thy | land ‖ thou hast turned away the cap | tivi | ty of | Jacob.

2 Thou hast forgiven the offence | of thy | people ‖ and | covered | all their | sins.

3 Thou hast taken away all | thy dis | pleasure ‖ and turned thyself from thy | wrathful | indig | nation.

4 Turn us then, O | God our | Saviour ‖ and let thine | anger | cease from | us.

5 Wilt thou be displeased at | us for | ever ‖ and wilt thou stretch out thy wrath from one gener | ation | to an | other?

6 Wilt thou not turn a | gain, and | quicken us ‖ that thy people | may re | joice in | thee?

7 Show us thy | mercy, O | Lord ‖ and | gra... us | thy sal | vation.

8 I will hearken what the Lord God will say con | cerning | me ‖ for he shall speak peace unto his people, and to his saints, | that they | turn not | again.

9 For his salvation is nigh | them that | fear him ‖ that glory may | dwell - | in our | land.

10 Mercy and truth are | met to | gether ‖ righteousness and | peace have | kissed each | other.

11 Truth shall flourish out | of the | earth ‖ and righteousnesss hath | looked | down from | heaven.

12 Yea, the Lord shall show | loving | kind-ness ‖ and our | land shall | give her | increase.

13 Righteousness shall | go be | fore him ‖ and he shall direct his | going | in the | way.

The Seventeenth Day.
MORNING PRAYER.

Psalm lxxxvi. *Inclina, Domine.*

BOW down thine ear, O | Lord, and | hear me ‖ for I am | poor, - | and in | misery.

2 Preserve thou my soul, for | I am | holy ‖ my God, save thy servant that | putteth his | trust in | thee.

3 Be merciful unto me | O - | Lord ‖ for I will | call - | daily up | on thee.

4 Comfort the soul | of thy | servant ‖ for unto thee, O Lord, | do I lift | up my | soul.

5 For thou, Lord, art | good and | gracious ‖ and of great mercy unto all | them that | call up | on thee.

6 Give ear, Lord, un | to my | prayer ‖ and ponder the voice | of my | humble de | sires.

7 In the time of my trouble I will | call up | on thee ‖ for | thou - | hearest | me.

8 Among the gods there is none like unto | thee, O | Lord ‖ there is not one that can | do as | thou - | doest.

9 All nations whom thou hast made shall come and worship | thee, O | Lord ‖ and shall | glori | fy thy | Name.

10 For thou art great, and doest | wondrous | things ‖ thou | - art | God a | lone.

11 Teach me thy way, O Lord, and I will walk | in thy | truth ‖ O knit my heart unto thee, that | I may | fear thy | Name.

12 I will thank thee, O Lord my God, with | all my | heart ‖ and will praise thy | Name for | ever | more.

13 For great is thy | mercy to | ward me ‖ and thou hast delivered my soul | from the | nethermost | hell.

14 O God, the proud are | risen a | gainst me ‖ and the congregations of naughty men have sought after my soul, and have not set | thee be | fore their | eyes.

15 But thou, O Lord God, art full of com | passion and | mercy ‖ long-suffering, plenteous in | good - | ness and | truth.

16 O turn thee then unto me, and have | mercy up | on me ‖ give thy strength unto thy servant, and help the | son - | of thine | hand-maid.

17 Show some token upon me for good ; that they who hate me may see it, and | be a | shamed ‖ because thou, Lord, hast holpen me, | and - | comforted | me.

Psalm lxxxvii. *Fundamenta ejus.*

HER foundations are upon the | holy | hills ‖ the Lord loveth the gates of Sion more than | all the | dwellings of | Jacob.

2 Very excellent things are | spoken of | thee ‖ thou | cit - | y of | God.

3 I will think upon Rahab | and - | Babylon ‖ with | them that | know - | me

4 Behold ye the | Phil | istines | also ‖ and they

of Tyre, with the Morians; lo, | there - | was he | born.

5 And of Sion it shall be reported that he was | born in | her ‖ and the Most | High shall | stablish | her.

6 The LORD shall rehearse it, when he writeth | up the | people ‖ that | he was | born - | there.

7 The singers also and trumpeters shall | he re | hearse ‖ All my fresh | springs shall | be in | thee.

PSALM lxxxviii. *Domine, Deus.*

O LORD God of my salvation, I have cried day and | night be | fore thee ‖ O let my prayer enter into thy presence, incline thine | ear un | to my | calling;

2 For my soul is | full of | trouble ‖ and my life draweth | nigh - | unto | hell.

3 I am counted as one of them that go down in | to the | pit ‖ and I have been even as a | man that | hath no | strength.

4 Free among the dead, like unto them that are wounded, and lie | in the | grave ‖ who are out of remembrance, and are cut a | way - | from thy | hand.

5 Thou hast laid me in the | lowest | pit ‖ in a place of darkness, | and - | in the | deep.

6 Thine indignation lieth | hard up | on me ‖ and thou hast vexed | me with | all thy | storms.

7 Thou hast put away mine acquaintance | far from | me ‖ and made me to | be ab | horred | of them.

8 I am so | fast in | prison ‖ that I | can - | not get | forth.

9 My sight faileth for | very | trouble ‖ Lord, I have called daily upon thee, I have stretched forth my | hands - | unto | thee.

10 Dost thou show wonders a | mong the | dead ‖ or shall the dead rise | up a | gain, and | praise thee?

11 Shall thy loving-kindness be showed | in the | grave ‖ or thy | faithfulness | in de | struction?

12 Shall thy wondrous works be | known in the | dark ‖ and thy righteousness in the land where | all things | are for | gotten?

13 Unto thee have I cried, | O - | Lord ‖ and early shall my | prayer | - come be | fore thee.

14 Lord, why abhorrest | thou my | soul ‖ and hidest | thou thy | face from | me?

15 I am in misery, and like unto him that is at the | point to | die ‖ even from my youth up thy terrors have I suffered | with a | troubled | mind.

16 Thy wrathful displeasure | goeth | over me ‖ and the fear of | thee - | hath un | done me.

17 They come round about me daily | like - | water ‖ and compassed me to | gether on | every | side.

18 My lovers and friends hast thou put a | way from | me ‖ and hid mine ac | quaintance | out of my | sight.

―――

EVENING PRAYER.

Psalm lxxxix. *Misericordias Domini.*

MY song shall be alway of the loving-kindness | of the | Lord ‖ with my mouth will I ever be showing thy truth from one gener | ation | to an | other.

2 For I have said, Mercy shall be set | up for | ever ‖ thy truth shalt thou | stablish | in the | heavens.

3 I have made a covenant | with my | chosen ‖ I have sworn | unto | David my | servant;

4 Thy seed will I | stablish for | ever ‖ and set up thy throne from one gener | ation | to an | other.

5 O Lord, the very heavens shall praise thy | wondrous | work ‖ and thy truth in the congre | gation | of the | saints.

6 For who is he a | mong the | clouds ‖ that shall be com | pared un | to the | Lord?

7 And what is he a | mong the | gods ‖ that shall be | like un | to the | Lord?

8 God is very greatly to be feared in the coun- cil of the | saints ‖ and to be had in reverence of all them that are | round a | bout him.

9 O Lord God of hosts, who is like | unto | thee ‖ thy truth, most mighty Lord, | is on | every | side.

10 Thou rulest the raging | of the | sea ‖ thou stillest the waves there | of when | they a | rise.

11 Thou hast subdued Egypt, | and de | stroyed it ‖ thou hast scattered thine enemies abroad | with thy | mighty | arm.

12 The heavens are thine, the earth | also is | thine ‖ thou hast laid the foundation of the round world, and all that | therein | is.

13 Thou hast made the north | and the |

south ‖ Tabor and Hermon shall re | joice - | in thy | Name.

14 Thou hast a | mighty | arm ‖ strong is thy hand, and | high is thy right | hand.

15 Righteousness and equity are the habitation | of thy | seat ‖ mercy and truth shall | go be | fore thy | face.

16 Blessed is the people, O Lord, that can re | joice in | thee ‖ they shall walk in the | light - | of thy | countenance.

17 Their delight shall be daily | in thy | Name ‖ and in thy righteousness | shall they | make their | boast.

18 For thou art the glory | of their | strength ‖ and in thy loving-kindness thou shalt | lift - | up our | horns.

19 For the Lord is | our de | fence ‖ the Holy One of | Israel | is our | King.

20 Thou spakest sometime in visions unto thy | saints, and | saidst ‖ I have laid help upon One that is mighty, I have exalted One | chosen | out of the | people.

21 I have found | David my | servant ‖ with my holy oil have | I a | nointed | him.

22 My hand shall | hold him | fast ‖ and my | arm shall | strengthen | him.

23 The enemy shall not be able to | do him | violence ‖ the son of | wickedness | shall not | hurt him.

24 I will smite down his foes be | fore his | face ‖ and | plague - | them that | hate him.

25 My truth also and my mercy | shall be |

with him ‖ and in my Name shall his | horn - | be ex | alted.

26 I will set his dominion also | in the | sea ‖ and his | right hand | in the | floods.

27 He shall call me, Thou | art my | Father ‖ my God, | and my | strong sal | vation.

28 And I will make | him my | First-born ‖ higher than the | kings - | of the | earth.

29 My mercy will I keep for him for | ever | more ‖ and my covenant shall | stand - | fast with | him.

30 His seed also will I make to en | dure for | ever ‖ and his throne | as the | days of | heaven.

31 But if his children for | sake my | law | and | walk not | in my | judgments ;

32 If they break my statutes, and keep not | my com | mandments ‖ I will visit their offences with the rod, | and their | sin with | scourges.

33 Nevertheless, my loving-kindness will I not utterly | take - | from him ‖ nor | suffer my | truth to | fail.

34 My covenant will I not break, nor alter the thing that is gone | out of my | lips ‖ I have sworn once by my holiness, that I | will not | fail - | David.

35 His seed shall en | dure for | ever ‖ and his seat is like | as the | sun be | fore me.

36 He shall stand fast for evermore | as the | moon ‖ and as the | faithful | witness in | heaven.

37 But thou hast abhorred and forsaken | thine A | nointed ‖ and | art dis | pleased | at him.

38 Thou hast broken the covenant | of thy | servant ‖ and cast his | crown - | to the | ground.

39 Thou hast overthrown | all his | hedges |
and broken down - | his strong | holds.

40 All they that go | by - | spoil him || and he
is become a re proach - | to his | neighbours.

41 Thou hast set up the right hand | of his |
enemies || and made all his | adversaries | to re |
joice.

42 Thou hast taken away the | edge of his |
sword || and givest him not | victory | in the |
battle.

43 Thou hast put | out his | glory || and cast
his | throne - | down to the | ground.

44 The day of his youth | hast thou | shortened || and | covered him | with dis | honour.

45 Lord, how long wilt thou hide thyself? |
for - | ever || and shall thy | wrath - | burn like |
fire ?

46 O remember how | short my | time is |
wherefore hast thou | made all | men for | nought?

47 What man is he that liveth, and shall | not
see | death || and shall he deliver his soul | from
the | hand of | hell ?

48 Lord. where are thy old | loving | kindnesses || which thou swarest unto | David | in thy |
truth ?

49 Remember, Lord, the rebuke that thy | servants | have || and how I do bear in my bosom the
re | bukes of | many | people ;

50 Wherewith thine enemies have blasphemed
thee, and slandered the footsteps of | thine A |
nointed || Praised be the Lord for evermore. |
Amen, | and A | men.

The Eighteenth Day.
MORNING PRAYER.
Psalm xc. *Domine, refugium.*

LORD, thou hast | been our | refuge ‖ from one | gener | ation | to an | other.

2 Before the mountains were brought forth, or ever the earth and the | world were | made ‖ thou art God from everlasting, and | world with | out - | end.

3 Thou turnest man | to de | struction ‖ again thou sayest, Come a | gain, ye | children of | men.

4 For a thousand years in thy sight are | but as | yesterday ‖ seeing that is past | as a | watch in the | night.

5 As soon as thou scatterest them they are even | as a | sleep ‖ and fade away | suddenly | like the | grass.

6 In the morning it is green, and | groweth | up ‖ but in the evening it is cut down, | dried | up, and | withered.

7 For we consume away in | thy dis | pleasure ‖ and are afraid at thy | wrathful | indig | nation.

8 Thou hast set our mis | deeds be | fore thee ‖ and our secret sins in the | light - | of thy | countenance.

9 For when thou art angry all our | days are | gone ‖ we bring our years to an end, as it | were a | tale that is | told.

10 The days of our age are threescore years and ten; and though men be so strong that they come to fourscore years, yet is their strength then but | labour and | sorrow ‖ so soon passeth it a | way, and we are | gone.

11 But who regardeth the power | of thy | wrath ¶ for even thereafter as a man feareth, | so is | thy dis | pleasure.

12 So teach us to | number our | days ‖ that we may apply our | hearts - | unto | wisdom.

13 Turn thee again, O LORD, | at the | last ¶ and be | gracious | unto thy | servants.

14 O satisfy us with thy mercy, and | that - | soon ‖ so shall we rejoice and be glad | all the | days of our | life.

15 Comfort us again now after the time that | thou hast | plagued us ‖ and for the years wherein | we have | suffered ad | versity.

16 Show thy | servants thy | work ‖ and their | chil - | dren thy | glory.

17 And the glorious Majesty of the LORD our God | be up | on us ‖ prosper thou the work of our hands upon us ; O prosper | thou our | handy | work.

PSALM xci. *Qui habitat.*

WHOSO dwelleth under the defence of the | Most - | High ‖ shall abide under the | shadow of | the Al | mighty.

2 I will say unto the LORD, Thou art my hope, and | my strong | hold ‖ my God, in | him - | will I | trust.

3 For he shall deliver thee from the snare | of the | hunter ‖ and | from the | noisome | pestilence.

4 He shall defend thee under his wings, and thou shalt be safe | under his | feathers ‖ his faithfulness and truth shall | be thy | shield and | buckler.

5 Thou shalt not be afraid for any | terror by | night ‖ nor for the | arrow that | flieth by | day;
6 For the pestilence that | walketh in | darkness ‖ nor for the sickness that de | stroyeth | in the | noon-day.
7 A thousand shall fall beside thee, and ten thousand at | thy right | hand ‖ but it shall | not come | nigh - | thee.
8 Yea, with thine eyes shalt | thou be | hold ‖ and see the re | ward of | the un | godly.
9 For thou, Lord, | art my | hope ‖ thou hast set thine house of de | fence - | very | high.
10 There shall no evil happen | unto | thee ‖ neither shall any | plague come | nigh thy | dwelling.
11 For he shall give his angels charge | over | thee ‖ to | keep thee in | all thy | ways.
12 They shall bear thee | in their | hands ‖ that thou hurt not thy | foot a | gainst a | stone.
13 Thou shalt go upon the | lion and | adder ‖ the young lion and the dragon shalt thou | tread - | under thy | feet.
14 Because he hath set his love upon me, therefore will | I de | liver him ‖ I will set him up, be | cause he hath | known my | Name.
15 He shall call upon me, and | I will | hear him ‖ yea, I am with him in trouble; I will deliver him, and | bring - | him to | honour.
16 With long life will I | satis ⋮ fy him ‖ and | show him | my sal | vation.

PSALM xcii. *Bonum est confiteri.*

IT is a good thing to give thanks un | to the | Lord ‖ and to sing praises unto thy | Name, - | O Most | Highest;

2 To tell of thy loving-kindness early | in the | morning ‖ and of thy truth | in the | night - | season;

3 Upon an instrument of ten strings, and up | on the | lute ‖ upon a loud instrument, | and up | on the | harp.

4 For thou, Lord, hast made me glad | through thy | works ‖ and I will rejoice in giving praise for the oper | ations | of thy | hands.

5 O Lord, how glorious | are thy | works ‖ thy | thoughts are | very | deep

6 An unwise man doth not well con | sider | this ‖ and a fool | doth not | under | stand it.

7 When the ungodly are green as the grass, and when all the workers of wickedness | do - | flourish ‖ then shall they be destroyed forever; but thou, Lord, art the Most | Highest for | ever | more.

8 For lo, thine enemies, O Lord, lo, thine enemies | shall - | perish ‖ and all the workers of wickedness | shall - | be de | stroyed.

9 But mine horn shall be exalted like the horn | of an | unicorn ‖ for I am a | nointed | with fresh | oil.

10 Mine eye also shall see his lust | of mine enemies ‖ and mine ear shall hear his desire of the wicked that a | rise - | up a | gainst me.

11 The righteous shall flourish | like a | palm

tree ‖ and shall spread abroad | like a | cedar in | Libanus.

12 Such as are planted in the house | of the | Lord ‖ shall flourish in the courts of the | house - | of our | God.

13 They also shall bring forth more fruit | in their | age ‖ and shall be | fat and | well - | liking;

14 That they may show how true the Lord my | strength - | is ‖ and that there is | no un | righteousness | in him.

EVENING PRAYER.

Psalm xciii. *Dominus regnavit.*

THE Lord is King, and hath put on | glorious ap | parel ‖ the Lord hath put on his apparel, and | girded him | self with | strength.

2 He hath made the round | world so | sure ‖ that it | can - | not be | moved.

3 Ever since the world began hath thy seat | been pre | pared ‖ thou | art from | ever | lasting.

4 The floods are risen, O Lord, the floods have lift | up their | voice ‖ the | floods lift | up their | waves.

5 The waves of the sea are mighty, and | rage - | horribly ‖ but yet the Lord, who | dwelleth on | high, is | mightier.

6 Thy testimonies, O Lord, are | very | sure ‖ holiness be | cometh thine | house for | ever.

Psalm xciv. *Deus ultionum.*

O LORD God, to whom | vengeance be | longeth ‖ thou God, to whom vengeance be | longeth, | show thy | self.

2 Arise, thou Judge | of the | world ‖ and re-
ward the proud | after | their de | serving.

3 Lord, how long shall | the un | godly ‖
how long shall | the un | godly | triumph?

4 How long shall all wicked doers speak | so
dis | dainfully ‖ and | make such | proud - | boast-
ing?

5 They smite down thy people | O - | Lord ‖
and | trouble | thine - | heritage.

6 They murder the widow | and the | stranger ‖
and put the | father | less to | death.

7 And yet they say, Tush, the Lord | shall
not | see ‖ neither shall the | God of | Jacob re |
gard it.

8 Take heed, ye unwise a | mong the | people ‖
O ye fools, | when will ye | under | stand?

9 He that planted the ear, shall | he not |
hear ‖ or he that made the | eye, shall | he not |
see?

10 Or he that | nurtureth the | heathen ‖ it is
he that teacheth man knowledge; | shall not |
he - | punish?

11 The Lord knoweth the | thoughts of |
man ‖ that | they - | are but | vain.

12 Blessed is the man whom thou chastenest, |
O - | Lord ‖ and | teachest him | in thy | Law;

13 That thou mayest give him patience in
time | of ad | versity ‖ until the pit be digged |
up for | the un | godly.

14 For the Lord will not | fail his | people ‖
neither will he for | sake - | his in | heritance.

15 Until righteousness turn again | unto |

judgment ‖ all such as are | true in | heart shall | follow it.

16 Who will rise up with me a | gainst the | wicked ‖ or who will take my part a | gainst the | evil | doers?

17 If the Lord | had not | helped me ‖ it had not failed, but my soul | had been | put to | silence.

18 But when I said, My | foot hath | slipped ‖ thy mercy, O | Lord, - | held me | up.

19 In the multitude of the sorrows that I had | in my | heart ‖ thy comforts | have re | freshed my | soul.

20 Wilt thou have anything to do with the | stool of | wickedness ‖ which imagineth | mischief | as a | law?

21 They gather them together against the soul | of the | righteous ‖ and con | demn the | innocent | blood.

22 But the Lord | is my | refuge ‖ and my God is the | strength - | of my | confidence.

23 He shall recompense them their wickedness, and destroy them in | their own | malice ‖ yea, the Lord our | God - | shall de | stroy them.

The Nineteenth Day.

MORNING PRAYER.

Psalm xcv. *Venite, exultemus.*

O COME, let us sing un | to the | Lord ‖ let us heartily rejoice in the | strength of | our sal | vation.

2 Let us come before his presence | with thanks | giving ‖ and show ourselves | glad in | him with | psalms.

3 For the LORD is a | great - | God ‖ and a great | King a | bove all | gods.

4 In his hand are all the corners | of the | earth ‖ and the strength of the | hills is | his - | also.

5 The sea is his, | and he | made it ‖ and his hands pre | pared the | dry - | land.

6 O come, let us worship | and fall | down ‖ and kneel be | fore the | LORD our | Maker.

7 For he is the | Lord our | God ‖ and we are the people of his pasture | and the | sheep of his | hand.

8 To-day if ye will hear his voice, harden | not your | hearts ‖ as in the provocation, and as in the day of temp | tation | in the | wilderness ;

9 When your fathers | tempted | me ‖ proved me, | and - | saw my | works.

10 Forty years long was I grieved with this gener | ation, and | said ‖ It is a people that do err in their hearts, for they | have not | known my | ways.

11 Unto whom I sware | in my | wrath ‖ that they should not | enter in | to my | rest.

PSALM xcvi. *Cantate Domino.*

O SING unto the LORD a | new - | song ‖ sing unto the LORD, | all the | whole - | earth.

2 Sing unto the LORD, and | praise his | Name ‖ be telling of his sal | vation from | day to | day.

3 Declare his honour un | to the | heathen ‖ and his | wonders | unto all | people.

4 For the Lord is great, and cannot worthily | be - | praised ‖ he is more to be | feared than | all - | gods

5 As for all the gods of the heathen, they | are but | idols ‖ but it is the | Lord that | made the | heavens.

6 Glory and worship | are be | fore him ‖ power and | honor are | in his | sanctuary.

7 Ascribe unto the Lord, O ye kindreds | of the | people ‖ ascribe unto the | Lord - | worship and | power.

8 Ascribe unto the Lord the honour due un | to his | Name ‖ bring presents, and | come in | to his | courts.

9 O worship the Lord in the | beauty of | holiness ‖ let the whole earth | stand in | awe of | him.

10 Tell it out among the heathen, that the | Lord is | King ‖ and that it is he who hath made the round world so fast that it cannot be moved; and how that he shall | judge the | people | righteously.

11 Let the heavens rejoice, and let the | earth be | glad ‖ let the sea make a noise, and | all that | therein | is.

12 Let the field be joyful, and all | that is | in it ‖ then shall all the trees of the wood re | joice be | fore the | Lord.

13 For he cometh, for he cometh to | judge the | earth ‖ and with righteousness to judge the world, and the | people ! with his | truth.

Psalm xcvii. *Dominus regnavit.*

THE Lord is King, the earth may be | glad
there | of || yea, the multitude of the isles |
may be | glad there | of.

2 Clouds and darkness are | round a | bout
him || righteousness and judgment are the habi |
tation | of his | seat.

3 There shall go a | fire be | fore him || and
burn up his enemies | on - | every | side.

4 His lightnings gave shine un | to the |
world || the earth | saw it, and | was a | fraid.

5 The hills melted like wax at the presence |
of the | Lord || at the presence of the Lord | of
the | whole - | earth.

6 The heavens have de | clared his | righte-
ousness || and all the | people have | seen his |
glory.

7 Confounded be all they that worship carved
images, and that delight in | vain - | gods || wor-
ship | him, - | all ye | gods.

8 Sion heard of it, | and re | joiced || and the
daughters of Judah were glad, because of thy |
judgments, | O - | Lord.

9 For thou, Lord, art higher than all that are |
in the | earth || thou art exalted | far a | bove
all | gods.

10 O ye that love the Lord, see that ye hate
the thing | which is | evil || the Lord preserveth
the souls of his saints; he shall deliver them
from the | hand of | the un | godly.

11 There is sprung up a light | for the | right-
eous || and joyful gladness for | such as | are true |
hearted.

12 Rejoice in the | Lord, ye | righteous ǁ and give thanks for a re | membrance | of his | holiness.

EVENING PRAYER.

Psalm xcviii. *Cantate Domino.*

O SING unto the Lord a | new - | song ǁ for he hath | done - | marvellous | things.

2 With his own right hand, and with his | holy | arm ǁ hath he | gotten him | self the | victory.

3 The Lord declared | his sal | vation ǁ his righteousness hath he openly showed | in the sight of the | heathen.

4 He hath remembered his mercy and truth toward the | house of | Israel ǁ and all the ends of the world have seen the sal | vation | of our | God.

5 Show yourselves joyful unto the Lord, | all ye | lands ǁ sing, re | joice, - | and give | thanks.

6 Praise the Lord up | on the | harp ǁ sing to the | harp with a | psalm of | thanksgiving.

7 With trumpets | also and | shawms ǁ O show yourselves joyful be | fore the | Lord, the | King.

8 Let the sea make a noise, and all that | therein | is ǁ the round world, and | they that | dwell there | in.

9 Let the floods clap their hands, and let the hills be joyful together be | fore the | Lord ǁ for he is | come to | judge the | earth.

10 With righteousness shall he | judge the | world ǁ and the | people | with - | equity.

PSALM xcix. *Dominus regnavit.*

THE Lord is King, be the people never | so im | patient ‖ he sitteth between the Cheru- bim, be the earth | never | so un | quiet.

2 The Lord is | great in | Sion ‖ and | high a | bove all | people.

3 They shall give thanks un | to thy | Name ‖ which is great, | wonder | ful, and | holy.

4 The King's power loveth judgment; thou hast pre | pared | equity ‖ thou hast executed judgment and | righteous | ness in | Jacob.

5 O magnify the | Lord our | God ‖ and fall down before his footstool; | for - | he is | holy.

6 Moses and Aaron among his priests, and Samuel among such as call up | on his | Name ‖ these called upon the | Lord, - | and he | heard them.

7 He spake unto them out of the | cloudy | pillar ‖ for they kept his testimonies, and the | law - | that he | gave them.

8 Thou heardest them, O | Lord our | God ‖ thou forgavest them, O God, and punishedst | their - | own in | ventions.

9 O magnify the Lord our God, and worship him upon his | holy | hill ‖ for the | Lord our | God is | holy.

PSALM c. *Jubilate Deo.*

O BE joyful in the Lord, | all ye ! lands ‖ serve the Lord with gladness, and come before his | presence | with a | song.

2 Be ye sure that the Lord | he is | God ‖ it is he that hath made us, and not we ourselves;

we are his people, | and the | sheep of his | pasture.

3 O go your way into his gates with thanksgiving, and into his | courts with | praise ‖ be thankful unto him, and speak | good - | of his | Name.

4 For the LORD is gracious, his mercy is | ever lasting ‖ and his truth endureth from gener | ation to | gener | ation.

PSALM ci. *Misericordiam et judicium.*

MY song shall be of | mercy and | judgment ‖ unto thee, O | LORD, - | will I | sing.

2 O let me have | under | standing ‖ in the | way of | godli | ness!

3 When wilt thou come | unto | me ‖ I will walk in my house | with a | perfect | heart.

4 I will take no wicked thing in hand; I hate the sins | of un | faithfulness ‖ there shall no such | cleave - | unto | me.

5 A froward heart shall de | part from | me ‖ I will not | know a | wicked | person.

6 Whoso privily | slandereth his | neighbour ‖ him | will - | I de | stroy.

7 Whoso hath also a proud look and | high - | stomach ‖ I | will not | suffer | him.

8 Mine eyes look upon such as are faithful | in the | land ‖ that | they may | dwell with | me.

9 Whoso leadeth a | godly | life ‖ he | shall - | be my | servant.

10 There shall no deceitful person dwell | in my | house ‖ he that telleth lies shall not | tarry | in my | sight.

11 I shall soon destroy all the ungodly that are | in the | land ‖ that I may root out all wicked doers from the | city ¦ of the | Lord.

The Twentieth Day.
MORNING PRAYER.
Psalm cii. *Domine, exaudi.*

HEAR my prayer, | O - | Lord ‖ and let my crying | come - | unto | thee.

2 Hide not thy face from me in the time | of my | trouble ‖ incline thine ear unto me when I call; O | hear me and | that right | soon.

3 For my days are consumed a | way like | smoke ‖ and my bones are burnt up | as it | were a | fire-brand.

4 My heart is smitten down, and | withered like | grass ‖ so that I for | get to | eat my | bread.

5 For the voice | of my | groaning ‖ my bones will scarce | cleave - ¦ to my | flesh.

6 I am become like a pelican | in the | wilderness ‖ and like an | owl that is | in the | desert.

7 I have watched, and am even as it | were a | sparrow ‖ that sitteth a | lone upon | the house | top.

8 Mine enemies revile me | all the day ¦ long ‖ and they that are mad upon me are | sworn to | gether a | gainst me.

9 For I have eaten ashes as it | were - | bread ‖ and | mingled my | drink with | weeping.

10 And that, because of thine indig | nation and | wrath ‖ for thou hast taken me | up, and | cast me | down.

11 My days are gone | like a | shadow ‖ and I am | withered | like - | grass.

12 But thou, O Lord, shalt en | dure for | ever ‖ and thy remembrance through | out all | gener | ations.

13 Thou shalt arise, and have mercy up | on - | Sion ‖ for it is time that thou have mercy upon her, | yea, the | time is | come.

14 And why? thy servants think up | on her | stones ‖ and it pitieth them to | see her | in the | dust.

15 The heathen shall fear thy | Name, O | Lord ‖ and all the kings of the | earth thy | Majes | ty;

16 When the Lord shall | build up | Sion ‖ and when his | glory | shall ap | pear;

17 When he turneth him unto the prayer of the | poor - | destitute ‖ and despiseth | not - | their de | sire.

18 This shall be written for those | that come | after ‖ and the people which shall be | born shall | praise the | Lord.

19 For he hath looked down | from his | sanctuary ‖ out of the heaven did the | Lord be | hold the | earth;

20 That he might hear the mourning of such as are | in cap | tivity ‖ and deliver the children ap | pointed | unto | death;

21 That they may declare the Name of the | Lord in | Sion ‖ and his | worship | at Je | rusalem :

22 When the people are | gathered to | gether ‖ and the kingdoms | also, to | serve the | Lord.

23 He brought down my strength | in my journey ‖ and | shortened | my - | days.

24 But I said, O my God, take me not away in the | midst of mine | age ‖ as for thy years, they endure through | out all | gener | ations.

25 Thou, Lord, in the beginning hast laid the foundation | of the | earth ‖ and the heavens are the | work - | of thy | hands.

26 They shall perish, but | thou shalt en | dure ‖ they all shall wax | old as | doth a | garment;

27 And as a vesture shalt thou change them, and they | shall be | changed ‖ but thou art the same, and thy | years - | shall not | fail.

28 The children of thy servants | shall con | tinue ‖ and their seed shall stand | fast - | in thy | sight.

Psalm ciii. *Benedic, anima mea.*

PRAISE the Lord, | O my | soul ‖ and all that is within me, | praise his | holy | Name.

2 Praise the Lord, | O my | soul ‖ and for | get not | all his | benefits :

3 Who forgiveth | all thy | sin ‖ and healeth | all - | thine in | firmities ;

4 Who saveth thy life | from de ' struction ‖ and crowneth thee with | mercy and | loving | kindness ;

5 Who satisfieth thy mouth with | good - | things ‖ making thee young and | lusty | as an | eagle.

6 The Lord executeth righteousness | and - |

judgment ‖ for all them that | are oppress | ed with | wrong.

7 He showed his ways | unto | Moses ‖ his works unto the | children of | Isra | el.

8 The Lord is full of com | passion and | mercy ‖ long-suffering | and of | great - | goodness.

9 He will not | alway be | chiding ‖ neither keepeth | he his | anger for | ever.

10 He hath not dealt with us | after our | sins ‖ nor rewarded us according | to our | wicked | nesses.

11 For look how high the heaven is in comparison | of the | earth ‖ so great is his mercy also to | ward - | them that | fear him.

12 Look how wide also the east is | from the | west ‖ so far hath he | set our | sins - | from us.

13 Yea, like as a father pitieth his | own - | children ‖ even so is the Lord merciful | unto | them that | fear him.

14 For he knoweth where | of we are | made ‖ he remembereth | that we | are but | dust.

15 The days of man are | but as | grass ‖ for he flourisheth as a | flower | of the | field.

16 For as soon as the wind goeth over it, | it is gone ‖ and the place there | of shall | know it no | more.

17 But the merciful goodness of the Lord endureth for ever and ever upon | them that | fear him ‖ and his righteousness up | on - | children's | children ;

18 Even upon such as | keep his | covenant ‖ and think upon | his com | mandments to | do them.

19 The Lord hath prepared his | seat in | heaven ‖ and his kingdom | ruleth | over | all.

20 O praise the Lord, ye angels of his, ye that ex | cel in | strength ‖ ye that fulfil his commandment, and hearken unto the | voice -ˈ of his | word.

21 O praise the Lord, all | ye his | hosts ‖ ye servants of | his that | do his | pleasure.

22 O speak good of the Lord, all ye works of his, in all places of | his do | minion ‖ praise thou the | Lord, - | O my | soul.

EVENING PRAYER.

Psalm civ. *Benedic, anima mea.*

PRAISE the Lord, | O my | soul ‖ O Lord my God, thou art become exceeding glorious; thou art clothed with | majes | ty and | honour.

2 Thou deckest thyself with light as it were | with a | garment ‖ and spreadest out the | heavens | like a | curtain.

3 Who layeth the beams of his chambers | in the | waters ‖ and maketh the clouds his chariot, and walketh upon the | wings - | of the | wind.

4 He maketh his | angels | spirits ‖ and his | ministers | a flaming | fire.

5 He laid the foundations | of the | earth ‖ that it never should | move at | any | time.

6 Thou coveredst it with the deep like as | with a | garment ‖ the waters | stand - | in the | hills.

7 At thy re | buke they | flee ‖ at the voice of thy | thunder they | are a | fraid.

8 They go up as high as the hills, and down to the | valleys be | neath ‖ even unto the place which thou | hast ap | pointed | for them.

9 Thou hast set them their bounds, which they | shall not | pass ‖ neither turn a | gain to | cover the | earth.

10 He sendeth the springs in | to the | rivers ⁞ which | run a | mong the | hills.

11 All the beasts of the field | drink there | of ‖ and the wild | asses | quench their | thirst.

12 Beside them shall the fowls of the air have their | habi | tation ‖ and | sing a | mong the | branches.

13 He watereth the hills | from a | bove ‖ the earth is filled with the | fruit - | of thy | works.

14 He bringeth forth grass | for the | cattle ‖ and green herb | for the | service of | men ;

15 That he may bring food out of the earth, and wine that maketh glad the | heart of | man ‖ and oil to make him a cheerful countenance, and | bread to | strengthen man's | heart.

16 The trees of the LORD also are | full of | sap ‖ even the cedars of Libanus | which - | he hath | planted ;

17 Wherein the birds | make their | nests ‖ and the fir-trees are a | dwell ng | for the | stork.

18 The high hills are a refuge | for the wild | goats ‖ and so are the | stony rocks | for the | conies.

19 He appointed the moon for | certain | seasons ‖ and the sun | knoweth his | going | down.

20 Thou makest darkness that it | may be | night ‖ wherein all the beasts | of the | forests do | move.

21 The lions, roaring | after their | prey ‖ do | seek their | meat from | God.

22 The sun ariseth, and they get them a | way to | gether ‖ and lay them | down - | in their | dens

23 Man goeth forth | to his | work ‖ and to his | labour, | until the | evening.

24 O Lord, how manifold | are thy | works ‖ in wisdom hast thou made them all; the earth is | full - | of thy | riches.

25 So is the great and wide | sea - | also ‖ wherein are things creeping innumerable, both | small and | great - | beasts.

26 There go the ships, and there is | that Le | viathan ‖ whom thou hast made to take his | pas- time | there - | in.

27 These wait | all up | on thee ‖ that thou mayest give them | meat in | due - | season.

28 When thou givest it them, they | gather | it ‖ and when thou openest thy hand, | they are | filled with | good.

29 When thou hidest thy face, | they are | troubled ‖ when thou takest away their breath, they die, and are turned a | gain - | to their | dust.

30 When thou lettest thy breath go forth, they | shall be | made ‖ and thou shalt re | new the | face of the | earth.

31 The glorious Majesty of the Lord shall en | dure for | ever ‖ the Lord shall re | joice - | in his | works.

32 The earth shall tremble at the | look of | him ‖ if he do but | touch the | hills they shall | smoke.

33 I will sing unto the Lord as | long as I |

live ‖ I will praise my God | while I | have my | being.

34 And so shall my | words - please him ‖ my | joy shall | be in the | Lord.

35 As for sinners, they shall be consumed out of the earth, and the ungodly shall come | to an | end ‖ Praise thou the Lord, O my | soul - | Praise the | Lord.

The Twenty-First Day.

MORNING PRAYER.

Psalm cv. *Confitemini Domino.*

O GIVE thanks unto the Lord, and call up | on his | Name ‖ tell the people what | things - | he hath | done.

2 O let your songs be of him, and | praise - | him ‖ and let your talking be of | all his | wondrous | works.

3 Rejoice in his | holy | Name ‖ let the heart of them re | joice that | seek the | Lord.

4 Seek the Lord | and his | strength ‖ seek his | face - | ever | more.

5 Remember the marvellous works that | he hath | done ‖ his wonders, and the | judgments | of his | mouth;

6 O ye seed of | Abraham his | servant ‖ ye children of | Jacob | his - | chosen.

7 He is the | Lord our | God ‖ his judgments | are in | all the | world.

8 He hath been alway mindful of his | covenant and | promise ‖ that he made to a | thousand | gener | ations;

9 Even the covenant that he | made with | Abraham ‖ and the oath that he | sware - | unto | Isaac ;

10 And appointed the same unto Jacob | for a | law ‖ and to Israel for an | ever | lasting | testament ;

11 Saying, Unto thee will I give the | land of | Canaan ‖ the | lot of | your in | heritance :

12 When there were yet | but a | few of them ‖ and they | strangers | in the | land ;

13 What time as they went from one nation | to an | other ‖ from one kingdom | to an | other | people ;

14 He suffered no man to | do them | wrong ‖ but reproved even | kings - | for their | sakes ;

15 Touch not | mine A | nointed ‖ and | do my | prophets no | harm.

16 Moreover, he called for a dearth up | on the | land ‖ and destroyed | all the pro | vision of | bread.

17 But he had sent a | man be | fore them ‖ even Joseph, who was sold to | be a | bond - | servant ;

18 Whose feet they hurt | in the | stocks ‖ the iron | entered | into his | soul ;

19 Until the time came that his | cause was | known ‖ the word of the | Lord - | tried | him.

20 The king sent, and de | livered | him ‖ the prince of the | people | let him go | free.

21 He made him lord also | of his | house ‖ and | ruler of | all his | substance ;

22 That he might inform his princes | after his | will ‖ and | teach his | senators | wisdom.

23 Israel also came | into | Egypt ‖ and Jacob was a stranger | in the | land of | Ham.

24 And he increased his | people ex | ceedingly ‖ and made them | stronger | than their | enemies;

25 Whose heart turned so, that they | hated his | people ‖ and dealt un | truly | with his | servants.

26 Then sent he | Moses his | servant ‖ and Aaron | whom - | he had | chosen.

27 And these showed his | tokens a | mong them ‖ and wonders | in the | land of | Ham.

28 He sent darkness, | and it was | dark ‖ and they were not o | bedient | unto his | word.

29 He turned their waters | into | blood ‖ and | slew - | their - | fish.

30 Their land | brought forth | frogs ‖ yea, even | in their | kings' - | chambers.

31 He spake the word, and there came all | manner of | flies ‖ and | lice in | all their | quarters.

32 He gave them | hailstones for | rain ‖ and | flames of | fire in their | land.

33 He smote their vines | also and | fig-trees ‖ and destroyed the | trees that were | in their | coasts.

34 He spake the word, and the grasshoppers came, and caterpillars in | numer | able ‖ and did eat up all the grass in their land, and devoured the | fruit - | of their | ground.

35 He smote all the first-born | in their | land ‖ even the | chief of | all their | strength.

36 He brought them forth also with | silver

and | gold ‖ there was not one feeble | person a | mong their | tribes.

37 Egypt was glad at | their de | parting ‖ for they | were a | fraid of | them.

38 He spread out a cloud to | be a | covering ‖ and fire to give | light - | in the | night-season.

39 At their desire he | brought - | quails ‖ and he filled them | with the | bread of | heaven.

40 He opened the rock of stone, and the | waters flowed | out ‖ so that rivers | ran in the | dry - | places.

41 For why? he remembered his | holy | promise ‖ and | Abra | ham his | servant.

42 And he brought forth his | people with | joy ‖ and his | cho - | sen with | gladness;

43 And gave them the lands | of the | heathen ‖ and they took the labors of the | people | in pos | session;

44 That they might | keep his | statutes ‖ and ob | serve - | his - | laws.

EVENING PRAYER.
PSALM cvi. *Confitemini Domino.*

O GIVE thanks unto the LORD; for | he is | gracious ‖ and his | mercy en | dureth for | ever.

2 Who can express the noble acts | of the | LORD ‖ or | show forth | all his | praise?

3 Blessed are they that alway | keep - | judgment ‖ and | do - | righteous | ness.

4 Remember me, O LORD, according to the favour that thou bearest un | to thy | people ‖ O visit | me with | thy sal | vation;

5 That I may see the felicity | of thy | chosen ‖ and rejoice in the gladness of thy people, and give | thanks with | thine in | heritance.

6 We have sinned | with our | fathers ‖ we have done a | miss, and | dealt - | wickedly.

7 Our fathers regarded not thy wonders in Egypt, neither kept they thy great goodness | in re | membrance ‖ but were disobedient at the sea, | even at the | Red - | Sea.

8 Nevertheless, he helped them for his | Name's - | sake ‖ that he might make his | power | to be | known.

9 He rebuked the Red Sea also, and it was | dried | up ‖ so he led them through the | deep, as | through a | wilderness.

10 And he saved them from the | adversary's | hand ‖ and delivered them from the | hand - | of the | enemy.

11 As for those that troubled them, the waters | over | whelmed them ‖ there was not | one - | of th m | left.

12 Then believed | they his | words ‖ and sang | praise - | unto | him.

13 But within a while they for | gat his | works ‖ and would | not a | bide his | counsel.

14 But lust came upon them | in the | wilderness | and they tempted | God - | in the | desert.

15 And he gave them | their de | sire ‖ and sent leanness with | al in | to their | soul.

16 They angered Moses also | in the | tents ‖ and Aaron the | saint - | of the | Lord.

17 So the earth opened, and | swallowed up |

Dathan ‖ and covered the congre | gation | of A | biram.

18 And the fire was kindled | in their | company ‖ the flame | burnt - | up the un | godly.

19 They made a | calf in | Horeb ‖ and | worshipped the | molten | image.

20 Thus they | turned their | glory ‖ into the similitude of a | calf that | eateth | hay.

21 And they forgat | God their | Saviour ‖ who had done so | great - | things in | Egypt;

22 Wondrous works in the | land of | Ham ‖ and | fearful things | by the Red | Sea.

23 So he said he would have destroyed them, had not Moses his chosen stood before him | in the | gap ‖ to turn away his wrathful indignation, | lest he | should de | stroy them.

24 Yea, they thought scorn of that | pleasant | land ‖ and gave no | credence un | to his | word;

25 But murmured | in their | tents ‖ and hearkened not unto the | voice - | of the | Lord.

26 Then lift he up his | hand a | gainst them ‖ to over | throw them | in the | wilderness;

27 To cast out their seed a | mong the | nations ‖ and to | scatter them | in the | lands.

28 They joined themselves unto | Baal | peor ‖ and ate the | offerings | of the | dead.

29 Thus they provoked him to anger with their | own in | ventions ‖ and the | plague was | great a | mong them.

30 Then stood up | Phinees, and | prayed ‖ and | so the | plague - | ceased.

31 And that was counted unto him for | right-

eous | ness ‖ among all posterities | for - | ever | more.

32 They angered him also at the | waters of | strife ‖ so that he punished | Moses | for their | sakes ;

33 Because they pro | voked his | spirit ‖ so that he spake unad | visedly | with his | lips.

34 Neither destroyed | they the | heathen ‖ as the | Lord com | manded | them ;

35 But were mingled a | mong the | heathen ‖ and | learned | their - | works.

36 Insomuch that they worshipped their idols, which turned to their | own de | cay ‖ yea, they offered their sons and their | daughters | unto | devils ;

37 And shed innocent blood, even the blood of their sons and | of their | daughters ‖ whom they offered unto the idols of Canaan ; and the | land was de | filed with | blood.

38 Thus were they stained with | their own | works ‖ and went a whoring | with their | own in | ventions.

39 Therefore was the wrath of the Lord kindled a | gainst his | people ‖ insomuch that he ab | horred his | own in | heritance.

40 And he gave them over into the hand | of the | heathen ‖ and they that hated them were | lords - | over | them.

41 Their enemies op | pressed | them ‖ and | had them | in sub | jection.

42 Many a time did | he de | liver them ‖ but they rebelled against him with their own inven-

tions, and were brought | down - | in their | wickedness.

43 Nevertheless, when he | saw their ad | versity ‖ he | heard - | their com | plaint.

44 He thought upon his covenant, and pitied them, according unto the multitude | of his | mercies ‖ yea, he made all those that led them away | captive to | pity | them.

45 Deliver us, O LORD our God, and gather us from a | mong the | heathen ‖ that we may give thanks unto thy holy Name, and make our | boast - | of thy | praise.

46 Blessed be the LORD God of Israel, from everlasting, and world with | out - | end ‖ and let all the | people | say, A | men.

The Twenty-Second Day.
MORNING PRAYER.

PSALM cvii. *Confitemini Domino.*

O GIVE thanks unto the LORD ; for | he is | gracious ‖ and his | mercy en | dureth for | ever.

2 Let them give thanks whom the LORD | hath re | deemed ‖ and delivered from the | hand - | of the | enemy.

3 And gathered them out of the lands, from the east, and | from the | west ‖ from the | north and | from the | south.

4 They went astray in the wilderness | out of the | way ‖ and | found no | city to | dwell in.

5 Hungry | and - | thirsty ‖ their | soul - | fainted | in them.

6 So they cried unto the Lord | in their | trouble ‖ and he delivered them | from - | their dis | tress.

7 He led them forth by the | right - | way ‖ that they might go to the | city | where they | dwelt.

8 O that men would therefore praise the Lord ; for his | goodness ‖ and declare the wonders that he doeth | for the | children of | men !

9 For he satisfieth the | empty | soul ‖ and filleth the | hungry | soul with | goodness.

10 Such as sit in darkness, and in the | shadow of | death ‖ being fast | bound in | misery and | iron.

11 Because they rebelled against the words | of the | Lord ‖ and lightly regarded the counsel | of the | Most - | Highest.

12 He also brought down their | heart through | heaviness ‖ they fell down, and | there was | none to | help them.

13 So when they cried unto the Lord | in their | trouble ‖ he delivered them | out of | their dis | tress.

14 For he brought them out of darkness, and out of the | shadow of | death ‖ and | brake their | bonds in | sunder.

15 O that men would therefore praise the Lord | for his | goodness ‖ and declare the wonders that he doeth | for the | children of | men !

16 For he hath broken the | gates of | brass ‖ and smitten the | bars of | iron in | sunder.

17 Foolish men are plagued for | their of | fence ‖ and be | cause - | of their | wickedness.

18 Their soul abhorred all | manner of | meat ‖ and they were even | hard - | at death's | door.

19 So when they cried unto the LORD | in their | trouble ‖ he delivered them | out of | their dis | tress.

20 He sent his word, and | healed | them ‖ and they were | saved from | their de | struction.

21 O that men would therefore praise the LORD | for his | goodness ‖ and declare the wonders that he doeth | for the | children of | men !

22 That they would offer unto him the sacrifice of | thanks - | giving ‖ and tell | out his | works with | gladness !

23 They that go down to the | sea in | ships ‖ and occupy their | business | in great | waters ;

24 These men see the | works of the | LORD ‖ and his | wonders | in the | deep.

25 For at his word the stormy | wind a | riseth ‖ which lifteth | up the | waves there- | of.

26 They are carried up to the heaven, and down again | to the | deep ‖ their soul melteth away be | cause - | of the | trouble.

27 They reel to and fro, and stagger like a | drunken | man ‖ and are | at their | wit's - | end.

28 So when they cry unto the LORD | in their | trouble ‖ he delivereth them | out of | their dis | tress.

29 For he maketh the | storm to | cease ‖ so that the | waves there | of are | still.

30 Then are they glad, because they | are at rest ‖ and so he bringeth them unto the | haven | where they | would be.

31 O that men would therefore praise the

Lord | for his | goodness ‖ and declare the wonders that he doeth | for the | children of | men!

32 That they would exalt him also in the congregation | of the | people ‖ and praise him in the | seat - | of the | elders!

33 Who turneth the floods in | to a | wilderness ‖ and drieth | up the | water | springs.

34 A fruitful land | maketh he | barren ‖ for the wickedness of | them that | dwell there | in.

35 Again, he maketh the wilderness a | standing | water ‖ and water-springs | of a | dry - | ground.

36 And there he | setteth the | hungry ‖ that they may | build them a | city to | dwell in.

37 That they may sow their land, and | plant - | vineyards ‖ to | yield them | fruits of | increase.

38 He blesseth them, so that they multi | ply ex | ceedingly ‖ and suffereth not their | cattle | to de | crease.

39 And again, when they are minished and | brought - | low ‖ through oppression, through | any | plague or | trouble;

40 Though he suffer them to be evil-entreated | through - | tyrants ‖ and let them wander out of the | way - | in the | wilderness;

41 Yet helpeth he the poor | out of | misery ‖ and maketh him households | like a | flock of | sheep.

42 The righteous will consider this, | and re | joice ‖ and the mouth of all | wickedness | shall be | stopped

43 Whoso is wise, will | ponder these | things ‖

and they shall understand the loving | kindness | of the | Lord.

EVENING PRAYER.

Psalm cviii. *Paratum cor meum.*

O GOD, my heart is ready, my | heart is | ready ‖ I will sing, and give praise with the best | member | that I | have.

2 Awake, thou | lute and | harp ‖ I myself | will a | wake right | early.

3 I will give thanks unto thee, O Lord, a | mong the | people ‖ I will sing praises unto | thee a | mong the | nations.

4 For thy mercy is greater | than the | heavens ‖ and thy truth reacheth | un - | to the | clouds.

5 Set up thyself, O God, a | bove the | heavens ‖ and thy | glory a | bove all the | earth;

6 That thy beloved may | be de | livered ‖ let thy right hand save them, and | hear - | thou - | me.

7 God hath spoken | in his | holiness ‖ I will rejoice therefore, and divide Sichem, and mete | out the | valley of | Succoth.

8 Gilead is mine, and Ma | nasses is | mine ‖ Ephraim also is the | strength - | of my | head;

9 Judah is my law-giver; Moab | is my | wash-pot ‖ over Edom will I cast out my shoe; upon Phi | listia | will I | triumph.

10 Who will lead me into the | strong - | city ‖ and who will | bring me | into | Edom?

11 Hast not thou forsaken us, | O - | God ‖ and wilt not thou, O God, go | forth - | with our | hosts?

12 O help us a | gainst the | enemy ‖ for | vain is the | help of | man.

13 Through God we shall | do great | acts ‖ and it is he that shall | tread - | down our | enemies.

Psalm cix. *Deus laudum.*

HOLD not thy tongue, O God | of my | praise ‖ for the mouth of the ungodly, yea, the mouth of the deceitful | is - | opened up | on me.

2 And they have spoken against me with | false - | tongues ‖ they compassed me about also with words of hatred, and fought a | gainst me with | out a | cause.

3 For the love that I had unto them, lo, they take now my | contrary | part ‖ but I give my | self - | unto | prayer.

4 Thus have they rewarded me | evil for | good ‖ and | hatred for | my good | will.

5 Set thou an ungodly man to be | ruler | over him ‖ and let Satan | stand at | his right | hand.

6 When sentence is given upon him, let him | be con | demned ‖ and let his prayer be | turned | into | sin.

7 Let his | days be | few ‖ and let an | other take his | office.

8 Let his | children be | fatherless ‖ and | his - | wife a | widow.

9 Let his children be vagabonds, and | beg their | bread ‖ let them seek it also | out of | desolate | places.

10 Let the extortioner consume | all that he | hath ‖ and let the | stranger | spoil his | labour.

11 Let there be no man to | pity | him ‖ nor to have compassion up | on his | fatherless | children.

12 Let his posterity | be de | stroyed ‖ and in the next generation let his | name be | clean put | out.

13 Let the wickedness of his fathers be had in remembrance in the sight | of the | Lord ‖ and let not the sin of his | mother be | done a | way.

14 Let them alway be be | fore the | Lord ‖ that he may root out the memorial | of them | from off the | earth ;

15 And that, because his mind was not | to do | good ‖ but persecuted the poor helpless man, that he might slay him that was | vexed | at the | heart.

16 His delight was in cursing, and it shall happen | unto | him ‖ he loved not blessing, therefore | shall it | be far | from him.

17 He clothed himself with cursing like as | with a | raiment ‖ and it shall come into his bowels like water, and like | oil in | to his | bones.

18 Let it be unto him as the cloak that he | hath up | on him ‖ and as the girdle that he is | always | girded with | al.

19 Let it thus happen from the Lord un | to mine | enemies ‖ and to those that speak | evil a | gainst my | soul.

20 But deal thou with me, O Lord God, according un | to thy | Name ‖ for | sweet - | is thy | mercy.

21 O deliver me, for I am | helpless and | poor ‖ and my heart is | wound - | ed with | in me.

22 I go hence like the shadow | that de | parteth ‖ and am driven a | way - | as the | grasshopper.

23 My knees are | weak through | fasting ‖ my flesh is dried | up for | want of | fatness.

24 I became also a reproach | unto | them ‖ they that looked up | on me | shaked their | heads.

25 Help me, O | Lord my | God ‖ O save me ac | cording | to thy | mercy;

26 And they shall know how that this is | thy - | hand ‖ and that | thou, - | Lord, hast | done it.

27 Though they curse, yet | bless - | thou ‖ and let them be confounded that rise up against me; but | let thy | servant re | joice.

28 Let mine adversaries be | clothed with | shame ‖ and let them cover themselves with their own con | fusion, as | with a | cloak.

29 As for me, I will give great thanks unto the Lord | with my | mouth ‖ and praise | him a | mong the | multitude;

30 For he shall stand at the right hand | of the | poor ‖ to save his soul | from un | righteous | judges.

<p align="center">The Twenty-Third Day.
MORNING PRAYER.
Psalm cx. <i>Dixit Dominus.</i></p>

THE Lord said un | to my | Lord ‖ Sit thou on my right hand, until I make thine | enemies | thy - | footstool.

[Morning.] THE PSALTER. [Day 23

2 The LORD shall send the rod of thy power | out of | Sion ‖ be thou ruler, even in the | midst a | mong thine | enemies.

3 In the day of thy power shall the people offer thee free-will offerings with an | holy | worship ‖ the dew of thy birth is | of the | womb of the | morning.

4 The LORD sware, and will | not re | pent ‖ Thou art a Priest for ever, after the | order | of Mel | chizedech.

5 The Lord upon | thy right | hand ‖ shall wound even kings in the | day - | of his | wrath.

6 He shall judge among the heathen; he shall fill the places | with the dead | bodies ‖ and smite in sunder the heads | over | divers | countries.

7 He shall drink of the brook | in the | way ‖ therefore | shall he | lift up his | head.

PSALM cxi. *Confitebor tibi.*

I WILL give thanks unto the LORD with my ‖ whole - | heart ‖ secretly among the faithful, and | in the | congre | gation.

2 The works of the | LORD are | great ‖ sought out of all them | that have | pleasure there | in.

3 His work is worthy to be praised and | had in | honour ‖ and his righteousness en | dureth | for - | ever.

4 The merciful and gracious LORD hath so done his | marvellous | works ‖ that they ought to be | had - | in re | membrance.

5 He hath given meat unto | them that | fear him ‖ he shall ever be | mindful | of his | cove- nant.

6 He hath showed his people the power | of

his | works ‖ that he may give them the | heritage | of the | heathen.

7 The works of his hands are verity | and - | judgment ‖ all his com | mand - | ments are | true.

8 They stand fast for | ever and | ever ‖ and are | done in | truth and | equity.

9 He sent redemption un | to his | people ‖ he hath commanded his covenant for ever; holy and | reverend | is his | Name.

10 The fear of the Lord is the be | ginning of | wisdom | a good understanding have all they that do thereafter; the praise of it en | dureth | for - | ever.

Psalm cxii. *Beatus vir.*

BLESSED is the man that | feareth the | Lord ‖ he hath great de | light in | his com | mandments.

2 His seed shall be | mighty upon | earth ‖ the generation of the | faithful | shall be | blessed.

3 Riches and plenteousness shall be | in his | house | and his righteousness en | dureth for - | ever.

4 Unto the godly there ariseth up light | in the | darkness ‖ he is merciful, | loving, | and - | righteous.

5 A good man is merciful, | and - | lendeth ‖ and will guide his | words - | with dis | cretion.

6 For he shall | never be | moved ‖ and the righteous shall be had in | ever | lasting re | membrance.

7 He will not be afraid of any | evil | tidings ‖

for his heart standeth fast, and be | lieveth | in the | Lord.

8 His heart is stablished, and | will not shrink ‖ until he see his de | sire up | on his enemies.

9 He hath dispersed abroad, and given | to the | poor ‖ and his righteousness remaineth for ever; his horn shall | be ex | alted with | honour.

10 The ungodly shall see it, and | it shall grieve | him ‖ he shall gnash with his teeth, and consume away; the desire of the un | godly | shall - | perish.

Psalm cxiii   *Laudate, pueri.*

PRAISE the | Lord, ye | servants ‖ O praise the | Name - | of the | Lord.

2 Blessed be the | Name of the | Lord ‖ from this time forth for | ever | more.

3 The Lord's | Name is | praised ‖ from the rising up of the sun unto the | going | down of the | same.

4 The Lord is high a | bove all | heathen ‖ and his | glory a | bove the | heavens.

5 Who is like unto the Lord our God, that hath his | dwelling so | high ‖ and yet humbleth himself to behold the things that | are in | heaven and | earth!

6 He taketh up the simple out | of the | dust ‖ and lifteth the | poor - | out of the | mire;

7 That he may set him | with the | princes ‖ even with the | princes | of his | people.

8 He maketh the barren woman to | keep - | house ‖ and to be a | joyful | mother of | children.

EVENING PRAYER.

Psalm cxiv. *In exitu Israel.*

WHEN Israel came | out of | Egypt ‖ and the house of Jacob from a | mong the | strange - | people,

Judah | was his | sanctuary ‖ and | Israel | his do | minion.

3 The sea saw | that, and | fled ‖ Jordan | was - | driven | back.

4 The mountains | skipped like | rams ‖ and the little | hills like | young - | sheep.

5 What aileth thee, O thou sea. | that thou | fleddest ‖ and thou Jordan, that | thou wast | driven | back?

6 Ye mountains, that ye | skipped like | rams ‖ and ye little | hills, like | young - | sheep?

7 Tremble, thou earth, at the presence | of the | Lord ‖ at the presence | of the | God of | Jacob;

8 Who turned the hard rock into a | standing | water ‖ and the flint-stone in | to a | springing | well.

Psalm cxv. *Non nobis, Domine.*

NOT unto us, O Lord, not unto us, but unto thy Name | give the | praise ‖ for thy loving mercy, and | for thy | truth's - | sake.

2 Wherefore shall the | heathen | say ‖ Where | - is | now their | God?

3 As for our God, | he is in | heaven ‖ he hath done whatso | ever | pleased | him.

4 Their idols are | silver and | gold ‖ even the | work of | men's - | hands.

5 They have | mouths, and | speak not ‖ eyes | have they | and - | see not.

6 They have | ears and | hear not ‖ noses | have they, | and - | smell not.

7 They have hands, and handle not; feet | have they, and | walk not ‖ neither | speak they | through their | throat.

8 They that make them are like | unto | them ‖ and so are all | such as | put their | trust in them.

9 But thou, house of Israel, trust | thou in the | Lord ‖ he is their | succour | and de | fence.

10 Ye house of Aaron, put your trust | in the | Lord ‖ he is their | helper | and de | fender.

11 Ye that fear the Lord, put your trust | in the | Lord ‖ he is their | helper | and de | fender.

12 The Lord hath been mindful of us, and | he shall | bless us ‖ even he shall bless the house of Israel, he shall | bless the | house of | Aaron.

13 He shall bless them that | fear the | Lord ‖ both | small - | and - | great.

14 The Lord shall increase you | more and | more ‖ you | and - | your - | children.

15 Ye are the blessed | of the | Lord ‖ who | made - | heaven and | earth.

16 All the whole heavens | are the | Lord's ‖ the earth hath he given | to the | children of | men.

17 The dead praise not | thee, O | Lord ‖ neither all they that go down - | into | silence.

18 But we will | praise the | Lord ‖ from this time forth for evermore. | Praise - | - the | Lord.

The Twenty-Fourth Day.

MORNING PRAYER.

Psalm cxvi. *Dilexi, quoniam.*

I AM | well - | pleased ‖ that the Lord hath heard the | voice - | of my | prayer ;

2 That he hath inclined his ear | unto | me ‖ therefore will I call upon him as | long - | as I | live.

3 The snares of death compassed me | round a | bout ‖ and the pains of | hell gat | hold up | on me.

4 I shall find trouble and heaviness, and I will call upon the | Name of the | Lord ‖ O Lord, I beseech | thee, de | liver my | soul.

5 Gracious is the | Lord, and | righteous ‖ yea, | our - | God is | merciful.

6 The Lord pre | serveth the | simple ‖ I was in misery | and he | helped | me.

7 Turn again then unto thy rest, | O my | soul ‖ for the Lord | hath re | warded | thee.

8 And why? thou hast delivered my | soul from | death ‖ mine eyes from tears, | and my | feet from | falling.

9 I will walk be | fore the | Lord ‖ in the | land - | of the | living.

10 I believed, and therefore will I speak ; but I was | sore - | troubled ‖ I said in my haste, | All - | men are | liars.

11 What reward shall I give un | to the | Lord ‖ for all the benefits that he hath | done - | unto | me ?

12 I will receive the cup | of sal | vation ‖ and call upon the | Name - | of the | Lord.

13 I will pay my vows now in the presence of

all his | people ‖ right dear in the sight of the Lord is the | death - | of his | saints.

14 Behold, O Lord, how that | I am thy | servant ‖ I am thy servant, and the son of thy handmaid; thou hast | broken my | bonds in | sunder.

15 I will offer to thee the sacrifice of | thanksgiving ‖ and will call upon the | Name - | of the | Lord.

16 I will pay my vows unto the Lord, in the sight of | all his | people ‖ in the courts of the Lord's house; even in the midst of thee, O Jerusalem. | Praise - | - the | Lord.

Psalm cxvii. *Laudate Dominum.*

O PRAISE the Lord, | all ye | heathen ‖ praise | him, - | all ye | nations.

2 For his merciful kindness is ever more and | more to | wards us ‖ and the truth of the Lord endureth for ever. | Praise - | - the | Lord.

Psalm cxviii. *Confitemini Domino.*

O GIVE thanks unto the Lord, for | he is | gracious ‖ because his | mercy en | dureth for | ever.

2 Let Israel now confess that | he is | gracious ‖ and that his | mercy en | dureth for | ever.

3 Let the house of Aaron | now con | fess ‖ that his | mercy en | dureth for | ever.

4 Yea, let them now that fear the | Lord con | fess ‖ that his | mercy en | dureth for | ever.

5 I called upon the | Lord in | trouble ‖ and the Lord | heard - | me at | large.

6 The Lord is on | my - | side ‖ I will not fear what man | doeth | unto | me.

7 The Lord taketh my part with | them that | help me ‖ therefore shall I see my de | sire up | on mine | enemies.

8 It is better to trust | in the | Lord ‖ than to put any | confi | dence in | man.

9 It is better to trust | in the | Lord ‖ than to put any | confi dence in | princes.

10 All nations compassed me | round a | bout ‖ but in the Name of the | Lord will | I de | stroy them.

11 They kept me in on every side, they kept me in, I say, on | every | side ‖ but in the Name of the | Lord will | I de | stroy them.

12 They came about me like bees, and are ex- tinct even as the fire a | mong the | thorns ‖ for in the Name of the | Lord I | will de | stroy them.

13 Thou hast thrust sore at me, that | I might | fall ‖ but the | Lord - | was my | help.

14 The Lord is my strength, | and my | song ‖ and is be | come - | my sal | vation.

15 The voice of joy and health is in the dwell- ings | of the | righteous ‖ the right hand of the Lord bringeth | mighty | things to | pass.

16 The right hand of the Lord hath | the pre | eminence ‖ the right hand of the Lord bringeth | mighty | things to | pass.

17 I shall not | die but | live ‖ and declare the | works - | of the | Lord.

18 The Lord hath chastened and cor | rected | me ‖ but he hath not given me | over | unto | death.

19 Open me the | gates of | righteousness ‖

that I may go into them, and give | thanks un | to the | Lord.

20 This is the gate | of the | Lord ‖ the righteous shall | enter | into it.

21 I will thank thee ; for | thou hast | heard me ‖ and art be | come - | my sal | vation.

22 The same stone which the | builders re | fused ‖ is become the | head-stone | in the | corner.

23 This is the | Lord's - | doing ‖ and it is | marvellous | in our | eyes.

24 This is the day which the | Lord hath | made ‖ we will rejoice | and be | glad in | it.

25 Help me | now, O | Lord, ‖ O Lord | send us | now pros | perity.

26 Blessed be he that cometh in the | Name of the | Lord ‖ we have wished you good luck, ye that are of the | house - | of the | Lord.

27 God is the Lord, who hath | showed us | light ‖ bind the sacrifice with cords, yea, even unto the | horns - | of the | altar.

28 Thou art my God, and | I will | thank thee ‖ thou art my God, | and - | I will | praise thee.

29 O give thanks unto the Lord ; for | he is | gracious ‖ and his | mercy en | dureth for | ever.

EVENING PRAYER.

Psalm cxix. *Beati immaculati.*

BLESSED are those that are undefiled | in the | way ‖ and walk in the | law - | of the | Lord.

2 Blessed are they that | keep his | testimo-
nies ‖ and seek him | with their | whole - | heart.

3 For they who | do no | wickedness ‖ walk |
in - | his - | ways.

4 Thou | hast - | charged ‖ that we shall dili-
gently | keep - | thy com | mandments.

5 O that my ways were made | so di | rect ‖
that | I might | keep thy | statutes!

6 So shall I not | be con | founded ‖ while I
have respect unto | all - | thy com | mandments.

7 I will thank thee with an un | feigned |
heart ‖ when I shall have learned the | judg-
ments | of thy | righteousness.

8 I will | keep thy | ceremonies ‖ O for | sake
- | me not | utterly.

In quo corriget?

WHEREWITHAL shall a young man | cleanse
his | way ‖ even by ruling him | self - | after
thy | word.

2 With my whole heart | have I | sought thee ‖
O let me not go wrong | out of | thy com | mand-
ments!

3 Thy words have I hid with | in my | heart ‖
that I | should not | sin a | gainst thee.

4 Blessed art | thou, O | Lord ‖ O | teach - | me
thy | statutes!

5 With my lips have | I been | telling ‖ of all
the | judgments | of thy | mouth.

6 I have had as great delight in the way | of
thy | testimonies ‖ as in | all - | manner of |
riches.

7 I will talk of | thy com | mandments ‖ and
have re | spect un | to thy | ways.

8 My delight shall be | in thy | statutes ‖ and I will | not for | get thy | word.

Retribue servo tuo.

O DO well un | to thy | servant ‖ that I may | live, and | keep thy | word.

2 Open | thou mine | eyes ‖ that I may see the | wondrous | things of thy | law.

3 I am a | stranger upon | earth ‖ O hide not | thy com | mandments | from me !

4 My soul breaketh out for the very | fervent de | sire ‖ that it hath | alway un | to thy | judgments.

5 Thou hast re | buked the | proud ‖ and cursed are they that do | err from | thy com | mandments.

6 O turn from me shame | and re | buke ‖ for | I have | kept thy | testimonies.

7 Princes also did sit and | speak a | gainst me ‖ but thy servant is | occupied | in thy | statutes.

8 For thy testimonies are | my de | light ‖ and | my - | counsel | lors.

Adhæsit pavimento.

MY soul cleaveth | to the | dust ‖ O quicken thou me, ac | cording | to thy | word.

2 I have acknowledged my ways, and thou | heardest | me ‖ O | teach - | me thy | statutes !

3 Make me to understand the way of | thy com | mandments ‖ and so shall I talk | of thy | wondrous | works.

4 My soul melteth away for | very | heavi-

ness ‖ comfort thou me ac | cording | unto thy | word.

5 Take from me the | way of | lying ‖ and cause thou me to make | much - | of thy | law.

6 I have chosen the | way of | truth ‖ and thy judgments | have I | laid be | fore me.

7 I have stuck un | to thy | testimonies ‖ O | Lord, con | found me | not!

8 I will run the way of | thy com | mandments ‖ when thou hast | set my | heart at | liberty.

The Twenty-Fifth Day.
MORNING PRAYER.

Legem pone.

TEACH me, O Lord, the way | of thy statutes ‖ and I shall | keep it | unto the | end.

2 Give me understanding, and I shall | keep thy | law ‖ yea, I shall keep it | with my | whole - | heart.

3 Make me to go in the path of | thy com | mandments ‖ for there | in is | my de | sire.

4 Incline mine heart un | to thy | testimonies ‖ and | not to | covetous | ness.

5 O turn away mine eyes, lest they be | hold - | vanity ‖ and quicken | thou me | in thy | way.

6 O stablish thy word | in thy | servant ‖ that | I may | fear - | thee.

7 Take away the rebuke that I | am a | fraid of ‖ for thy | judg - | ments are | good.

8 Behold, my delight is in | thy com | mandments ‖ O | quicken me | in thy | righteousness.

Et veniat super me.

LET thy loving mercy come also unto | me, O | Lord || even thy salvation, ac | cording | unto thy | word.

2 So shall I make answer unto | my blas | phemers || for my | trust is | in thy | word.

3 O take not the word of thy truth utterly out | of my | mouth || for my | hope is | in thy | judgments.

4 So shall I alway | keep thy | law || yea, | for - | ever and | ever.

5 And I will | walk at | liberty || for I | seek - | thy com | mandments.

6 I will speak of thy testimonies also, | even before | kings || and | will not | be a | shamed.

7 And my delight shall be in | thy com | mandments || which | I - | have - | loved.

8 My hands also will I lift up unto thy commandments, which | I have | loved || and my | study shall | be in thy | statutes.

Memor esto servi tui.

O THINK upon thy servant, as con | cerning thy | word || wherein thou hast caused | me to | put my | trust.

2 The same is my comfort | in my | trouble || for thy | word hath | quickened | me.

3 The proud have had me exceedingly | in de | rision || yet have I not | shrinked | from thy | law.

4 For I remembered thine everlasting judgments, | O - | Lord || and | re - | ceived | comfort.

5 I am | horribly a | fraid || for the ungodly | that for | sake thy | law.

6 Thy statutes have | been my | songs ‖ in the | house - | of my | pilgrimage.

7 I have thought upon thy Name, O Lord in the | night - | season ‖ and | have - | kept thy | law.

8 This | - I | had ‖ because I | kept - | thy com | mandments.

Portio mea, Domine.

THOU art my | portion, O | Lord ‖ I have | promised to | keep thy | law.

2 I made my humble petition in thy presence with my | whole - | heart ‖ O be merciful unto me, ac | cording | to thy | word.

3 I called mine own ways | to re | membrance ‖ and turned my | feet un | to thy | testimonies.

4 I made haste, and prolonged | not the | time ‖ to | keep - | thy com | mandments.

5 The congregations of the ungodly have | robbed | me ‖ but I have | not for | gotten thy | law.

6 At midnight I will rise to give thanks | unto | thee ‖ because | of thy | righteous | judgments.

7 I am a companion of all | them that | fear thee ‖ and | keep - | thy com | mandments.

8 The earth, O Lord, is full | of thy | mercy ‖ O teach - | me thy | statutes!

Bonitatem fecisti.

O LORD, thou hast dealt graciously | with thy | servant ‖ ac | cording un | to thy | word.

2 O learn me true understanding | and - |

knowledge : for I have be | lieved | thy com | mandments.

3 Before I was troubled, | I went | wrong : but | now have I | kept thy | word.

4 Thou art | good and | gracious ‖ O | teach - | me thy | statutes!

5 The proud have imagined a | lie a | gainst me ‖ but I will keep thy commandments | with my | whole - | heart.

6 Their heart is as | fat as | brawn ‖ but my de | light hath | been in thy | law.

7 It is good for me that I have | been in | trouble ‖ that | I may | learn thy | statutes.

8 The law of thy mouth is dearer | unto | me ‖ than | thousands of | gold and | silver.

EVENING PRAYER.

Manus tuæ fecerunt me.

THY hands have made me and | fashioned | me ‖ O give me understanding, that I may | learn - | thy com | mandments.

2 They that fear thee will be glad | when they | see me ‖ because I have put my | trust - | in thy | word.

3 I know, O LORD, that thy | judgments are | right ‖ and that thou of very faithfulness hast | caused me | to be | troubled.

4 O let thy merciful kindness | be my | comfort ‖ according to thy | word un | to thy | servant.

5 O let thy loving mercies come unto me, that | I may | live ‖ for thy | law is | my de | light.

6 Let the proud be confounded, for they go wickedly about | to de | stroy me ‖ but I will be occupied | in - | thy com | mandments.

7 Let such as fear thee, and have | known thy | testimonies ‖ be | turned | unto | me.

8 O let my heart be sound | in thy | statutes ‖ that | I be | not a | shamed.

Deficit anima mea.

MY soul hath longed for | thy sal | vation ‖ and I have a good hope be | cause - | of thy | word.

2 Mine eyes long sore | for thy | word ‖ saying, O | when - | wilt thou | comfort me?

3 For I am become like a bottle | in the | smoke ‖ yet do I | not for | get thy | statutes.

4 How many are the days | of thy | servant ‖ when wilt thou be avenged of | them that | per- secute | me?

5 The proud have digged | pits for | me ‖ which | are not | after thy | law.

6 All thy com | mandments are | true ‖ they persecute me falsely; | O be | thou my | help.

7 They had almost made an end of me up | on - | earth ‖ but I for | sook not | thy com | mandments.

8 O quicken me after thy | loving | kindness ‖ and so shall I keep the | testimonies | of thy | mouth.

In æternum, Domine.

O LORD, | thy - | word ‖ en | dureth for | ever in | heaven.

2 Thy truth also remaineth from one genera-

tion | to an | other ‖ thou hast laid the foundation of the | earth, and | it a | bideth.

3 They continue this day according | to thine | ordinance ‖ for | all things | serve - | thee.

4 If my delight had not been | in thy ׳ law ‖ I should have | perished | in my | trouble.

5 I will never forget | thy com | mandments ‖ for with them | thou hast | quickened | me.

6 I am | thine ; O | save me ‖ for I have | sought - | thy com | mandments.

7 The ungodly laid wait for me, | to de | stroy me ‖ but I will con | sider thy | testi | monies.

8 I see that all things come | to an | end ‖ but thy commandment | is ex | ceeding | broad.

Quomodo dilexi !

LORD, what love have I un | to thy | law ‖ all the day long | is my | study | in it.

2 Thou, through thy commandments, hast made me wiser | than mine | enemies ‖ for | they are | ever | with me.

3 I have more understanding | than my | teachers ‖ for thy | testimonies | are my | study.

4 I am wiser | than the | aged ‖ because I | keep - | thy com | mandments.

5 I have refrained my feet from every | evil | way ‖ that | I may | keep thy | word.

6 I have not shrunk | from thy | judgments ‖ for | thou - | teachest | me.

7 O how sweet are thy words un | to my | throat ‖ yea, sweeter than | honey | unto my | mouth !

8 Through thy commandments I get | under | standing ‖ therefore I | hate all | evil | ways.

The Twenty-Sixth Day.

MORNING PRAYER.

Lucerna pedibus meis.

THY word is a lantern un | to my | feet : and a | light un | to my | paths.

2 I have sworn, and am | steadfastly | purposed ‖ to | keep thy | righteous | judgments.

3 I am troubled a | bove - | measure ‖ quicken me, O Lord, ac | cording | to thy | word.

4 Let the free-will offerings of my mouth please | thee, O | Lord ‖ and | teach - | me thy | judgments.

5 My soul is alway | in my | hand ‖ yet do I | not for | get thy | law.

6 The ungodly have laid a | snare for | me ‖ but yet I swerved | not from | thy com | mandments.

7 Thy testimonies have I claimed as mine heritage | for - | ever ‖ and why? they are the very | joy - | of my | heart.

8 I have applied my heart to fulfil thy | statutes | alway ‖ even | un - | to the | end.

Iniquos odio habui.

I HATE them that imagine evil | things ‖ but thy | law - | do I | love.

2 Thou art my de | fence and | shield ‖ and my | trust is | in thy | word.

3 Away | from me, ye | wicked ‖ I will keep the com | mandments | of my | God.

4 O stablish me according to thy word, that | I may | live ‖ and let me not be disap | pointed | of my | hope.

5 Hold thou me up, and I | shall be | safe ‖ yea, my delight shall be | ever | in thy | statutes.

6 Thou hast trodden down all them that depart | from thy | statutes ‖ for they im | agine | but de | ceit.

7 Thou puttest away all the ungodly of the | earth like | dross ‖ there | fore I | love thy | testimonies.

8 My flesh trembleth for | fear of | thee ‖ and I am a | fraid - | of thy | judgments.

Feci judicium.

I DEAL with the thing that is | lawful and | right ‖ O give me not over | unto | mine op | pressors!

2 Make thou thy servant to delight in that | which is | good ‖ that the | proud do | me no | wrong.

3 Mine eyes are wasted away with looking | for thy | health ‖ and for the word | of thy | righteous | ness.

4 O deal with thy servant according unto thy | loving | mercy ‖ and | teach - | me thy | statutes!

5 I am thy servant: O grant me | under | standing ‖ that | I may | know thy | testimonies.

6 It is time for thee, LORD, to lay | to thine | hand ‖ for they | have de | stroyed thy | law.

7 For I love | thy com | mandments ‖ above | gold and | precious | stones.

8 Therefore hold I straight | all thy com | mandments ‖ and all false | ways I | utterly ab | hor.

Mirabilia.

THY testimonies are | wonder | ful ‖ therefore | doth my | soul - | keep them.

2 When thy word | goeth | forth ‖ it giveth light and under | standing | unto the | simple.

3 I opened my mouth, and drew | in my | breath ‖ for my delight | was in | thy com | mandments.

4 O look upon me, and be merciful | unto | me ‖ as thou usest to do unto | those that | love thy | Name.

5 Order my steps | in thy | word ‖ and so shall no wickedness | have do | minion | over me.

6 O deliver me from the wrongful | dealings of | men ‖ and so shall I | keep - | thy com | mandments.

7 Show the light of thy countenance up | on thy | servant ‖ and | teach - | me thy | statutes.

8 Mine eyes gush | out with | water ‖ because men | keep - | not thy | law.

Justus es, Domine.

RIGHTEOUS art | thou, O | Lord ‖ and | true - | is thy | judgment.

2 The testimonies that thou | hast com | mand-ed ‖ are ex | ceeding | righteous and | true.

3 My zeal hath | even con | sumed me ‖ because mine enemies | have for | gotten thy | words.

4 Thy word is tried to the | utter | most ‖ and thy | servant | loveth | it.

5 I am small and of | no repu | tation ‖ yet do I not for | get - | thy com | mandments.

6 Thy righteousness is an ever | lasting | right-eousness ‖ and thy | law - | is the | truth.

7 Trouble and heaviness have taken | hold up- | on me ‖ yet is my de | light in | thy com | mand-ments.

8 The righteousness of thy testimonies is | ever | lasting ‖ O grant me under | standing, and | I shall | live.

EVENING PRAYER.

Clamavi in toto corde meo.

I CALL with my | whole - | heart ‖ hear me, O Lord: | I will | keep thy | statutes.

2 Yea, even unto thee | do I | call ‖ help me, and | I shall | keep thy | testimonies.

3 Early in the morning do I cry | unto | thee ‖ for in thy | word - | is my | trust.

4 Mine eyes prevent the | night - | watches ‖ that I might be | occupied | in thy | words.

5 Hear my voice, O Lord, according unto thy | loving | kindness ‖ quicken me, ac | cording as | thou art | wont.

6 They draw nigh that of malice | persecute | me ‖ and are | far - | from thy | law.

7 Be thou nigh at | hand, O | Lord ‖ for all | thy com | mandments are | true.

8 As concerning thy testimonies, I have | known long | since ‖ that thou hast | grounded | them for | ever.

Vide humilitatem.

O CONSIDER mine adversity, | and de | liver me ‖ for I do | not for | get thy | law.

2 Avenge thou my cause, | and de | liver me | quicken me ac | cording | to thy | word.

3 Health is far from | the un | godly ‖ for they re | gard - | not thy | statutes.

4 Great is thy mercy, | O - | Lord ‖ quicken me, | as - | thou art | wont.

5 Many there are that trouble me, and | per- secute | me ‖ yet do I not | swerve - | from thy | testimonies.

6 It grieveth me when I | see the trans | gress- ors ‖ because they | keep - | not thy | law.

7 Consider, O Lord, how I | love thy com | mandments ‖ O quicken me, according | to thy | loving | kindness.

8 Thy word is true from | ever | lasting ‖ all the judgments of thy righteousness en | dure for | ever | more.

Principes persecuti sunt.

PRINCES have persecuted me with | out a | cause ‖ but my heart standeth in | awe - | of thy | word.

2 I am as glad | of thy | word ‖ as one that | findeth | great - | spoils.

3 As for lies, I hate | and ab | hor them ‖ but thy | law - | do I | love.

4 Seven times a day | do I | praise thee ‖ be- cause | of thy | righteous | judgments.

5 Great is the peace that they have who | love thy | law ‖ and they are | not of | fended | at it.

6 Lord, I have looked for thy | saving | health ‖ and done | after | thy com | mandments.

7 My soul hath | kept thy | testimonies ‖ and | loved | them ex | ceedingly.

8 I have kept thy commandments | and - | testimonies ‖ for all my | ways - | are be | fore thee.

Appropinquet deprecatio.

LET my complaint come before | thee, O | Lord ‖ give me understanding ac | cording to thy | word.

2 Let my supplication | come be | fore thee ‖ deliver me ac | cording | to thy | word.

3 My lips shall speak | of thy | praise ‖ when thou hast | taught - | me thy | statutes.

4 Yea, my tongue shall sing | of thy | word ‖ for all | thy com | mandments are | righteous.

5 Let thine | hand - | help me ‖ for I have | chosen | thy com | mandments.

6 I have longed for thy saving health, | O - | Lord ‖ and in thy | law is | my de | light.

7 O let my soul live, and | it shall | praise thee ‖ and thy | judg - | ments shall | help me.

8 I have gone astray like a sheep | that is | lost ‖ O seek thy servant, for I do not for | get - | thy com | mandments.

𝕮𝖍𝖊 𝕿𝖜𝖊𝖓𝖙𝖞-𝕾𝖊𝖇𝖊𝖓𝖙𝖍 𝕯𝖆𝖞.

MORNING PRAYER.

PSALM CXX. *Ad Dominum.*

WHEN I was in trouble, I called up | on the | Lord ‖ and | he - | heard - | me.

2 Deliver my soul, O Lord, from | lying | lips ‖ and | from a de | ceitful | tongue.

3 What reward shall be given or done unto thee, | thou false | tongue ‖ even mighty and sharp arrows, with | hot - | burning | coals.

4 Woe is me, that I am constrained to | dwell with | Mesech ‖ and to have my habitation a | mong the | tents of | Kedar!

5 My soul hath long | dwelt among | them ∎ that are | enemies | unto | peace.

6 I labor for peace: but when I speak unto | them there | of ‖ they | make them | ready to | battle.

Psalm cxxi. *Levavi oculos meos.*

I WILL lift up mine eyes un | to the | hills ∎ from | whence - | cometh my | help.

2 My help cometh even | from the | Lord ∎ who hath | made - | heaven and | earth.

3 He will not suffer thy foot | to be | moved ‖ and he that | keepeth thee | will not | sleep.

4 Behold, he that | keepeth | Israel ‖ shall | neither | slumber nor | sleep.

5 The Lord himself | is thy | keeper ‖ the Lord is thy defence up | on thy | right - | hand;

6 So that the sun shall not | burn thee by | day ‖ neither the | moon - | by - | night.

7 The Lord shall preserve thee | from all | evil ‖ yea, it is even | he that shall | keep thy | soul.

8 The Lord shall preserve thy going out, and thy | coming | in ‖ from this time | forth for | ever | more.

Psalm cxxii. *Lætatus sum.*

I WAS glad when they said | unto | me ‖ We will go into the | house - | of the | Lord.

2 Our feet shall stand | in thy | gates ∎ O | Je - | rusa | lem.

[Morning.] THE PSALTER. [Day 27

3 Jerusalem is built | as a | city ‖ that is at | unity | in it | self.
4 For thither the tribes go up, even the tribes | of the | Lord ‖ to testify unto Israel, to give thanks unto the | Name - | of the | Lord.
5 For there is the | seat of | judgment ‖ even the seat | of the | house of | David.
6 O pray for the peace | of Je | rusalem ‖ they shall | pros - | per that | love thee.
7 Peace be with | in thy | walls ‖ and plenteous | ness with | in thy | palaces.
8 For my brethren and com | panions' | sakes ‖ I will | wish - | thee pros | perity.
9 Yea, because of the house of the | Lord our | God ‖ I will | seek to | do thee | good.

Psalm cxxiii. *Ad te levavi oculos meos.*

UNTO thee lift I | up mine | eyes ‖ O Thou that | dwellest | in the | heavens.
2 Behold, even as the eyes of servants look unto the hand of their masters, and as the eyes of a maiden unto the hand | of her | mistress ‖ even so our eyes wait upon the Lord our God, until | he have | mercy up | on us.
3 Have mercy upon us, O Lord, have | mercy up | on us ‖ for we are | utter | ly de | spised.
4 Our soul is filled with the scornful reproof | of the | wealthy ‖ and with the de | spitefulness | of the | proud.

Psalm cxxiv. *Nisi quia Dominus.*

IF the Lord himself had not been on our side, now may | Israel | say ‖ if the Lord himself had not been on our side, when | men rose | up a | 'gainst us :

2 They had swallowed | us up | quick ‖ when they were so wrathfully | dis - | pleased | at us.

3 Yea, the waters had | drowned | us ‖ and the stream | had gone | over our | soul.

4 The deep waters | of the | proud ‖ had gone | even | over our | soul.

5 But praised | be the | Lord ‖ who hath not given us over for a | prey un | to their | teeth.

6 Our soul is escaped even as a bird out of the snare | of the | fowler ‖ the snare is broken, | and we | are de | livered.

7 Our help standeth in the Name | of the | Lord ‖ who hath | made - | heaven and | earth.

Psalm cxxv. *Qui confidunt.*

THEY that put their trust in the Lord shall be even as the | Mount - | Sion ‖ which may not be removed, but | standeth | fast for | ever.

2 The hills stand a | bout Je | rusalem ‖ even so standeth the Lord round about his people, from this time | forth for | ever | more.

3 For the rod of the ungodly cometh not into the lot | of the | righteous ‖ lest the righteous put their | hand - | unto | wickedness.

4 Do | well, O | Lord ‖ unto those that are | good and | true of | heart.

5 As for such as turn back unto | their own | wickedness ‖ the Lord shall lead them forth with the evil doers ; but | peace shall | be upon | Israel.

EVENING PRAYER.

Psalm cxxvi. *In convertendo.*

WHEN the Lord turned again the captivity | of - | Sion ‖ then were we like | unto | them that | dream.

2 Then was our mouth | filled with | laughter ‖ and | our - | tongue with | joy.

3 Then said they a | mong the | heathen ‖ The Lord hath | done - | great things | for them.

4 Yea, the Lord hath done great things for | us al | ready ‖ where | of - | we re | joice.

5 Turn our captivity, | O - | Lord ‖ as the | rivers | in the | south.

6 They that | sow in | tears ‖ shall | reap - | in - | joy.

7 He that now goeth on his way weeping, and beareth forth | good - | seed ‖ shall doubtless come again with joy, and | bring his | sheaves - | with him.

Psalm cxxvii. *Nisi Dominus.*

EXCEPT the Lord | build the | house ‖ their labour | is but | lost that | build it.

2 Except the Lord | keep the | city ‖ the watchman | waketh | but in | vain.

3 It is but lost labour that ye haste to rise up early, and so late take rest, and eat the | bread of | carefulness ‖ for so he giveth | his be | loved | sleep.

4 Lo, children, and the fruit | of the | womb ‖ are an heritage and gift that | cometh | of the | Lord.

5 Like as the arrows in the hand | of the | giant ‖ even | so are the | young - | children.

6 Happy is the man that hath his | quiver | full of them ‖ they shall not be ashamed when they speak with their | enemies | in the | gate.

PSALM cxxviii. *Beati omnes.*

BLESSED are all they that | fear the | LORD ‖ and | walk - | in his | ways.
  2 For thou shalt eat the labour | of thine | hands ‖ O well is thee, and | happy | shalt thou | be !
  3 Thy wife shall be as the | fruitful | vine ‖ upon the | walls - | of thine | house.
  4 Thy children like the | olive | branches ‖ round a | bout - | thy - | table.
  5 Lo, thus shall the | man be | blessed ‖ that | fear - | eth the | LORD.
  6 The LORD from out of Sion | shall so | bless thee ‖ that thou shalt see Jerusalem in prosperity | all thy | life - | long.
  7 Yea, that thou shalt see thy | children's | children ‖ and | peace up | on - | Israel.

PSALM cxxix. *Sæpe expugnaverunt.*

MANY a time have they fought against me from my | youth - | up ‖ may | Israel | now - | say ;
  2 Yea, many a time have they vexed me from my | youth - | up ‖ but they have | not pre | vailed a | gainst me.
  3 The plowers plowed up | on my | back ‖ and | made - | long - | furrows.
  4 But the | righteous | LORD ‖ hath hewn the snares of the un | god - | ly in | pieces.
  5 Let them be confounded and | turned | back ward ‖ as many as have | evil | will at | Sion.

6 Let them be even as the grass growing up | on the | house tops ‖ which withereth a | fore it be | plucked | up ;

7 Whereof the mower filleth | not his | hand ‖ neither he that bindeth | up the | sheaves his | bosom.

8 So that they who go by say not so much as, The Lord | prosper | you ‖ we wish you good luck in the | Name - | of the | Lord.

Psalm cxxx. *De profundis.*

OUT of the deep have I called unto | thee, O | Lord ‖ Lord, | hear - | my - | voice.

2 O let thine ears con | sider | well ‖ the | voice of | my com | plaint.

3 If thou, Lord, wilt be extreme to mark what is | done a | miss ‖ O Lord, | who - | may a | bide it ?

4 For there is | mercy with | thee ‖ therefore | shalt - | thou be | feared.

5 I look for the Lord ; my | soul doth | wait for him ‖ in his | word - | is my | trust.

6 My soul fleeth un | to the | Lord ‖ before the morning watch ; I say, be | fore the | morning | watch.

7 O Israel, trust in the Lord ; for with the Lord | there is | mercy ‖ and with | him is | plenteous re | demption.

8 And he shall re | deem - | Israel ‖ from | all - | his - | sins.

Psalm cxxxi. *Domine, non est.*

LORD, I am | not high | minded ‖ I | have no | proud - | looks.

2 I do not exercise myself in | great - | mat‑
ters ‖ which | are - | too high | for me.

3 But I refrain my soul, and keep it low, like
as a child that is weaned | from his | mother ‖
yea, my soul is even | as a | weaned | child.

4 O Israel, | trust in the | Lord ‖ from this
time | forth for | ever | more.

The Twenty-Eighth Day.

MORNING PRAYER.

Psalm cxxxii. *Memento, Domine.*

LORD, re | member | David ‖ and | all - | his - | trouble :

2 How he sware un | to the | Lord ‖ and vowed
a vow unto the Al | mighty | God of | Jacob;

3 I will not come within the tabernacle | of
mine | house ‖ nor | climb up | into my | bed;

4 I will not suffer mine eyes to sleep, nor
mine | eyelids to | slumber ‖ neither the temples
of my head to | take - | any | rest;

5 Until I find out a place for the temple | of the |
Lord ‖ an habitation for the | mighty | God of |
Jacob.

6 Lo, we heard of the | same at | Ephrata ‖
and | found it | in the | wood.

7 We will go in | to his | tabernacle ‖ and fall
low on our | knees be | fore his | footstool.

8 Arise, O Lord, into thy | resting | place |
thou, and the | ark - | of thy | strength.

9 Let thy priests be | clothed with | righteous‑
ness ‖ and let thy | saints - | sing with | joyful‑
ness.

10 For thy servant | David's | sake ‖ turn not away the | presence of | thine A | nointed.
11 The LORD hath made a faithful oath | unto | David ‖ and he | shall not | shrink - | from it ;
12 Of the fruit | of thy | body ‖ shall I | set up on thy | seat.
13 If thy children will keep my covenant, and my testimonies that | I shall | learn them ‖ their children also shall sit upon thy | seat for | ever | more.
14 For the LORD hath chosen Sion to be an habitation | for him | self ‖ he | hath - | longed | for her.
15 This shall be my | rest for | ever ‖ here will I dwell, for I | have a de | light there | in.
16 I will bless her | victuals with | increase ‖ and will satis | fy her | poor with | bread.
17 I will deck her | priests with | health ‖ and her | saints shall re | joice and | sing.
18 There shall I make the horn of | David to | flourish ‖ I have ordained a | lantern for | mine A | nointed.
19 As for his enemies, I shall | clothe them with | shame ‖ but upon himself | shall his | crown - | flourish.

PSALM cxxxiii. *Ecce, quam bonum!*

BEHOLD, how good and joyful a | thing it | is ‖ brethren, to | dwell to | gether in | unity !
2 It is like the precious ointment upon the head, that ran down un | to the | beard ‖ even unto Aaron's beard, and went down to the | skirts - | of his | clothing.

3 Like as the | dew of | Hermon ‖ which fell up | on the | hill of | Sion.

4 For there the Lord | promised his | blessing ‖ and | life for | ever | more.

Psalm cxxxiv. *Ecce nunc.*

BEHOLD now, | praise the | Lord ‖ all ye | servants | of the | Lord;

2 Ye that by night stand in the house | of the | Lord ‖ even in the courts of the | house - | of our | God.

3 Lift up your hands | in the | sanctuary ‖ and | praise - | - the | Lord.

4 The Lord, that made | heaven and | earth ‖ give thee | blessing | out of | Sion.

Psalm cxxxv. *Laudate Nomen.*

O PRAISE the Lord, laud ye the | Name of the | Lord ‖ praise it, O ye | servants | of the | Lord;

2 Ye that stand in the house | of the | Lord ‖ in the courts of the | house - | of our | God.

3 O praise the Lord, for the | Lord is | gracious ‖ O sing praises unto his | Name, for | it is | lovely.

4 For why? the Lord hath chosen Jacob un | to him | self ‖ and Israel | for his | own pos | session.

5 For I know that the | Lord is | great ‖ and that our | Lord is a | bove all | gods.

6 Whatsover the Lord pleased, that did he in heaven, | and in | earth ‖ in the sea, | and in | all deep | places.

7 He bringeth forth the clouds from the ends | of the | world ‖ and sendeth forth lightnings with the rain, bringing the | winds out | of his | treasures.

8 He smote the | first-born of | Egypt ‖ both | - of | man and | beast.

9 He hath sent tokens and wonders into the midst of thee, O thou | land of | Egypt ‖ upon | Pharaoh, an' all his | servants.

10 He smote | divers | nations ‖ and | slew - | mighty | kings;

11 Sehon, king of the Amorites; and Og, the | king of | Basan ‖ and | all the | kingdoms of | Canaan;

12 And gave their land to | be an | heritage ‖ even an heritage unto | Isra | el his | people.

13 Thy Name, O Lord, en | dureth for | ever ‖ so doth thy memorial, O Lord, from one gener | ation | to an | other.

14 For the Lord will a | venge his | people ‖ and be | gracious un | to his | servants.

15 As for the images of the heathen, they are but | silver and | gold ‖ the | work of | men's - | hands.

16 They have | mouths, and | speak not ‖ eyes | have they, | but they | see not.

17 They have ears, and | yet they | hear not ‖ neither is there any | breath - | in their | mouths.

18 They that make them are like | unto | them ‖ and so are all | they that | put their | trust in them.

19 Praise the Lord, ye | house of | Israel ‖ praise the | Lord, ye | house of | Aaron.

20 Praise the Lord, ye | house of | Levi ‖ ye that fear the Lord, | praise - | - the | Lord.

21 Praised be the Lord | out of | Sion ‖ who | dwelleth | at Je | rusalem.

EVENING PRAYER.

Psalm cxxxvi. *Confitemini Domino.*

O GIVE thanks unto the Lord, for | he is | gracious ‖ and his | mercy en | dureth for | ever.

2 O give thanks unto the God | of all | gods ‖ for his | mercy en | dureth for | ever.

3 O thank the Lord | of all | lords ‖ for his | mercy en | dureth for | ever.

4 Who only | doeth great | wonders ‖ for his | mercy en | dureth for | ever.

5 Who by his excellent wisdom | made the | heavens ‖ for his | mercy en | dureth for | ever.

6 Who laid out the earth a | bove the | waters ‖ for his | mercy en | dureth for | ever.

7 Who hath made | great - | lights ‖ for his | mercy en | dureth for | ever :

8 The sun to | rule the | day ‖ for his | mercy en | dureth for | ever :

9 The moon and the stars to | govern the | night ‖ for his | mercy en | dureth for | ever.

10 Who smote Egypt, | with their | first-born ‖ for his | mercy en | dureth for | ever :

11 And brought out Israel | from a | mong them ‖ for his | mercy en | dureth for | ever :

12 With a mighty hand and | stretched-out | arm ‖ for his | mercy en | dureth for | ever.

13 Who divided the Red Sea | in two | parts ‖ for his | mercy en | dureth for | ever :

14 And made Israel to go | through the | midst of it ‖ for his | mercy en | dureth for | ever.
15 But as for Pharaoh and his host, he overthrew them | in the Red | Sea ‖ for his | mercy en | dureth for | ever:
16 Who led his people | through the | wilderness ‖ for his | mercy en | dureth for | ever.
17 Who | smote great | kings ‖ for his | mercy en | dureth for | ever :
18 Yea, and slew | mighty | kings ‖ for his | mercy en | dureth for | ever:
19 Sehon, king | of the | Amorites ‖ for his | mercy en | dureth for | ever :
20 And Og, the | king of | Basan ‖ for his | mercy en | dureth for | ever.
21 And gave away their land | for an | heritage ‖ for his | mercy en | dureth for | ever.
22 Even for an heritage unto Israel, | his - | servant ‖ for his | mercy en | dureth for | ever.
23 Who remembered us when we | were in | trouble ‖ for his | mercy en | dureth for | ever.
24 And hath delivered us | from our | enemies ‖ for his | mercy en | dureth for | ever.
25 Who giveth food | to all | flesh ‖ for his | mercy en | dureth for | ever.
26 O give thanks unto the | God of | heaven ‖ for his | mercy en | dureth for | ever.
27 O give thanks unto the | Lord of | lords ‖ for his | mercy en | dureth for | ever.

PSALM cxxxvii. *Super flumina.*

BY the waters of Babylon we sat | down and | wept ‖ when we remembered | thee, - | O - | Sion.

2 As for our harps, we | hanged them | up ‖ upon the | trees that | are there | in.

3 For they that led us away captive, required of us then a song, and melody | in our | heaviness ‖ Sing us one of the | songs - | of - | Sion.

4 How shall we sing the | Lord's - | song | in a | strange - | - - | land?

5 If I forget thee, | O Je | rusalem ‖ let my right | hand for | get her | cunning.

6 If I do not remember thee, let my tongue cleave to the roof | of my | mouth ‖ yea, if I prefer not Je | rusalem | in my | mirth.

7 Remember the children of Edom, O Lord, in the day | of Je | rusalem ‖ how they said, Down with it, down with it, | even | to the | ground.

8 O daughter of Babylon, | wasted with | misery ‖ yea, happy shall he be that rewardeth thee as | thou hast | served | us.

9 Blessed shall he be that | taketh thy | children ‖ and throweth | them a | gainst the | stones.

PSALM cxxxviii *Confitebor tibi.*

I WILL give thanks unto thee, O Lord, with my | whole - | heart ‖ even before the gods will I sing | praise - | unto | thee.

2 I will worship toward thy holy temple, and praise thy Name, because of thy loving | kindness and | truth ‖ for thou hast magnified thy Name, and thy | Word, a | bove all | things.

3 When I called upon thee, thou | heardest | me ‖ and enduedst my | soul - | with much | strength.

4 All the kings of the earth shall praise | thee

O | Lord ‖ for they have heard the | words - | of thy | mouth.

5 Yea, they shall sing in the ways | of the | Lord ‖ that great is the | glory | of the | Lord.

6 For though the Lord be high, yet hath he respect un | to the | lowly ‖ as for the proud, he be | holdeth | them afar | off.

7 Though I walk in the midst of trouble, yet shalt | thou re | fresh me ‖ thou shalt stretch forth thy hand upon the furiousness of mine enemies, and | thy right | hand shall | save me.

8 The Lord shall make good his loving | kindness to | ward me ‖ yea, thy mercy, O Lord, endureth for ever; despise not then the | works of | thine own | hands.

The Twenty-Ninth Day.

MORNING PRAYER.

Psalm cxxxix. *Domine, probasti.*

O LORD, thou hast searched me | out, and | known me ‖ Thou knowest my down-sitting, and mine up-rising; thou understandest my | thoughts - | long be | fore.

2 Thou art about my path, and a | bout my | bed ‖ and | spiest out | all my | ways.

3 For lo, there is not a word | in my | tongue ‖ but thou, O Lord, | knowest it | alto | gether.

4 Thou hast fashioned me behind | and be | fore ‖ and | laid thine | hand up | on me.

5 Such knowledge is too wonderful and | excellent | for me ‖ I cannot at | tain - | unto | it.

6 Whither shall I go then | from thy | Spirit ‖ or whither shall I | go then | from thy | presence?

7 If I climb up into heaven, | thou art | there ‖ if I go down to hell, | thou art | there - | also.

8 If I take the wings | of the | morning ‖ and remain in the uttermost | parts - | of the | sea;

9 Even there also shall | thy hand | lead me ‖ and thy | right - | hand shall | hold me.

10 If I say, Peradventure the | darkness shall | cover me ‖ then shall my | night be | turned to | day.

11 Yea, the darkness is no darkness with thee, but the night is as clear | as the | day ‖ the darkness and light to | thee are | both a | like.

12 For my | reins are | thine ‖ thou hast covered me | in my | mother's | womb.

13 I will give thanks unto thee, for I am fearfully and | wonderfully | made ‖ marvellous are thy works, and that my soul | knoweth | right - | well.

14 My bones are not | hid from | thee ‖ though I be made secretly, and fashioned be | neath - | in the | earth.

15 Thine eyes did see my substance, yet | being im | perfect ‖ and in thy book were | all my | members | written;

16 Which day by | day were | fashioned ‖ when as | yet - | there was | none of them.

17 How dear are thy counsels unto | me, O | God ‖ O how | great - | is the | sum of them!

18 If I tell them, they are more in number | than the sand ‖ when I wake up, | I am | present | with thee.

19 Wilt thou not slay the | wicked, O | God ‖ Depart from me, | ye blood | thirsty | men.

20 For they speak unrighteously a | gainst - | thee ‖ and thine enemies | take thy | Name in | vain.

21 Do not I hate them, O Lord, | that hate | thee ‖ and am not I grieved with those that | rise - | up a | gainst thee.

22 Yea, I | hate them right | sore ‖ even as | though they | were mine | enemies.

23 Try me, O God, and seek the ground | of my | heart ‖ prove me, | and ex | amine my | thoughts.

24 Look well if there be any way of wickedness | in - | me ‖ and lead me in the | way - | ever | lasting.

Psalm cxl. *Eripe me, Domine.*

DELIVER me, O Lord, from the | evil | man ‖ and preserve me | from the | wicked | man;

2 Who imagine mischief | in their | hearts ‖ and stir up | strife - | all the day | long.

3 They have sharpened their tongues | like a | serpent ‖ adder's | poison is | under their | lips.

4 Keep me, O Lord, from the hands of | the un | godly ‖ preserve me from the wicked men, who are purposed to | over | throw my | goings.

5 The proud have laid a snare for me, and spread a net a | broad with | cords ‖ yea, and set traps - in my | way.

6 I said unto the Lord. | Thou art my | God ‖ hear the voice | of my | prayers, O | Lord.

7 O Lord God, thou strength | of my | health ‖

thou hast covered my head | in the | day of | battle.

8 Let not the ungodly have his de | sire, O | Lord ‖ let not his mischievous imagination pros- per, | lest they | be too | proud.

9 Let the mischief of their own lips fall upon the | head of | them ‖ that | compass | me a | bout.

10 Let hot burning coals | fall up | on them ‖ let them be cast into the fire, and into the pit, that they | never | rise up a | gain.

11 A man full of words shall not prosper up | on the | earth ‖ evil shall hunt the wicked | per- son to | over | throw him.

12 Sure I am that the Lord will a | venge the | poor ‖ and maintain | the cause | of the | helpless

13 The righteous also shall give thanks un | to thy | Name ‖ and the just shall con | tinue | in thy | sight.

Psalm cxli. *Domine, clamavi.*

LORD, I call upon thee; haste thee | unto | me ‖ and consider my voice, | when I | cry unto | thee.

2 Let my prayer be set forth in thy sight | as the | incense ‖ and let the lifting up of my hands | be an | evening | sacrifice.

3 Set a watch, O Lord, be | fore my | mouth ‖ and keep the | door - | of my | lips.

4 O let not mine heart be inclined to any | evil | thing ‖ let me not be occupied in ungodly works with the men that work wickedness, lest I | eat of such | things as | please them.

5 Let the righteous rather | smite me | friend- ly ‖ and | - re | prove - | me.

6 But let not their precious balms | break my | head ‖ yea, I will pray | yet a | gainst their | wickedness.

7 Let their judges be overthrown in | stony | places ‖ that they may hear my | words; for | they are | sweet.

8 Our bones lie scattered be | fore the | pit ‖ like as when one breaketh and heweth | wood up | on the | earth.

9 But mine eyes look unto thee, | O Lord | God ‖ in thee is my trust; O | cast not | out my | soul.

10 Keep me from the snare that they have | laid for | me ‖ and from the traps | of the | wicked | doers.

11 Let the ungodly fall into their own | nets to | gether ‖ and | let me | ever es | cape them.

EVENING PRAYER.

Psalm cxlii. *Voce mea ad Dominum.*

I CRIED unto the Lord | with my | voice ‖ yea, even unto the Lord did I | make my | suppli | cation.

2 I poured out my com | plaints be | fore him ‖ and | showed him | of my | trouble.

3 When my spirit was in heaviness, thou | knewest my | path ‖ in the way wherein I walked, have they privily | laid a | snare - | for me.

4 I looked also upon my | right - | hand ‖ and saw there was | no man | that would | know me.

5 I had no place to | flee un | to ‖ and no man cared | for my | soul.

6 I cried unto thee, O | Lord, and | said ‖ Thou art my hope, and my portion in the | land - | of the | living.

7 Consider | my com | plaint ‖ for I am | brought - | very | low.

8 O deliver me | from my | persecutors ‖ for | they - | are too | strong for me.

9 Bring my soul out of prison, that I may give thanks un | to thy | Name ‖ which thing if thou wilt grant me, then shall the righteous re | sort un | to my | company.

Psalm cxliii. *Domine, exaudi.*

HEAR my prayer, O Lord, and consider | my de | sire ‖ hearken unto me for thy | truth and | righteousness' | sake.

2 And enter not into judgment | with thy | servant ‖ for in thy sight shall | no man | living be | justified.

3 For the enemy hath persecuted my soul; he hath smitten my life | down to the | ground ‖ he hath laid me in the darkness as the men | that have | been long | dead.

4 Therefore is my spirit | vexed with | in me ‖ and my | heart with | in me is | desolate.

5 Yet do I remember the time past; I muse upon | all thy | works ‖ yea, I exercise myself in the | works - | of thy | hands.

6 I stretch forth my hands | unto | thee ‖ my soul gaspeth unto thee | as a | thirsty | land.

7 Hear me, O Lord, and that soon; for my spirit | waxeth | faint ‖ hide not thy face from me, lest I be like unto them that go | down in | to the | pit.

8 O let me hear thy loving-kindness betimes in the morning; for in | thee is my | trust ‖ show thou me the way that I should walk in ; for I lift up my | soul - | unto | thee.

9 Deliver me, O LORD, | from mine | enemies |' for I flee | unto | thee to | hide me.

10 Teach me to do the thing that pleaseth thee; for thou | art my | God ‖ let thy loving Spirit lead me forth in | to the | land of | righteousness.

11 Quicken me, O LORD, for thy | Name's - | sake | and for thy righteousness' sake bring my | soul - | out of | trouble.

12 And of thy goodness | slay mine | enemies ‖ and destroy all them that vex my soul; | for I | am thy | servant.

The Thirtieth Day.

MORNING PRAYER.

PSALM cxliv. *Benedictus Dominus.*

BLESSED be the | LORD my | strength ‖ who teacheth my hands to war, | and my | fingers to | fight:

2 My hope and my fortress, my castle and deliverer, my defender in | whom I | trust ‖ who subdueth my | people | that is | under me.

3 LORD, what is man, that thou hast such respect | unto | him ‖ or the son of man, that thou | so re | gardest | him!

4 Man is like a | thing of | nought ‖ his time passeth a | way - | like a | shadow.

5 Bow thy heavens, O Lord, | and come | down ‖ touch the | mountains, and | they shall | smoke.

6 Cast forth thy | lightning, and | tear them ‖ shoot out thine | arrows, | and con | sume them.

7 Send down thine hand | from a | bove ‖ deliver me, and take me out of the great waters, from the | hand of | strange - | children ;

8 Whose mouth | talketh of | vanity ‖ and their right hand is a | right - | hand of | wickedness.

9 I will sing a new song unto | thee, O | God ‖ and sing praises unto thee up | on a | ten-stringed | lute.

10 Thou hast given victory | unto |. kings ‖ and hast delivered David thy servant from the | peril | of the | sword.

11 Save me, and deliver me from the hand of | strange - | children ‖ whose mouth talketh of vanity, and their right hand is a | right hand | of in | iquity :

12 That our sons may grow up as the | young - | plants ‖ and that our daughters may be as the polished | corners | of the | temple :

13 That our garners may be full and plenteous with all | manner of | store ‖ that our sheep may bring forth thousands, and ten | thousands | in our | streets :

14 That our oxen may be strong to labour; that there be | no de | cay ‖ no leading into captivity, and no com | plaining | in our | streets.

15 Happy are the people that are in | such a | case ; yea, blessed are the people who have the | Lord - | for their | God.

PSALM cxlv. *Exaltabo te, Deus.*

I WILL magnify thee, O | God, my | King ‖ and I will praise thy | Name for | ever and | ever.

2 Every day will I give thanks | unto | thee ‖ and praise thy | Name for | ever and | ever.

3 Great is the LORD, and marvellous worthy | to be | praised ‖ there is no | end - | of his | greatness.

4 One generation shall praise thy works un | to an | other ‖ and de | clare - | thy - | power.

5 As for me, I will be talking | of thy | worship ‖ thy glory, thy | praise and | wondrous works ;

6 So that men shall speak of the might of thy | marvellous | acts ‖ and I will also | tell - | of thy | greatness.

7 The memorial of thine abundant kindness | shall be | showed ‖ and men shall | sing - | of thy | righteousness.

8 The LORD is gracious | and | merciful ‖ longsuffering, | and of | great - | goodness.

9 The LORD is loving unto | every | man ‖ and his mercy is | over | all his | works.

10 All thy works | praise thee, O | LORD ‖ and thy saints give | thanks - | unto | thee.

11 They show the glory | of thy | kingdom ‖ and | talk - | of thy | power ;

12 That thy power, thy glory, and mightiness | of thy | kingdom ‖ might be | known - | unto | men.

13 Thy kingdom is an ever | lasting | king-

dom ‖ and thy dominion en | dureth through | out all | ages.

14 The Lord upholdeth all | such as | fall ‖ and lifteth up all | those - | that are | down.

15 The eyes of all wait upon | thee, O | Lord ‖ and thou givest them their | meat in | due - | season.

16 Thou openest | thine - | hand ‖ and fillest all things | living with | plenteous | ness.

17 The Lord is righteous in | all his | ways ‖ and | holy in | all his | works.

18 The Lord is nigh unto all them that | call up | on him ‖ yea, all such as | call up | on him | faithfully.

19 He will fulfil the desire of | them that | fear him ‖ he also will hear their | cry, - | and will | help them.

20 The Lord preserveth all | them that | love him ‖ but scattereth a | broad all | the un | godly.

21 My mouth shall speak the praise | of the | Lord ‖ and let all flesh give thanks unto his holy | Name for | ever and | ever.

Psalm cxlvi. *Lauda, anima mea.*

PRAISE the Lord, O my soul; while I live, will I | praise the | Lord ‖ yea, as long as I have any being, I will sing | praises | unto my | God.

2 O put not your trust in princes, nor in any | child of | man ‖ for | there is | no help | in them.

3 For when the breath of man goeth forth, he shall turn again | to his | earth ‖ and then | all his | thoughts - | perish.

4 Blessed is he that hath the God of Jacob |

for his | help ‖ and whose hope is | in the | Lord his | God :

5 Who hath made heaven and earth, the sea, and all that | therein | is ‖ who | keepeth his | promise for | ever :

6 Who helpeth them to right that | suffer | wrong ‖ who | feed - | eth the | hungry.

7 The Lord looseth men | out of | prison ‖ the Lord giveth | sight - | to the | blind.

8 The Lord helpeth them | that are | fallen ‖ the Lord | careth | for the | righteous.

9 The Lord careth for the strangers; he defendeth the fatherless | and - | widow ‖ as for the way of the ungodly, he | turneth it | upside | down.

10 The Lord thy God, O Sion, shall be King for | ever | more ‖ and throughout | all - | gener | ations.

EVENING PRAYER.

Psalm cxlvii. *Laudate Dominum.*

O PRAISE the Lord, for it is a good thing to sing praises un | to our | God ‖ yea, a joyful and pleasant | thing it | is to be | thankful.

2 The Lord doth build | up Je | rusalem ‖ and gather together the | out - | casts of | Israel.

3 He healeth those that are | broken in | heart ‖ and giveth medicine to | heal - | their - | sickness.

4 He telleth the number | of the | stars ‖ and calleth them | all - | by their | names.

5 Great is our Lord, and | great is his | power ‖ yea, and his | wisdom | is - | infinite.

6 The Lord setteth | up the | meek || and bringeth the ungodly | down - | to the | ground.

7 O sing unto the | Lord with | thanksgiving || sing praises upon the | harp un | to our | God;

8 Who covereth the heaven with clouds, and prepareth rain | for the | earth || and maketh the grass to grow upon the mountains, and | herb for the | use of | men;

9 Who giveth fodder un | to the | cattle || and feedeth the young | ravens that | call up | on him.

10 He hath no pleasure in the strength | of an | horse || neither delighteth | he in | any man's | legs.

11 But the Lord's delight is in | them that | fear him || and put their | trust - | in his | mercy.

12 Praise the Lord, | O Je | rusalem || praise thy | God, - | O - | Sion.

13 For he hath made fast the bars | of thy | gates || and hath | blessed thy | children with | in thee.

14 He maketh peace | in thy | borders || and filleth thee | with the | flour of | wheat.

15 He sendeth forth his commandment up | on - | earth || and his word | runneth | very | swiftly.

16 He giveth | snow like | wool || and scattereth the | hoar-frost | like - | ashes.

17 He casteth forth his | ice like | morsels || who is able | to a | bide his | frost?

18 He sendeth out his word, and | melteth | them || he bloweth with his wind, | and the | waters | flow.

19 He showeth his word | unto | Jacob ‖ his statutes and ordinances | unto | Isra | el.

20 He hath not dealt so with | any | nation ‖ neither have the heathen | knowledge | of his | laws.

PSALM cxlviii. *Laudate Dominum.*

O PRAISE the | LORD of | heaven ‖ praise - | him | in the | height.

2 Praise him, all ye | angels of | his ‖ praise - | him, | all his | hosts.

3 Praise him, | sun and | moon ‖ praise him, | all ye | stars and | light.

4 Praise him, | all ye | heavens ‖ and ye waters that | are a | bove the | heavens.

5 Let them praise the | Name of the | LORD ‖ for he spake the word, and they were made; he commanded, | and they were | cre | ated.

6 He hath made them fast for | ever and | ever ‖ he hath given them a law | which shall | not be | broken.

7 Praise the | LORD upon | earth ‖ ye | dragons, | and all | deeps :

8 Fire and hail, | snow and | vapours ‖ wind and | storm, ful | filling his | word :

9 Mountains | and all | hills ‖ fruitful | trees - | and all | cedars :

10 Beasts | and all | cattle ‖ worms | and - | feathered | fowls :

11 Kings of the earth | and all | people ‖ princes and all | judges | of the | world :

12 Young men and maidens, old men and children, praise the | Name of the | LORD ‖ for his

Name only is excellent, and his praise a | bove - | heaven and | earth.

13 He shall exalt the horn of his people : all his | saints shall | praise him ‖ even the children of Israel, even the | people that | serveth | him.

Psalm cxlix. *Cantate Domino.*

O SING unto the Lord a | new - | song ‖ let the congre | gation of | saints - | praise him.

2 Let Israel rejoice in | him that | made him ‖ and let the children of Sion be | joyful | in their | King.

3 Let them praise his | Name in the | dance ‖ let them sing praises unto | him with | tabret and | harp.

4 For the Lord hath pleasure | in his | people ‖ and | helpeth | the meek | hearted.

5 Let the saints be | joyful with | glory ‖ let them re | joice - | in their | beds.

6 Let the praises of God | be in their | mouth ‖ and a two-edged | sword - | in their | hands ;

7 To be avenged | of the | heathen ‖ and | to re | buke the | people.

8 To bind their | kings in | chains ‖ and their | nobles with | links of | iron.

9 That they may be avenged of them ; | as it is | written ‖ Such | honour have | all his | saints.

Psalm cl. *Laudate Dominum.*

O PRAISE God | in his | holiness ‖ praise him in the | firmament | of his | power.

2 Praise him in his | noble | acts ‖ praise him according | to his | excellent | greatness.

3 Praise him in the | sound of the | trumpet ||
praise him up | on the | lute and | harp.
4 Praise him in the | cymbals and | dances ||
praise him up | on the | strings and | pipe.
5 Praise him upon the | well-tuned | cymbals |
praise him up | on the | loud - | cymbals.
6 Let every thing | that hath | breath ¶ praise |
. . | - the | Lord.

The Nicene Creed.

I BELIEVE in one God, the | Father Al | mighty ‖ Maker of heaven and earth, and of all things | visible | and - | invisible ‖

And in one Lord, | Jesus | Christ ‖ the only begotten Son of God, begotten of His Father before - | all - | worlds. God of God, Light of Light, very God | of very | God ‖ Be | gotten | not - | made ‖ Being of one substance | with the | Father ‖ by | whom all | things were | made. Who, for us men, and for our salvation, came | down from | Heaven ‖ And was incarnate by the Holy Ghost | of the | Virgin | Mary ‖ And was | made - | man ‖ and was crucified also for us | under | Pontius | Pilate. He suffered and was buried: and the third | day He | rose again ‖ according to the scriptures: and a | scended | into | Heaven ‖ and sitteth on the right hand | of the | Father ‖ And he shall come again with glory to judge both the quick and the dead; whose | kingdom shall | have no | end.

And I believe in the Holy Ghost, the Lord, and | Giver of | Life ‖ who proceedeth from the | Father | and the | Son ‖ who, with the Father and the Son together, is worshipped and | glori | fied ‖ Who | spake - | by the | prophets.

And I believe one Catholic and Apos | tolic | Church ‖ I acknowledge one Baptism | for the re | mission of | sins ‖ And I look for the Resurrection of the | dead, ‖ and the | Life of the | world to | come. | A | men.

APPENDIX.

Hymns from Holy Scripture

N.B.—The authority for the use of these anthems (which restores to us a privilege of the English Church) is found in the following extract from the Journal of the House of Bishops in General Convention, 1811:

"There was laid before the House an address from the Rev. WM. SMITH, of Connecticut, together with surdry Anthems, selected from Holy Scripture, and adapted to certain Festivals and Fasts of the Church. The object of the address is to induce the establishment of the said Anthems as part of the Liturgy: Whereupon—*Resolved*, That it is not expedient, during the present Convention, to go into a review, either in whole or in part, of the Book of Common Prayer. It could not, however, but give satisfaction to the Bishops to recollect that Anthems taken from Scripture, and judiciously arranged, may, according to the known usage of this Church, be sung in congregations at the discretion of their respective ministers."

HYMNS FROM HOLY SCRIPTURE.

I.
For Unto Us.
Isaiah ix. 6, 7.

FOR unto us a | child is | born ‖ unto | us a | Son is | given.

And the government shall be up | on his | shoulder ‖ and His | name - | shall be | called:

Wonderful, Counsellor, the Mighty God, the Ever | lasting | Father ‖ the | Prince - | of - | Peace.

Of the increase of his government and peace there shall | be no | end ‖ upon the throne of David | and up | on his | kingdom;

To order it and to establish it with judgment | and with | justice ‖ from | henceforth | even for | ever.

The zeal of the | Lord of | Hosts ‖ will | per - | form - | this.

II.
The Wilderness.
Isaiah xxxv.

THE wilderness and the solitary place | shall be | glad for them ‖ and the desert shall rejoice and | blossom | as the | rose.

SCRIPTURE HYMNS.

It shall | blossom a | bundantly ‖ and rejoice | even with | joy and | singing.

The glory of Lebanon shall be given unto it, the excellency of | Carmel and | Sharon ‖ they shall see the glory of the Lord and the | excellency | of our | God.

Then the eyes of the blind | shall be | opened ‖ and the ears of the | deaf shall | be un | stopped.

Then shall the lame man | leap as an | hart ‖ and the | tongue of the | dumb - | sing.

For in the wilderness shall | waters break | out ‖ and | streams - | in the | desert.

And the ransomed of the Lord shall return, and | come to | Zion ‖ with songs and everlasting | joy up | on their | heads.

They shall obtain | joy and | gladness ‖ and sorrow and sighing | shall - | flee a | way.

III.

He Was Wounded.

Isaiah liii.

HE was wounded for | our trans | gressions ‖ He was | bruised for | our in | iquities.

The chastisement of our peace | was upon | Him ‖ and with | his stripes | we are | healed.

All we like sheep have | gone a | stray ‖ we have turned every | one to | his own | way.

And the Lord hath | laid on | Him ‖ the in | iquity | of us | all.

He was oppressed and He | was af | flicted ‖ yet He | opened | not his | mouth.

He is brought as a lamb to the slaughter, and
as a sheep before her | shearer is | dumb ‖ so He |
openeth | not his | mouth.

Rev. i. and v.

UNTO Him that | loved | us ‖ and washed us
from our | sins in | his own | blood.
And hath made us kings and priests unto God |
and His | Father ‖ to Him be glory and dominion
for | ever and | ever. A | men
Worthy is the Lamb | that was | slain ‖ to
re | ceive - | Power, | and Riches,
And | Wisdom, and | Strength ‖ and Honor,
and Glory, and | Blessing | A - | men.

IV.
How Beautiful.
Isaiah lii. 7–10.

HOW beautiful up | on the | mountains ‖ are the
feet of him that bringeth good tidings, | that - |
publisheth | peace.
That bringeth good tidings of good, that pub-
lisheth | sal - | vation ‖ that saith unto Zion |
Thy - | God - | reigneth.
Thy watchmen shall lift | up the | voice ‖ with
the voice to | gether | shall they | sing.
For they shall see | eye to | eye ‖ when the
Lord shall | bring a | gain - | Zion.
Break forth into joy, sing together ye waste
places | of Je | rusalem ‖ for the Lord hath com-

forted his people, he | hath re | deemed Je | ru-
salem.

The Lord hath made bare his holy arm in the eyes of | all the | nations ‖ and all the ends of the earth shall see the sal | vation | of our | God.

V.

Arise, Shine.

Isaiah lx.

ARISE, shine, for thy | light is | come ‖ and the glory of the | Lord is | risen up | on thee.

The Gentiles shall come | to thy | light ‖ and kings to the | brightness | of thy | rising.

Lift up thine eyes round a | bout and | see ‖ all they gather themselves together, | they - | come to | Thee.

Thy sons shall | come from | far ‖ and thy daughters shall be | nursed | at thy | side.

Thy gates shall be | open con | tinually ‖ they shall not be | shut - | day nor | night;

That men may bring unto thee the forces | of the | Gentiles ‖ and that their | kings - | may be | brought.

For the nation and kingdom that will not serve | Thee shall | perish ‖ yea, those nations | shall be | utterly | wasted.

Violence shall no more be heard | in thy | land ‖ wasting nor destruction | with - | in thy | borders.

But thou shalt call thy | walls sal | vation ‖ and | thy - | gates - | praise.

The sun shall be no more thy | light by | day ‖ neither for brightness shall the | moon give | light unto | thee.

But the Lord shall be unto thee an ever | lasting light ‖ and thy | God - | thy - | glory.

VI.

Magnificat.

[*As in the English Prayer Book.*]

St. Luke i.

MY soul doth magni | fy the | Lord ‖ and my spirit hath re | joiced in | God my | Saviour.

For He | hath re | garded ‖ the lowli | ness of | his hand | maiden;

For behold, | from hence | forth ‖ all gene | rations shall | call me | blessed.

For He that is mighty hath magnified me, and holy | is his | Name ‖ and his mercy is on them that fear Him, through | out all | gener | ations.

He hath shewed strength | with his | arm ‖ He hath scattered the proud in the imagi | nation | of their | hearts.

He hath put down the mighty | from their | seats ‖ and hath exalted the | humble | and the | meek.

He hath filled the hungry | with good | things ‖ and the rich He | hath sent | empty a | way.

He remembering his mercy hath holpen his | servant | Israel ‖ as He promised to our **forefathers**, Abraham | and his | seed, for | ever.

VII.

Nunc Dimittis.
St. Luke ii.

LORD, now lettest thou thy servant de | part in | peace ‖ ac | cording | to thy | word,
 For | mine - | eyes ‖ have | seen - | thy sal | va tion.
 Which thou | hast pre | pared ▌ before the | face - | of all | people.
 To be a light to | lighten the | Gentiles ‖ and the glory | of thy | people | Israel.

VIII.
In the Beginning.
St. John i.

IN the beginning | was the | Word ▌ and the | Word was with God, | and the | Word was | God.
 The same was in the be | ginning with | God ‖ all things were made by him; and without him was not any thing | made - | that was | made.
 In | him was | life ‖ and the life | was the | light of | men.
 And the light | shineth in | darkness ‖ and the darkness | compre | hended | it not;
 That was the | true - | Light ‖ which lighteth every man that | cometh | into the | world.
 He was in the world, and the world was | made by | him ‖ and the | world - | knew him | not.
 He came | unto his | own ‖ and his | own re | ceived him | not.

But as many | as re | ceived him ‖ to them gave he power to become the sons of God, even to them | that be | lieve on his | name :

Which were born | not of | blood ‖ nor of the will of the flesh, nor of the will of man | but - | of - | God.

And the Word was made flesh, and | dwelt a | mong us ‖ and we beheld his glory, the glory as of the only begotten of the Father | full of | grace and | truth.

And of his fulness have all | we re | ceived ‖ and | grace - | for - | grace.

For the law was | given by | Moses ‖ but grace and truth | came by | Jesus | Christ.

IX.

God so Loved.

St. John iii.

FOR God so loved the world, that he gave his only be | gotten | Son ‖ that whosoever believeth in him should not perish, but have | ever | lasting | life.

For God sent not his Son into the world to con | demn the | world ‖ but that the world through | him - | might be | saved.

He that believeth on him is | not con | demned ‖ but he that believeth not is condemned already, because he hath not believed in the name of the only be | gotten | Son of | God

And this is the condemnation, that light is come | into the | world ‖ and men loved darkness

SCRIPTURE HYMNS.

rather than light, be | cause their | deeds were | evil.

For every one that doeth evil hateth the light, neither cometh | to the | light ‖ lest his | deeds should | be re | proved :

But he that doeth truth cometh | to the | light ₤ that his deeds may be made manifest that | they are | wrought in | God.

X.
Lord, Thou art God.
Acts iv.

LORD, | thou art | God ‖ which hast made heaven, and earth, and the sea, and | all that | in them | is :

Who by the mouth of thy servant | David hast | said ‖ Why did the heathen rage, and the people im | agine | vain - | things?

The kings of the earth stood up, and the rulers were | gathered to | gether ‖ against the Lord, | and a | gainst his | Christ.

For of a truth against thy holy child Jesus, whom thou | hast a | nointed ‖ both Herod, and Pontius Pilate, with the Gentiles, and the people of Israel, | were - | gathered to | gether.

For to do whatsoever thy hand | and thy | counsel ‖ determined be | fore - | to be | done.

And now, Lord, be | hold their | threatenings ‖ and grant unto thy servants, that with all boldness | they may | speak thy | word,

By stretching forth thy | hand to | heal ‖ and that signs and wonders may be done by the name of thy | holy | child - | Jesus.

XL.

Though I Speak.

1 Corinthians xiii.

THOUGH I speak with the tongues of men and of angels, and | have not | charity ‖ I am become as sounding brass, | or a | tinkling | cymbal.

And though I have the gift of prophecy, and understand all mysteries, | and all | knowledge ‖ and though that I have all faith, so that I could remove mountains, and have not | charity, | I am | nothing.

And though I bestow all my goods to feed the poor, and though I give my body | to be | burned ‖ and have not | charity, | I am | nothing.

Charity suffereth long, | and is | kind ‖ charity envieth not; charity vaunteth not itself, | is not | puffed | up;

Doth not behave it | self un | seemly ‖ secketh not her own, is not easily pro | voked, | thinketh no | evil;

Rejoiceth | not in in | iquity ‖ but re | joiceth | in the | truth;

Beareth all things, be | lieveth | all things ‖ hopeth all things, en | dureth | all - | things.

Charity | never | faileth ‖ but whether there be prophecies, they shall fail; whether there be tongues, they shall cease; whether there be knowledge, | it shall | vanish a | way.

For we | know in | part ‖ and we | prophe | sy in | part;

But when that which is | perfect is | come ‖

then that which is in | part shall be | done a | way.

When I was a child, I spake as a child, I understood as a child, I | thought as a | child ‖ but when I became a man, I | put away | childish | things.

For now we see through a glass, darkly; but then | face to | face ‖ now I know in part; but then shall I know even as | also | I am | known.

And now abideth | faith, hope, | charity ‖ these three; but the | greatest of | these is | charity.

XII.

If God be for Us.

ROMANS viii.

IF | God be | for us ‖ who | can - | be a | gainst us?

He that spared not his own Son, but delivered him up | for us | all ‖ how shall he not with him also | freely | give us | all things?

Who shall lay any thing to the charge of | God's e | lect ‖ It is | God that | justi | fieth.

Who is he that condemneth? It is Christ that died, yea rather, that is | risen a | gain ‖ who is even at the right hand of God, who also maketh | inter | cession | for us.

Who shall separate us from the | love of | Christ ‖ Shall tribulation, or distress, or persecution, or famine, or nakedness, or | peril, | or - | sword?

Nay, in all these things we are | more than | conquerors ‖ through | him that | loved | us.

For I am persuaded that neither death, nor life, nor angels, nor | princi | palities ‖ nor powers, nor things present, | nor - | things to | come.

Nor height, nor depth, nor any | other | crea- ture ‖ shall be able to separate us from the love of God, which is in | Christ - | Jesus our | Lord.

XIII.
Easter Benedictus.
1 St. Peter i.

BLESSED be the God and Father of our Lord | Jesus | Christ ‖ who, according to | His a | bundant | mercy,

Hath begotten us again unto a | lively | hope ‖ by the resurrection of | Jesus Christ | from the | dead.

To an inheritance incorruptible and | unde | filed ‖ and that fadeth not away, re | served in | Heaven | for us.

Who are kept by the power of God, through faith un | to sal | vation ‖ ready to be revealed | in the | last - | time.

XIV.
We shall not all Sleep.
1 Cor. xv.

WE shall not | all - | sleep ‖ but we | shall - | all be | changed,

In a moment, in the twinkling of an eye, | at the last | trump ‖ for the trumpet shall sound, and the dead shall be raised incorruptible, | and we | shall be | changed

SCRIPTURE HYMNS.

For this corruptible must put on | incor | rup- tion ‖ and this mortal must | put on | immor | tality.

So when this corruptible shall have put on in | corrup | tion ‖ and this mortal shall have | put on | immor | tality,

Then shall be brought to pass the saying | that is | written ‖ Death is | swallowed | up in | victory.

O death, | where is thy | sting ‖ O | grave, where | is thy | victory?

The sting of | death is | sin ‖ and the | strength of | sin is the | law.

But | thanks be to | God ‖ which giveth us the victory through our | Lord - | Jesus | Christ.

XV.
God, who is Rich.
Ephesians ii.

GOD, who is | rich in | mercy ‖ for his great love where | with he | loved | us,

Even when we were | dead in | sins ‖ hath quickened us together with Christ, by | grace - | we are | saved;

And hath raised us | up to | gether ‖ and made us sit together in heavenly | places in | Christ - | Jesus:

That in the ages to come he might shew the ex- ceeding riches | of his | grace ‖ in his kindness toward us, | through - | Christ - | Jesus.

For by grace are we saved | through - | faith ‖ and that not of ourselves: it | is the | gift of | God:

No - | t of | works ‖ lest | any | man should | boast.

For we are his workmanship, created in Christ Jesus | unto good | works ‖ which God hath before ordained that | we should | walk in | them

XVI.

God, who at Sundry Times.
HEBREWS i.

GOD, who at sundry times and in | divers | manners ‖ spake in time past unto the | fathers | by the | prophets,

Hath in these last days spoken unto us | by his | Son ‖ whom he hath appointed heir of all things, by whom | also he | made the | worlds ;

Who, being the brightness of his glory and the express image | of his | person ‖ and upholding all things by the | word - | of his | power ;

When he had by himself | purged our | sins ‖ sat down on the right hand of the | Majes | ty on | high ;

Being made so much better | than the | angels ‖ as he hath by inheritance obtained a more | excellent | name than | they.

For unto which of the angels said he at any time, Thou art my Son, this day have | I be | gotten thee ‖ And again, I will be to him a Father, and he shall | be to | me a | Son ?

And again, when he bringeth in the First-begotten into the | world, he | saith ‖ And let all the | angels of | God - | worship him.

And of the | angels he | saith ‖ Who maketh

his angels spirits, and his | ministers a | flame of | fire.

But unto the Son he saith, Thy throne, O God, is for | ever and | ever ‖ a sceptre of righteousness is the | sceptre | of thy | kingdom:

Thou hast loved righteousness, and | hated iniquity ‖ therefore God, even thy God, hath anointed thee with the oil of | gladness a | bove thy | fellows.

And, Thou, Lord, in the beginning hast laid the foundation | of the | earth ‖ and the heavens | are the | works of thy | hands:

They shall perish, but | thou re | mainest ‖ and they all shall wax | old as | doth a | garment;

And as a vesture shalt thou fold them up, and they | shall be | changed ‖ but thou art the same, and | thy years | shall not | fail.

But to which of the angels said he at | any | time ‖ Sit on my right hand, until I make thine | ene | mies thy | footstool?

Are they not all | ministering | spirits ‖ sent forth to minister for them who shall be | heirs - | of sal | vation?

XVII
Seeing Then.
HEBREWS iv.

SEEING then that we have a great High Priest, that is passed in | to the | heavens ‖ Jesus the Son of God, let us hold | fast - | our pro | fession

For we have not a high priest which cannot be touched with the feeling of | our in | firmities ‖

but was in all points tempted like as we are, | yet with | out - | sin.

Let us therefore come boldly unto the | throne of | grace ‖ that we may obtain mercy, and find grace to | help in | time of | need.

XVIII.
Behold what Manner.
1 St. John iii.

BEHOLD, what manner of love the Father hath be | stowed up | on us, ‖ that we should be | called the | sons of | God.

Therefore the world | knoweth us | not ‖ be | cause it | knew him | not.

Beloved, now are we the | sons of | God ‖ and it doth not yet ap | pear - | what we | shall be.

But we know that, when | he shall ap | pear ‖ we shall be like him; for we shall | see him | as he | is.

And every man that | hath this | hope in him ‖ purifieth himself, | even as | he is | pure.

XIX.
Beloved, if our Heart.
1 St. John iii. 21-24.

BELOVED, if our heart con | demn us | not ‖ then have we | confidence to | ward - | God.

And whatsoever we ask, | we re | ceive of him ‖ because we keep his commandments, and do those things that are | pleasing | in his | sight.

And this is his commandment, that we should

believe on the name of his Son | Jesus | Christ ‖ and love one another, | as he | gave us com | mandment.

And he that keepeth | his com | mandments, ‖ dwelleth in | him, and | he in | him.

And hereby we know that he a | bideth | in us ‖ by the Spirit | which - | he hath | given us.

XX.
Beloved, let Us.
1 St. John iv.

BELOVED, let us | love one a | nother ‖ for love is of God; and every one that loveth, is born of | God, and | knoweth | God.

He that loveth not, | knoweth not | God ‖ for | God - | is - | love.

In this was manifested the love of | God toward | us, ‖ because that God sent his only begotten Son into the world, that | we might | live through | him.

Herein is love, not that we loved God, but that | he loved | us ‖ and sent his Son to be the propiti | ation | for our | sins.

Beloved, if God so | loved | us ‖ we ought also to | love - | one a | nother.

XXI.
Whosoever Believeth.
1 St. John v.

WHOSOEVER believeth that Jesus is the Christ, is | born of | God ‖ and every one that loveth him that begat, loveth him also that | is be | gotten | of him.

By this we know that we love the | children of | God || when we love God, and | keep - | his com | mandments.

For this is the love of God, that we | keep his com | mandments || and his com | mandments | are not | grievous.

For whatsoever is born of God, over | cometh the | world || and this is the victory that overcometh the | world, - | even our | faith.

Who is he that over | cometh the | world || but he that believeth that Jesus | is the | Son of | God?

This is he that came by water and blood, even | Jesus | Christ || not by water only, but by | water | and - | blood.

And it is the Spirit that | beareth | witness || be | cause the | Spirit is | truth.

For there are three that bear record in heaven, the Father, the Word, and the | Holy | Ghost |: and | these - | three are | one.

XXII.

Christmas Cantate.

O SING unto the Lord a | new - | song || let the congre | gation of | saints - | praise Him.

Let Israel rejoice in | Him that | made him || and let the children of Zion be | joyful | in their | King.

SCRIPTURE HYMNS.

In Him, the First | and the | Last || the same yesterday, to | day, - | and for | ever.

The Angel | of the | Covenant || the | An - | cient of Days.

The Desire | of all | Nations || The glory | of his | people | Israel.

The Root and | Offspring of | David || The | Bright and | Morning Star.

The | Son of | Mary || The Only Begotten of the Father, | full of | grace and | truth.

The Day Spring | from on | high || The Sun of Righteousness risen with | healing | in his | wings.

The | Rose of | Sharon || and the | Lily | of the | Valley.

The | Crown of | Glory || The Diadem of | Beauty un | to his | people.

The Author and Finisher | of our | Faith || the Shepherd and | Bishop | of our | souls.

The Lamb slain from the foundation | of the | world || High Priest forever, after the | order | of Mel | chizedec.

The Propitiation for the Sins | of the | world || the Only Name under Heaven given among men where | by we | must be | saved.

The Prophet, | Priest and | King || The | Lord our | Righteous | ness.

The Judge of the | Quick and the | Dead || He that hath the | keys of | Death and | Hell.

God manifest | in the | Flesh || Image | of the in | visible | God.

The Brightness of the | Father's | Glory || The express | Image | of his | Person.

King of Kings and | Lord of | Lords || God over all | blessed for | ever | more.

In the following Music, which, it will be observed, runs across the opposite pages, the four vocal parts are written on two staves, in their usual order. Of the Gregorian Chants, on the first two pages, only the melody is given, as they are designed to be sung by a congregation in unison, the organ filling up the harmony.

In Nos. 1, 5, and 7 of these Gregorian Chants, the double notes signify that the melody may be finished with either the upper or lower notes. If taken alternately, they make double chants, suitable for antiphonal singing.

GREGORIAN CHANTS.

No. 1.

No. 2.

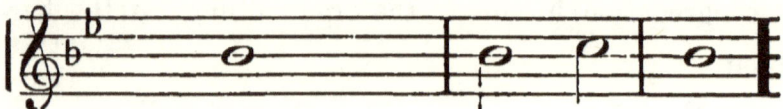

No. 3.

No. 4.

No. 5.

No. 6.

No. 7.

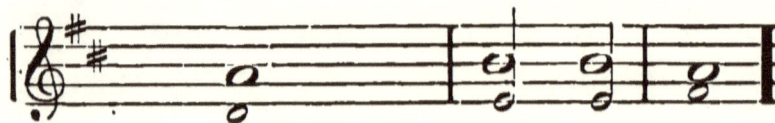

No. 8.

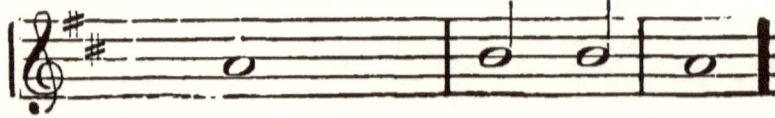

GREGORIAN CHANTS.

Continued.

No. 9.

No. 10.

No. 11.

No. 12.

Continued.

SINGLE CHANTS.

SINGLE CHANTS.

SINGLE CHANTS.

No 17.

No. 18.

No. 19.

No. 20.

SINGLE CHANTS.

Continued.

SINGLE CHANTS.

No. 21.

No. 22.

No. 23.

No. 24.

SINGLE CHANTS.

DOUBLE CHANTS.

No. 25.

No. 26.

DOUBLE CHANTS.

Continued.

Continued.

DOUBLE CHANTS.

DOUBLE CHANTS. 319

Continued.

320 DOUBLE CHANTS.

DOUBLE CHANTS.

Continued.

DOUBLE CHANTS.

No. 33.

No. 34.

Continued.

DOUBLE CHANTS.

No. 35.

No. 36.

DOUBLE CHANTS.

Continued.

DOUBLE CHANTS.

No. 37.

No. 38.

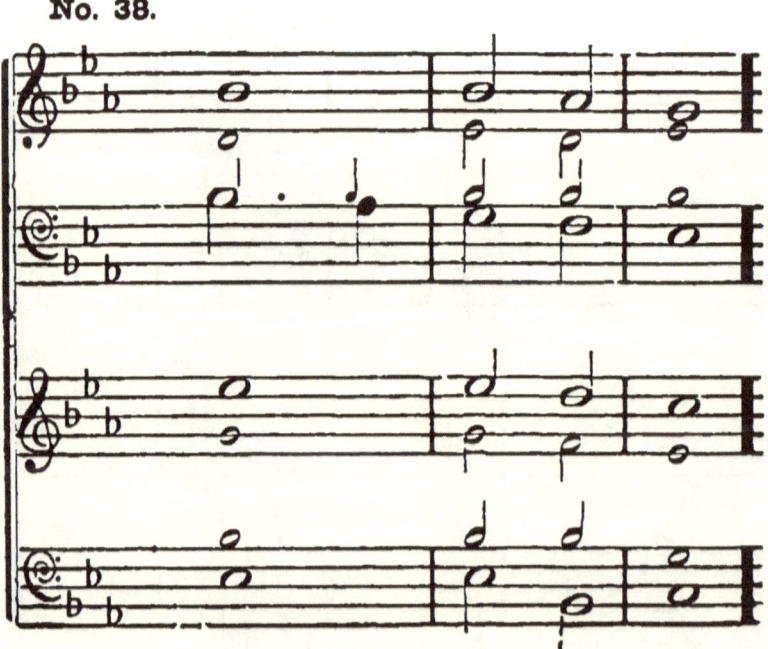

DOUBLE CHANTS. 32.

Continued

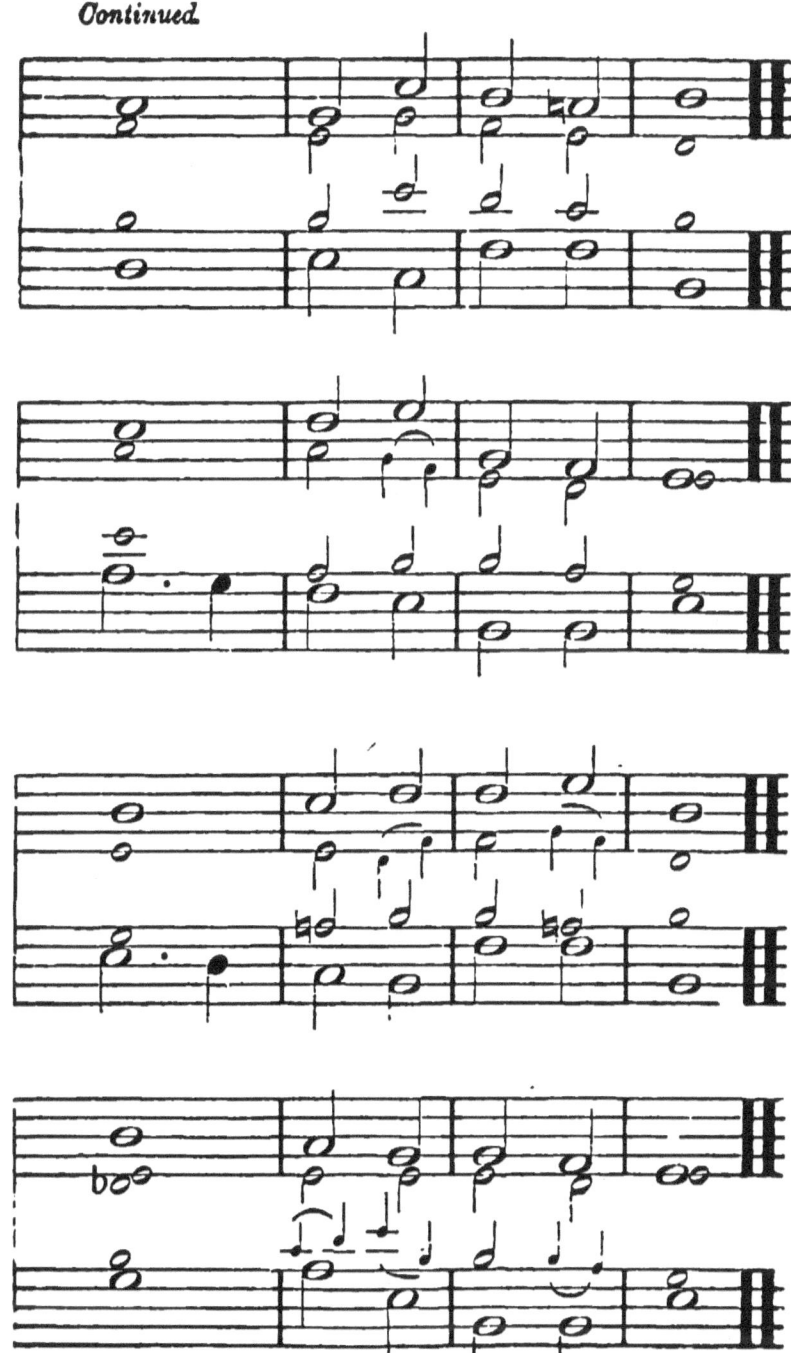

DOUBLE CHANTS.

No. 39.

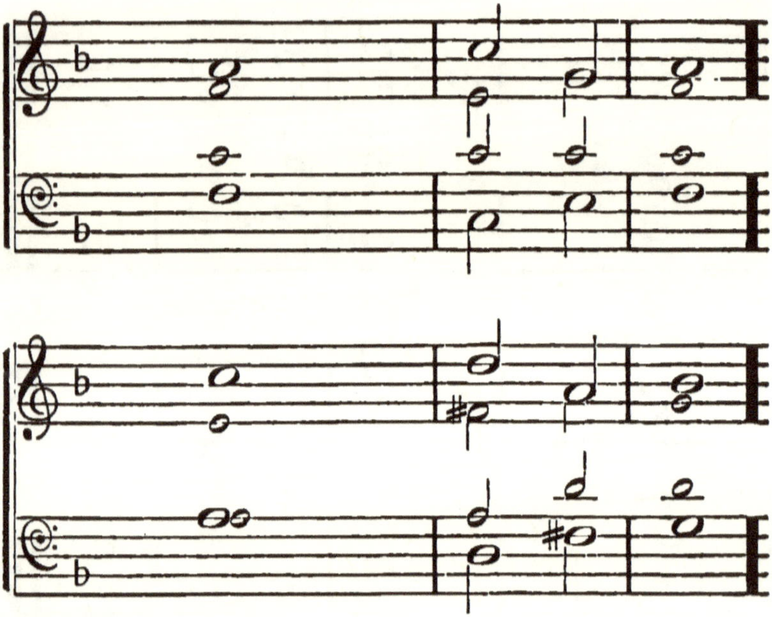

No. 40.

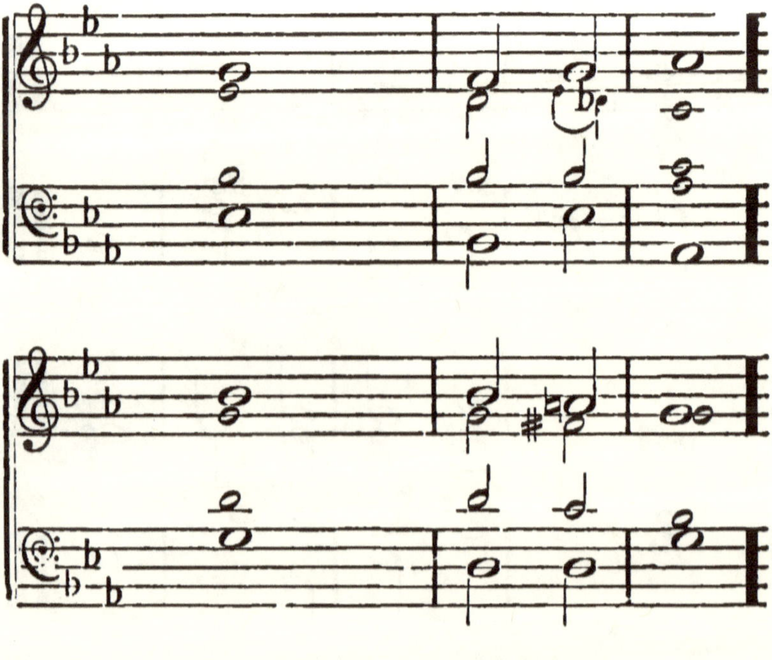

DOUBLE CHANTS.

Continued.

No. 41.

No. 42.

DOUBLE CHANTS.

Continued.

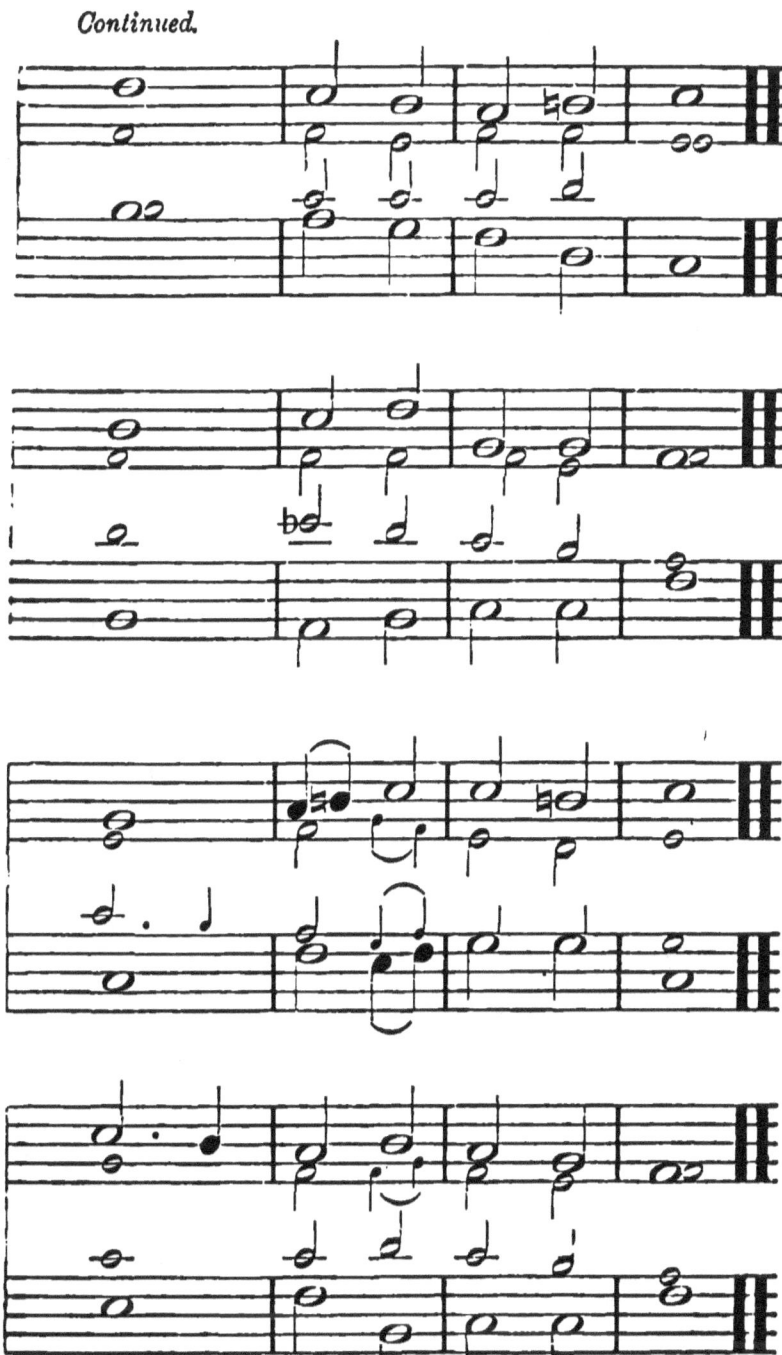

DOUBLE CHANTS.

No. 43.

No. 44.

DOUBLE CHANTS. 333

Continued.

APPENDIX OF SINGLE CHANTS.

Continued.

www.ingramcontent.com/pod-product-compliance
Lightning Source LLC
Chambersburg PA
CBHW030007240426
43672CB00007B/859